W9-AED-242

THE LAND AND PEOPLE OF NORTHEAST BRAZIL

THE LAND AND PEOPLE OF NORTHEAST BRAZIL

Manuel Correia de Andrade

Translated by Dennis V. Johnson

For Review in:

Contemporary Sociology
University of Connecticut
Storrs, CT 06268
_____300_____ words
Date ___5-1-81___

UNIVERSITY OF NEW MEXICO PRESS

Albuquerque

Library of Congress Cataloging in Publication Data

Andrade, Manuel Correia de Oliveira.
  The land and people of northeast Brazil.

  Translation of A terra e o homen no Nordeste.
  Bibliography: p. 233
    1. Land tenure—Brazil, Northeast.   2. Agriculture—
Economic aspects—Brazil, Northeast.   I. Title.
HD496.A713   338.1'0981'3   79-2309
ISBN 0-8263-0520-2

© 1980 by the University of New Mexico Press. All rights reserved.
Manufactured in the United States of America. Library of
Congress Catalog Card Number 79-2309. International Standard
Book Number 0-8263-0520-2.
First English edition.

Contents

Translator's Introduction   vii

Preface   ix

Foreword   xiii

1. Introduction   1

2. The Northeast: Region of Contrast   6

3. Land Tenure and Labor in the Zona da Mata
   and Eastern Littoral   41

4. Property, Polyculture, and Labor in the Agreste   111

5. Latifundia, Division of Land, and Labor Systems
   in the Sertão and Northern Littoral   141

6. The Middle North: Maranhão and Piauí   178

7. Tentative Solutions to the Agrarian Problem   190

Glossary   219

Notes   223

Bibliography   233

Index   241

Translator's Introduction

Brazilian readers have long been familiar with the writings of Manuel Correia de Andrade; his works are indispensable sources of information on the conditions and problems of the rural sector of the burgeoning Northeast region. Best known of his more than thirty publications is *A Terra e o Homem no Nordeste*, translated here as *The Land and People of Northeast Brazil*.

Manuel Correia de Andrade has established himself as a respected academic geographer, in his role of professor at the Federal University of Pernambuco at Recife, and as a respected applied geographer, through his participation in numerous research projects for most of the major governmental agencies operating in the Northeast. He bridges the gap between academic and applied geography and brings to this book the best of both. He is insightful and probing, yet never forgets the practical relation of a condition or a problem to real people.

Certainly the theme of man-land-labor is fundamental to understanding the nation-sized region of the Brazilian Northeast, and it should be carefully weighed with respect to the development of the region. That has not been the case over the past thirty years, for, as this book shows, the standard of living of rural people in the Northeast has declined, not simply because of the sharp increase in population, but because agricultural systems have been modified and the old paternalistic systems have given way to a predominance of wage labor. Although seemingly a mark of progress, this transformation has largely benefited the large private or corporate landowner. The rural laborer has been shortchanged because minimum wages were not established at levels that equitably compensate for the benefits enjoyed under the former paternalistic arrangement. Most assuredly, no one would argue for a reversion to paternalism. But one can and should argue for agricultural land and labor systems that provide income levels that give workers a decent standard of living. This book provides stark evidence of the unforeseen social consequences of changes, direct or indirect, in the agricultural production systems.

The foreword by Caio Prado Júnior and the author's preface together ably describe the importance and background of this book. I need only add that, as far as the international community of researchers and scholars is concerned, one can select any random study concerned with rural Northeast Brazil and find reference to several of Andrade's studies. It is appropriate that his major work be made available to those who do not read Portuguese.

The first Brazilian edition of this book was published in 1963; a second edition, virtually unchanged, appeared in 1964; a third, revised edition was published in 1973. This translation represents more than the separate efforts of author and translator. Rather, it is the result of a close collaboration between two professional geographers with a shared interest in Northeast Brazil. In this instance, we have worked together to produce what is in reality a fourth edition. The introductory chapter is new and the middle chapters have been updated. The concluding chapter, originally contained in the first and second editions, but dropped from the third edition with the inclusion of a new chapter on the Middle North, has been revised and reinstated. The revisions have been solely the work of the author. I have contributed the glossary and index.

Dennis Johnson

Preface

This book is the result of many years of study, research, and thought. In fact, for more than thirty years, since my student days, I have been engrossed with the problems of Brazil in general and those of the Northeast in particular. Also, teaching geography and history, first in secondary school and for more than twenty years at the university, has given me an opportunity to debate the Brazilian reality with the new generation, getting to the roots of the problems that concern young people and seeking solutions that can solve our national problems.

When I began my university teaching in 1952, I had the opportunity to conduct research for new institutions being founded in the Northeast: the Joaquim Nabuco Institute of Social Research, the Rural Social Service Agency, and the Bank of the Northeast. That research, as well as active participation in meetings of the Association of Brazilian Geographers, provided me the opportunity to travel over nearly all of Brazil, by the most varied forms of transportation. Travel by water ranged from small boats on the upper Amazon, to Brazilian Navy ships (which made possible visits to São Sebastião Island off the coast of the state of São Paulo, and to the Fernando de Noronha Archipelago and Roca Atoll in the open Atlantic). Travel by land has taken me as far south as the city of Santana do Livramento on the Uruguayan border. Excursions with colleagues and students provided an opportunity to gain first-hand awareness of the numerous problems that afflict the Brazilian people and seriously hinder the national development. Such problems are sometimes

geographic, including climatic and soil conditions; sometimes
historic, involving archaic traditions that require major modification but that resist the changes warranted by the passage of
time; sometimes social; sometimes technical; but above all
economic—low productivity, lack of planning, poor distribution,
and so forth.

I have had an opportunity to analyze these types of problems
in a number of earlier studies carried out for scientific research
institutions and governmental agencies involved in planning the
delivery of services to certain communities, as well as in two
theses and in papers presented at scientific meetings. In these
works I have always given special attention to man, to the problems that plague him, to his relationship with the land, and to
the relationships that exist among men with regard to the utilization of land. The land-tenure system, the system of crop cultivation and livestock raising, and their respective relationships to
labor in rural areas, were always aspects that interested me in
earlier studies.

Labor relationships, especially in rural areas, attracted the attention of historian and economist Caio Prado Júnior. He
suggested, in June 1961, that I write an essay on the subject for
the publisher Editôra Brasiliense. Because of the warm invita-
tion and encouragement I received from Caio Prado Júnior, I
wrote this book, which comes to grips with the problem of labor
relationships between landowners and landless workers in the
Brazilian Northeast. It goes without saying that in a study of this
type little would be revealed if only the relationships between
landowners and wage laborers, sharecroppers and renters were
analyzed without correlation to the existing relationships between the system of land use and the environmental conditions.

In the elaboration of this study I have tried above all to be
objective in the analysis of relationships, pointing out their
causes and their implications: that is, only attempting to describe
and analyze objectively the facts. Also, although I am a geographer, I have not tried to carry out a study that is purely and
methodically geographic, because the problem being analyzed is
not only geographic, but historic, social, and, above all,
economic.

I hope that this book, revised for the English-language translation, is well received, that it contributes to a greater divulgence

of knowledge of one of the most important and interesting areas of Brazil, where more than thirty million people live, and that it serves as material for comparative studies of the various parts of the tropical world. I believe, therefore, that I am providing a contribution to a better relationship between Brazil and other countries and a better understanding of the problems of the Third World, whose process of industrialization, most often called "development," is coming to aggravate the problems of rural peoples. I believe that in the Northeast and in Brazil as a whole, as well as in the entire world, the agrarian problem is one that must receive greater priority: agriculture is an economic activity that occupies the largest area, provides work for the greatest number of people, and produces the necessary food-stuffs and a large portion of the raw materials for industry. We live in a time during which there is the prospect of widespread starvation on earth, and during which there is an awareness of the need for ecological preservation, preservation that is not dependent upon agricultural productivity and the use of econometric models, but, chiefly, on the type of land use and the conditions of well-being in which rural people live.

Foreword

Certainly no region of Brazil has a more abundant bibliography than the Northeast. At first glance, this book by Manuel Correia de Andrade might seem to be merely one more study to add to the already very large number. One finds in the book, however, something genuinely original. Strange as it seems, among the extensive bibliography on the Northeast, the relationship between production and labor is almost always overlooked, despite undoubtedly constituting a very important topic and one more worthy of attention than any other.

It would be difficult to disagree that the subject is vital since it involves the relationship between men and their productive activities; the way in which men relate to one another and to the community as a whole in the carrying out of their economic functions. What is involved is the most important, or at least the fundamental, part of the life of any community. It is clear that an analysis such as this immediately reveals perspectives of the social structure and living conditions of the different population groups; only such an analysis can do so. Therefore, it is not necessary to reiterate the importance of the subject that Manuel Correia de Andrade assuredly comes to grips with for the first time by presenting a rigorous and systematic analysis of the complex whole.

But the information found in this book is not only of general scientific interest. At this time, when agrarian reform is being debated in Brazil, and profound changes, which must be made in the structure and relationship of production in the rural areas of the country, are imminent, this book is fundamental. Unfortunately, many of the debates on the subject arise from inadequate knowledge of Brazilian reality, from the presupposition that to arrive at satisfactory conclusions it suffices to use doctrinal and juridical principles, and general, sociological and agricultural economic knowledge. This is not so; the agrarian structure and the relationship of production in the rural areas is in many instances extremely complex. This is especially the case in Northeast Brazil, where, over the years, very specialized economic systems were formed. These systems must be considered in the formulation of required reforms in the current state of economic and social affairs in Brazil. It will be clear after reading this book that it is not possible to reform economic and labor relationships without taking into account specific situations that present themselves, since the latter are precisely what are to be reformed, and to do so in a productive manner, taking heed of the interests and aspirations of the rural population in Brazil.

Manuel Correia de Andrade is one of the most knowledgable specialists on the subjects of agricultural production and labor who has, through patient and exhaustive fieldwork as a professional geographer, observed and studied the agricultural economics of the Northeast. He has made a great number of contributions to the subject, which complement the extensive geographic, economic, and general sociological information about the region. *The Land and People of Northeast Brazil* once again substantiates the great competence of the author. For the first time an analysis of high scientific merit has been produced on the agricultural economics of the Northeast. If there were studies of this nature and caliber for all of Brazil, the work of economists, jurists, and legislators, on whom it is incumbent to formulate the guidelines for Brazilian agrarian reform, would be greatly facilitated. It is hoped that specialists from other regions of Brazil will follow the example of Manuel Correia de Andrade and attain the same level of rigorous scientific probity that characterizes this book.

Caio Prado Júnior

1

Introduction

Brazil is a country of continental dimensions, having an area of more than 8,500,000 square kilometers, and possessing a population of more than a hundred million. It has great potential resources and is still in the process of settling its territory; extensive areas in the Central-West and North regions, still covered by great forests, are now being opened up by road building and by the establishment of agricultural and livestock projects. The differences in levels of regional development are highly accentuated: there is the Southeast region, where the two principal and highly industrialized cities of the country, São Paulo and Rio de Janeiro, are found; the North region, Amazonia, just mentioned, still in the settlement phase; and the Northeast region, of fairly old settlement, slightly industrialized but still dependent upon traditional agriculture, and oriented toward foreign markets. In the Northeast the large-scale cultivation of products for export, now in the process of being modernized, still predominates.

The agrarian problem is one of the most serious the country has, because of the great concentration of land ownership and the low level of utilization by the large and medium property owners. A majority of the rural population receives very low wages, which practically puts them outside the consumer market. This helps account for the tremendous degree of rural poverty and the high rate of migration from the country to the city, provoking a disorderly growth of the cities and the marginalization of great numbers of people. The phenomena of unemploy-

ment, underemployment, lack of food, and poor sanitary conditions have created an urban problem that has been worrying
government officials and gaining great salience in the Second
National Development Plan.

The agrarian problem little concerned the Brazilian government in the 1940s, when policies were originated to protect
urban workers and the system of unions was consolidated under
the protection of the Ministry of Labor; that legislation, however, did not apply to rural workers. In fact, the agricultural
worker, isolated, living on a large holding, remaining directly
dependent upon the landowner, without being able to organize
or to demand his rights, was not able to call attention to his
needs because of a lack of access to communication.

Only in the decade 1951–60, when the country was stimulated
by development programs, when the means of communication,
through transistor radios, reached the interior, and when the
opening of new roads made more possible the exchange of information between rural and urban peoples, did the landless
rural workers, small property owners, sharecroppers, and renters
begin to organize into associations and unions. The agrarian
question was debated in the press, spoken and written about by
populist political leaders, as well as by those with socialist leanings; they all began to address themselves to the rural segment
of the population, trying to channel, by legal means, their demand for rights. The agrarian question, in the period during
which there was a succession of populist presidents (Getúlio
Vargas, Juscelino Kubitschek, Jânio Quadros, and João Goulart),
became the order of the day and pressure for agrarian reform,
from bottom to top, began to be exerted. In Congress tens of
projects were presented that had doctrinal leanings varying
from the leftist to the quite conservative. Popular pressure increased and the holders of property organized and offered serious resistance, as much in the press and in governmental agencies as through their own organizations.

With the recognition of the right of union organization for
rural workers and the recognition of their unions by the government, the dispute between property owners and peasants was
accentuated. It reached its peak in 1963 with the approval of the
Rural Labor Statute, introduced by Deputy Fernando Ferrari of
Rio Grande do Sul, which in practice extended to the rural

workers the rights granted urban workers by the Consolidated Labor Laws of 1943. Thus there arrived in the countryside, twenty years behind time, social labor legislation. In order to implement it, rural workers began to exert pressure on the property owners, who, to a great majority, affirmed that they were not in a position to accept its implementation. The situation reached a critical point, chiefly when the federal government created SUPRA (Superintendency of Agrarian Reform), which, among other things, intended to expropriate land in areas opened up by major paved roads, so that the land could be subdivided into farms and sold to families. At the same time, in furtherance of their rights, the agricultural workers began to make public protests and strikes, to exert pressure for implementation of the law.

Agrarian reform was, in 1962, being discussed by technicians, politicians, and union leaders in newspaper articles, in studies published in magazines, in radio programs, in street demonstrations, and so forth, but little was known about the actual rural conditions to be reformed for some, and maintained for others.

The overthrow of President João Goulart in 1964, and the succeeding constitutional changes of 1967 and 1969, led the Brazilian government to concentrate greater power in the hands of the president and to opt for capitalist development. The government began to search for ways that would bring an entrepreneurial capitalist organization to the agricultural production of the rural areas, confirming the rights assured by the Rural Labor Statute and bringing to the countryside social assistance programs, with a guarantee of retirement, pensions, and so on. The enactment of the Land Statute, by President Castelo Branco, created two agencies: IBRA (Brazilian Institute of Agrarian Reform) and INDA (National Institute of Agricultural Development). In 1969 these two agencies were united to form INCRA (National Institute of Colonization and Agrarian Reform), which was responsible for agricultural policy. Various programs, such as PROTERRA (Program of Land Redistribution and Stimulus to Agroindustry in the North and Northeast), have been formulated, but the surveys made in 1968 by IBRA and in 1972 by INCRA, confirmed the predominance of latifundium and the continued underutilization of rural land. At the same time, the modernization of agriculture has been destroying subsistence agriculture and, consequently, accentuating the proletarization of the rural workers.

These factors, the permanence of agriculture turned toward the export market, and the low income level of the rural people, indicate that the agrarian problem is becoming more and more serious, with disastrous repercussions for the economy and society of Brazil. It is evident that Brazil, opting for a capitalist process of development, has been trying to institute measures that more characterize an agrarian reformulation than an agrarian reform. These measures maintain existing land-tenure structure, make modest programs of land distribution, and try to give to the rural workers the full rights recognized for urban workers. That policy is accompanied by the development of commercial agriculture with the application of capital on a large scale, requiring, naturally, little manual labor, and thus provoking unemployment and the movement of the unemployed to the small- and medium-sized cities. The unemployed become itinerant workers, not tied to any land. They offer themselves as laborers on a day-to-day basis to an entrepreneur, going to the fields in the morning, bringing with them their meals, and only returning to their houses at nightfall.

This study divides the Northeast into four large subregions and analyzes the evolution of the system of settlement and the production methods from the sixteenth century to the present. This division is indispensable because of the territorial extent of the Northeast (more than 1,500,000 square kilometers), the natural diversity that exists there, and the economic systems that have been established.

These four subregions, in terms of the extent of penetration of the capitalistic modes of production, are at various stages, but the penetration is complementary to the organization and maintenance of a colonial export system, dependent upon external markets and, to a lesser degree, upon the more developed Southeast region of Brazil. Thus, on the coastal strip of the Zona da Mata and Eastern Littoral, the cultivation of sugarcane, coconuts, and cacao predominates. There are found the two principal cities of the Northeast, Salvador and Recife, both sizable industrial centers. In the Agreste, to the west, there is semiintensive cattle raising with improved stock for milk production, as well as the cultivation of cotton and foodstuffs for the urban centers. The third major subregion is the Sertão, with a semiarid climate, where cattle raising, aimed at meat production, and cotton growing predominate. On the banks of the Rio São Francisco large irrigation projects are being developed. Finally, there is the Middle North, a transition zone between the Northeast and Amazonia. Settled since the seventeenth century, but for a long period in stagnation, this area is now being touched by the process of modernization. It is devoted chiefly to rice growing, extensive cattle raising, and exploitation of carnauba wax and babassu nuts.

This study considers the process of settlement in each subregion, the establishment of the systems of land use, the evolution of the labor relationships, from slave labor to the wage labor dominant today, and attempts to schematize the causes of the low standard of living of the people, calling attention to possible solutions.

In the last chapter, I try to show how the agrarian problem has been regarded by intellectuals and by the government, and demonstrate the indecision that exists between the realization of agrarian reform (which would bring, naturally, major modifications to the land-tenure and political power structures of the rural areas) and what has been called agrarian reformulation (which seeks to modernize agriculture, transforming the units of production into economically efficient rural enterprises, while maintaining the existing agrarian structure). Hence the use of examples, such as the analysis of two programs, one developed by the state of Pernambuco, from 1958 to 1961, and another developed by SUDENE (Superintendency for Development of the Northeast) on lands then being settled in western Maranhão. In contrast to these official programs, there were the struggles of the rural workers organized into the Peasant Leagues under the leadership of Francisco Julião, the unions put together by priests like Antônio Melo with a Catholic orientation, and the unions planned by Communists and Socialists of various leanings. Because of the doctrines of each entity, a diversity of orientation arose: there were those who demanded land by division of the latifundia, and those who merely demanded wages and workers' rights.

The Northeast: Region of Contrast

The Concept of the Northeast as a Region

The Northeast is one of the most discussed, but least known, geographic regions of Brazil. According to any given author's point of view, the Northeast is shown: as an area of drought, something that has plagued the region since the colonial period and, in periods of crisis, prompted the attention and financial support of the government; as an area of extensive surgarcane fields that enrich a half-dozen at the expense of the majority of the population; as an area essentially underdeveloped because of the low per-capita income of the inhabitants; or even as a region of libertarian revolutions of which poet Manuel Bandeira speaks in his "Memories of Recife."

Researchers have had great difficulty defining the Northeast. If one analyzes the efforts made to date to divide Brazil into natural regions, one observes that some authors place within the Northeast only the states of Ceará, Rio Grande do Norte, Paraíba, Pernambuco, and Alagoas; others extend the region south to include the state of Sergipe and part of Bahia, generally to the area of the Recôncavo. In 1941, however, the CNG (National Council of Geography), through the efforts of geographer Fábio Macedo Soares Guimarães,[1] produced a classification for administrative purposes and, under that classification, the Northeast was defined as extending from Maranhão to Alagoas.

Despite its official standing, the CNG classification was not totally accepted; even the governmental organizations operating in the region did not adopt it. SUDENE extended its planning area from Maranhão to northern Minas Gerais, whereas the Bank of the Northeast had an area of operation limited to the drought polygon (Fig. 1), excluding Maranhão but including part of Minas Gerais (the São Francisco River basin). Today the Bank of the Northeast also operates in Maranhão. Since 1968 the IBGE (Brazilian Institute of Geography and Statistics) has created a new geographic division of the country and considers the Northeast to include the states of Maranhão, Piauí, Ceará, Rio Grande do Norte, Paraíba, Pernambuco, Alagoas, Sergipe, Bahia, and the territory of Fernando de Noronha.

Environmental Conditions and Regional Diversity

Having an area of 1,542,271 square kilometers, the Brazilian Northeast is characterized by, as is any other geographic region, the influence of a series of factors. Among them, to use the terminology employed by Cholley,[2] the physical features (geologic structure, relief, climate, and hydrography), the biological milieu (flora and fauna), and the spatial organization of man stand out. These factors influence each other and interact to produce the physical and cultural landscapes.

The origin of geographic landscapes being very complex, no one would dare to admit to the *exclusive* influence of a single element in their development; it would be difficult to prove such an influence in a scientific manner. In each region, however, a single element stands out, leading the experienced man who tills the soil to mention it, provided that he wishes to distinguish the various components of the regional mosaic. Thus, in the Amazon, there is constant reference to the river and the water level. In fact, it is "the river that rules life," as emphasized by Leandro Tocantins,[3] and man is always distinguishing the floodplain, which is inundated every year, from the *terra firme*, which is safe from flooding. In São Paulo, where coffee cultivation is the principal source of agricultural wealth, the peasant, technician, and even the scientist are always concerned with soil type; the areas where rich *terra roxa* soils are dominant are distinguished from those where soils derive from sandstone or crystalline rock. There is also a constant preoccupation to

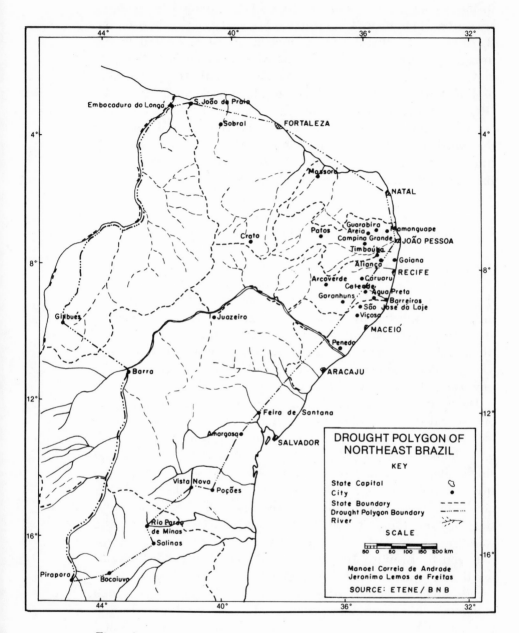

Figure 1.

identify the areas capable of producing coffee well, from those suited for other, less profitable agricultural activities. In the Northeast, the element that most leaves its mark on the landscape and most concerns man is the climate, the pattern of rainfall, and the natural vegetation. Since colonial times, areas within the region have been differentiated: the Zona da Mata, with its hot, humid climate and two well-defined seasons, one rainy the other dry; and the Sertão, also hot but dry, where droughts have periodically destroyed the vegetation, wreaked havoc on the animals, and forced the people to migrate. The climatic diversity has produced a duality recognized by the Northeasterners. In the colonial period this duality produced two diverse systems of agriculture (sugarcane and cattle raising), systems that are more economically complementary than politically and socially compatible.[4] Between one area and the other is a transition zone, with some stretches of land almost as humid as the Zona da Mata and others as dry as the Sertão. This is the Agreste with its small landholdings and mixed farming. The Middle North, still an area of forest gathering and ranching, lies to the far west.

In a study such as this, which tries to synthesize the Northeast, four major areas, both natural and geographic, can be delineated with traditionally recognized names: these are the Zona da Mata, Agreste, Sertão, and Middle North.

The Zona da Mata

The Zona da Mata region and the Eastern Littoral extend from Rio Grande do Norte to southern Bahia, occupying the eastern lands of the Northeast. The Rio Grande do Norte and Paraíba areas are small, being restricted to the lowlands of the rivers that empty into the Atlantic. On the slopes and level interfluves that separate the river basins, the dominant vegetation is similar to the locally called tableland (*tabuleiro*) vegetation.

On the low tablelands, because of higher annual precipitation,[5] uneven distribution of rainfall, and the influence of the geologic structure (Tertiary period clay pits predominate on the interfluves and Holocene epoch alluvial deposits on the lowlands), the coastal forests develop fully only in the alluvial areas, whereas on the interfluves the dominant vegetation is similar to that of the Brazilian Plateau.

When man settled the region he cut down the forest, drained the swampy lowlands, planted sugarcane, and built houses and sugar mills. Cities sprang up on the slopes above the rivers because of the fear that locations near the river would be flooded during high water. Flooding was always swift and violent. Since such rivers primarily run through the semiarid areas of the Agreste and Sertão, they therefore have the irregular regime typical of rivers in the *caatinga* area. This irregularity is manifested by the absence of water in the riverbeds during the summer, and by the overflowing of the banks and the inundation of the floodplains and cane fields during the rainy season.

On the extensive interfluves, the tableland vegetation is still present (since man has concentrated his activities on the lowlands), and settlement is extremely dispersed. Along the roads, with gaps of several kilometers, one finds a peasant house, a field of cotton, or a few head of cattle grazing. These areas were not suitable for cultivation of sugarcane; they were used during the colonial period for extensive cattle raising and, when cotton prices were high, for cultivation of that fiber by those who did not have better land available. Thus one can appropriately speak of "sugar rivers"[6] in Rio Grande do Norte and Paraíba since the canefields and sugar mills are concentrated on the lowlands of the rivers.[7]

In Pernambuco the circumstances are quite different. The Zona da Mata is continuous, covering almost all of the area between the Borborema Plateau and the Atlantic Ocean. The tablelands remain isolated, appearing in parts of the clay formation that extends a short distance from the littoral, between the cities of Goiana and Recife. In the southern part of the state, where the slope of the Borborema Plateau runs in an approximately northeast-southwest direction, the forest growth is lush and covers the slopes to high elevations. Only in the places where the slope is protected from the influence of the trade winds, as in Limoeiro, is the situation reversed: instead of the forest climbing the slopes, it is the *caatinga* of the Agreste that descends the slopes to the plains and foothills of the Borborema Plateau.

The amount of atmospheric moisture and the average annual precipitation diminish as one moves westward toward the interior, but on reaching the edge of the Borborema Plateau they increase once again because of orographic precipitation. This is shown by a comparison of annual precipitation averages of the meteorological stations of Mamanguape (1,854 millimeters), Guarabira (1,042 millimeters), and Areia (1,291 millimeters) in Paraíba, as well as the weather stations at Goiana (1,981 millimeters), Aliança (724 millimeters), and Cruanji (882 millimeters) in northern Pernambuco.[8] In southern Pernambuco, however, rainfall decreases gradually in proportion to distance from the coast, in areas less under the influence of the Borborema Plateau; this can be seen by comparing the statistics of the weather stations at Barreiros (2,464 millimeters), Catende (1,042 millimeters), Água Branca (965 millimeters), and Garanhuns (850 millimeters). Also, precipitation is higher in the southern part of the state, which Bernardes[9] and Guerra[10] classify as having tropical monsoon climates (*Am* and *Amí*, respectively), than in the north, where they classify the climate *Aś* (hot tropical with rains in fall and winter). The climatic difference between the south and the north of the state in the Zona da Mata has perceptibly influenced topography, natural vegetation, hydrography, land use, and socioeconomic evolution. Thus, in the north the lesser amount of rainfall permitted the conservation of large portions of plateau areas eroded during the Tertiary period, which alternate with hills and fluvial valleys, just the opposite of what can be observed in the south. Naturally, climate has influenced vegetation, permitting the evergreen forest, or the "humid forest" as the botanist Vasconcelos Sobrinho[11] prefers to call it, to dominate the south. The trees there are evergreen. At the same time, in the north during the summer (January, February, and March), the forest has a gray color, with many deciduous trees, inducing the same botanist mentioned above to give it the name of "dry forest." The climatic influence makes itself felt even more in the hydrography, since the rivers in the southern part of the state have greater volume and a more regular regime than those of the north. In land use the climate favored sugarcane cultivation, which, from the sixteenth century on, developed more rapidly in the south than in the north of the state. Sugarcane dominated other agricultural enterprises, industrialized more rapidly, used advanced agricultural processes, and resulted in concentration of land ownership as the Pernambucan sugar factory* evolved. For that reason, in previous studies,[12] I have tried to characterize the existence of two geographic subregions within the forests of Pernambuco: dry and humid.

In Alagoas, the conditions found in southern Pernambuco become modified, since the average annual precipitation figures decrease (1,616 millimeters in Maceió, 1,285 millimeters in Viçosa, and 1,247 millimeters at Usina Serra Grande in São José da Laje), and there are tablelands cut by the wide valleys of the Manguaba, Camaragibe, Santo Antônio, Mundaú, Paraíba do Meio, São Miguel, Jiquiá, and Coruripe rivers. These lowlands must always be drained for cultivation. Near the mouth of the river, they are submerged or flooded for a distance of some several kilometers. These fluvial valleys were, at times, authentic estuaries like those in Santo Antônio, or enclosed by sand banks and transformed into lagoons, like those of the Mundaú, Manguaba, and Jiquiá rivers. The wide interfluves eroded and became level, though slightly tilted from west to east, with elevations that vary between 120 and 60 meters above sea level. On these interfluves, where the sandy layer at the surface is thicker, as in Junqueiro, typical sparse tableland vegetation appears. There are small trees with extremely twisted trunks like the cashew, wild cashew, pumpwood, *mangabeira*, and so forth. In other areas, however, where the sandy surface layer is thinner (20–40 centimeters thick), the humid forest develops, the most luxuriant and most important forest on these crystalline-derived soils. Since these humus-poor soils are not suited to extensive sugarcane cultivation, the forests were preserved until very recently. Today, however, with the generalized use of fertilizer and the introduction of hardier varieties of sugarcane, the famous forests of Alagoas are fast being cut down and replaced with sugarcane fields.

The tablelands offer the sugar factories a series of advantages over the slopes and the lowlands. It is not necessary to contour

*Translator's note: The term *engenho* refers specifically to an old-fashioned sugar mill or generally to the entire landholding of which the mill is a part; *usina* refers specifically to a modern sugar factory or generally to the entire landholding of which the factory is a part. Both terms can be translated as "plantation." However, the distinction between the two would be lost. Therefore, *engenho* has been translated as "mill" or "sugar mill" and *usina* as "factory" or "sugar factory." Their meanings in English, as used in this book, have the same connotations as the Portuguese terms. The term "plantation" is used only where the author has used it in the original as a foreign term.

the fields or to drain them; since they are level, mechanization is facilitated; and, since they are closer to the factories, transportation of the cane, chiefly by truck, is cheaper. Other factories have imitated the practice initiated by the Sinimbu factory (*município* of São Miguel de Campos), abandoning the slopes to cattle-raising and to reforestation, in order to concentrate cane fields on the lowlands and tablelands, including Santa Clotilde (*município* of Rio Largo). The movement to cut the forest is intense and sugarcane is cultivated amidst stumps and burned tree trunks, and the cane field framed by as yet uncut forest, a picture of a pioneer landscape in an area settled more than three centuries ago. This practice constitutes an expansion of the sugarcane area, but contributes greatly to the intensified forest removal that has been ruthlessly carried on in the Northeast since the sixteenth century.

To the west of the tablelands is an area of the Zona da Mata marked by soils derived from crystalline rock and drained by the two principal rivers in Alagoas: the Mundaú and the Paraíba do Meio. Located there is the largest concentration of sugar factories in the state, especially the larger ones like the Serra Grande, the Brasileiro (today shut down), and the Central Leão. Cane fields occupy the fluvial valleys, ascending the hills and the slopes of the Borborema Plateau. Intensive erosion and lack of water constitute, in the dry years, serious problems for the sugar factory owners, who must do contour plowing and build dams to store water during the rainy season in order to irrigate the cane fields during the dry season.

Near the mouth of the Rio São Francisco, in areas where there were formerly cattle raising and sugar mills, the sandy surface formed of dunes and sand banks becomes wider and the valleys of the tributaries that discharge into the main river are, at times, entirely flooded, as in Marituba. The lagoons along the largest river of the Northeast, which receive waters from the summer floods, and return them to the river as the water level recedes, are the areas chosen for rice cultivation by the people who live along the river.

In Sergipe the relationship between the sea and the land is even closer. About 20 or 25 kilometers from the mouths of the small rivers that come from the interior—the Sergipe, the Jacarecica, the Vaza Barris, and the Piauí—the old lowlands are flooded by sea water, transforming them into majestic water-courses tens of meters in width. There the mangrove penetrates the continent to the limit reached by salt water. On the extensive sandy areas the famous coconut groves of Sergipe abound. Sugarcane cultivation is concentrated in small areas of calcareous soils, where the cities of Maruim and Laranjeiras are located. Cattle raising, however, which was the determining economic activity in the conquest of Sergipe at the end of the sixteenth century, has today become the dominant economic activity, surpassing sugarcane. Cane fields are gradually being replaced by cultivated pasture, causing serious trouble for the poor rural population. Unemployed, they take refuge in small cities.

To the south is the Recôncavo of Todos os Santos Bay, occupied since the sixteenth century, and famous for its production of sugar and tobacco. It is an area of traditional sugar mills and of old cities rich in historical monuments, like Cachoeira and Santo Amaro. Still farther south are the areas of more humid climates (*Af* type), where there has developed since the eighteenth century, cacao and, more recently, rubber tree cultivation. The extreme south of Bahia is still in the settlement phase, with intensive forest exploitation and active cattle raising. The opening of Highway BR-101, cutting the area from north to south, is increasing tourism and bringing back to life such historic cities as Porto Seguro, Belmonte, and Caravelas, until recently oriented toward the sea.[13]

The Zona da Mata and Eastern Littoral region can be considered the most important in the Northeast. Within it are a major portion of the population (29.8 percent), and the most important industrial parks and plantation agriculture. As seen in Figure 2, however, the region represents only a small portion of the entire Northeast (less than 18.2 percent of the total area), and occupies no more than 128,000 square kilometers.

The Agreste

The Agreste, as previously emphasized, is transitional between the Zona da Mata and the Sertão. Sometimes it is clearly characterized, but on other occasions it can be confused with the Zona da Mata in its more humid stretches, and with the Sertão in its more arid. There are areas in the Agreste, such as the *muni-*

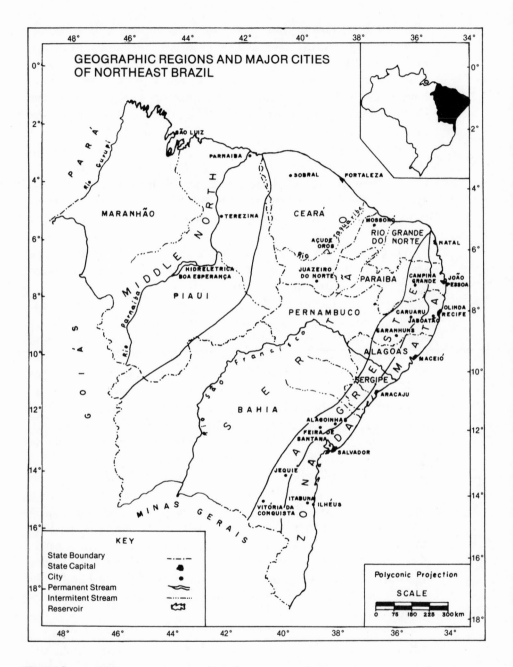

Figure 2.

cípios of Bom Jardim and Orobó in Pernambuco, that originally were covered by the coastal forest. Today they are considered part of the Agreste, more because of human occupance and land use than environmental conditions. In other places, generally of higher elevation and exposed to the moisture-laden winds of the southeast, there are moist areas (*brejos*) that enjoy moisture and rainfall conditions similar to those of the Zona da Mata, though temperatures, because of elevation, are lower. This has brought about the development of a spatial pattern based on agriculture. On the leeward side of these elevations, where the rainfall averages are much lower, *caatinga* is present over wide expanses, but is of lower stature and sparser density than is typical of the Agreste.

What characterizes the Agreste is the diversity of the landscape over short distances; it is almost the Northeast in miniature, with very dry and very humid areas.

The Agreste occupies the eastern portion of the Borborema Plateau, and extends toward the mountains of Rio Grande do Norte and the southern part of Alagoas.[14] The western portion of the Borborema Plateau is part of the Sertão (in Paraíba on the interfluves formed by the Rio Mamanguape and the tributaries of the Rio Curimataú, and in Pernambuco, where the Mimoso Serra separates the drainage basin of the Ipanema from that formed by the tributaries of the Rio Moxotó). The eastern portion of the Borborema Plateau, from Rio Grande do Norte to Alagoas, presents, in the residual massifs (more elevated and exposed to the trade winds), regions that benefit from the remaining moisture in the winds from the southeast—moisture not precipitated out in the Zona da Mata— and presents, in general, a pattern of rainfall that occurs in the fall and winter; that is, predominantly between March and August. In the westernmost portions, such as Pesqueira, São Bento do Una, and Brejo da Madre de Deus, summer rains occur in the months of January and February, brought on by the arrival there of the equatorial continental air mass.

At times, in those stretches where the Borborema Plateau is farther from the coast, or where one of the spurs that runs east-west from the plateau puts a portion of the slope in a sheltered location from the southeast winds, the Agreste descends the plateau and expands over the vast leveled surfaces to its east and northeast. This occurs in Taipu, Rio Grande do Norte; Guarabira, Paraíba; and Limoeiro, Pernambuco. Thus the balance that maintains the transition zone between the Zona da Mata and the Agreste is very unstable. This equilibrium appears to have been broken in the Serra das Russas, toward the end of the last century. The existing forest there was ravaged to meet demands for fuel for the railroad locomotives then being developed, and for charcoal for domestic use in Recife. This caused the *caatinga* to advance toward the city of São João dos Pombos.

In Alagoas, the Agreste surrounds the Borborema Plateau to the south, extending deeply into the interior; one finds only level surfaces, with elevations ranging from 150 to 300 or 400 meters, interrupted by a scattered residual relief. Thus, the winds that move up the valley of the Rio São Francisco and the adjoining nearly level areas, bring moisture as far into the interior as the Mata Grande and Água Branca mountains. Hence the Sertão in Alagoas has popularly been called the "fillet of the Northeast." It is, by and large, much more humid than the Sertão of Pernambuco, Paraíba, Rio Grande do Norte, Ceará, or Bahia, has a smaller semiarid area, and offers, in general, better conditions for agriculture than those of the semiarid areas of the other states of the Northeast.

In Sergipe, one could designate as Agreste the *município* of Itabaiana (the CNG places it in the central zone),[15] those in the Rio São Francisco Valley from Propriá to Aquidamã, and the entire designated western zone. These areas have characteristics similar to the Agreste of Alagoas, Pernambuco, and Paraíba. In the Sergipe Agreste there is too little moisture for sugarcane cultivation, but enough for intensive cultivation of manioc, vegetables, and tobacco (usually only found in the Sertão). In the foothills of the Itabaiana Mountains, in the moist areas of Moita Bonita and Bom Jardim, there is an appreciable division of land, maintained thanks to an agriculture devoted to subsistence and cash crops, carried out intensively by peasants for the food supply of the large cities of the coast, chiefly Aracaju and Salvador.

In Bahia, the Agreste extends north-south, possessing areas traditionally considered Sertão and dry forest. Thus, one can consider part of the Agreste the *municípios* of Alagoinhas and Feira de Santana, devoted to cattle raising and mixed farming, as well as those situated farther south, and at times reaching elevations of 600 meters, such as Jequié, Vitória da Conquista, and Itapetinga. In these latter, where there is cultivated pasture, the raising of high quality beef cattle has developed. The boundary between the Zona da Mata and the Agreste can be traced by a line that separates the raising of cacao from the raising of beef cattle.

The Agreste occupies, therefore, an area equivalent to that occupied by the Zona da Mata. It has a greater number of wet areas *(brejos)*[16] n Paraíba and in Pernambuco. In Paraíba, however, the residual massifs where Areia, Bananeiras, and other cities are located, form a wet area that occupies, in continuous territory, more than 120,000 hectares.[17] In it there are two sugar factories—Santa Maria in the most elevated part, and Tanque in the foothills—with an annual production of more than 520,000 sacks. There are also tens of sugar mills producing brown sugar, and small farms devoted to the production of tobacco, white potatoes, and bananas and other fruits.

In Pernambuco, most of the humid Agreste is found on the Garanhuns Plateau, the highest part of the Borborema, with elevations reaching more than 750 meters. From that area come the principal rivers of Alagoas—the Mundaú, Paraíba do Meio, and Coruripe. Thanks to existing moisture, a tall forest dominated the area in the past,[18] but was cut down toward the end of the last and the early part of the present centuries, and replaced by large coffee fazendas. Until the application of the policy of coffee tree removal, this zone constituted the principal producer of coffee in Pernambuco. But in 1970 this state produced fewer than 15,000 sixty-kilogram sacks.[19] Beside this plateau, the wet areas occupy the crests with elevations above 500 meters, and are located on the interfluves of the basins of the Rio Una and the Rio Ipojuca,[20] the interfluves of the Rio Ipojuca and the Rio Capibaribe, and the crests with elevations above 700 meters, to the north of the cities of Bezerros in the Serra Negra, and Pesqueira in the Serra de Ororobá.[21]

In fact, these wet areas result from two factors operating together: elevation and the exposure to the moisture-laden winds of the southeast. The elevation makes temperature conditions more pleasant, decreases the rate of evaporation, and brings about condensation of the moisture brought in by the wind. Thus the rainfall average by itself does not reveal the degree of moisture which exists in the mountains, where, in winter, during the early hours of the day, until 8:00 or 9:00 A.M., heavy mists limit visibility to a few meters. Also, the humid area is found at points quite a bit lower on the leeward than on the windward side of the wet area.

Besides these wet areas, which in previous studies were called wet areas of elevation and exposure, there exist others, smaller, less important, that are a consequence of them. These are called valley wet areas, ciliary wet areas, and piedmont wet areas.

The first type is found in valleys extending from the crest toward the leveled surface of the Borborema,[22] or from the slope toward the base of that plateau, in a northwest-southeast direction. Because of the direction, these valleys are open to the moist winds of the southeast and in the past a forest developed there that extended to the top of the crest. Today, cleared of forests, these areas are cultivated from the bed of the main stream to the highest point of the crest, being occupied, almost always, by bananas, coffee trees, and in the lower part by vegetables.

When the perennial and nearly perennial streams flow from the mountains, in a direction that is not toward the moist winds, there is formed what is called a ciliary wet area, because formerly a gallery forest would have been there. One can see, therefore, in the midst of the driest and most forbidding *caatinga,* a green ribbon, long and narrow, that follows the small river like a line. This green ribbon is formed by a gallery forest of fruit trees or cane fields that extend down to where moisture is provided by passing small streams, in search of the larger rivers of the Agreste, rivers that remain dry, with only a few wells in their beds seven or eight months of the year.

The piedmont wet areas, toward which the eroded material brought down by the streams is carried, almost always have a mantle of heavier soil, which permits better conservation of the moisture from the rainy season. These can be considered wet areas and are generally used by farmers in the regions of semiarid climate.

Away from the wet areas, where formerly there was forest but today there is agriculture, is the *caatinga. Caatinga* is not a word that describes a uniform vegetation formation, as already demonstrated by the biogeographer Walter Egler in a study done in Pernambuco,[23] but an enormous range of associations, now more, now less dense, some of greater, others of lesser height. In the most favorable zones and where the population density is higher, agriculture predominates. In those zones where the mantle of decomposed rock is thinner and agriculture cannot be developed, cattle raising predominates and the population density is less. It is interesting that, in the semiarid portions, the areas of sandy soils constitute a veritable magnet for population and are densely occupied by cultivators of fruit (in Surubim and Vertentes, Pernambuco); of manioc (in Lajedo and in Jurema, Pernambuco); of tobacco (in Arapiraca, Alagoas, and in Lagarto, Sergipe); and of manioc and vegetables (in Itabaiana, Sergipe).

In that way, the Agreste, formerly colonized by cattle raisers, today is more devoted to agriculture. In contrast to the Zona da Mata, it has mixed farming and generally produces for the internal market. The Zona da Mata is monocultural and chiefly preoccupied with export products—sugar, cacao, and tobacco. It is also distinguished from the Sertão by its greater population density, by the great importance of agriculture, and because cattle raising, though not the dominant economic activity, is carried out more efficiently than in the Sertão, where open grazing of cattle still is dominant and there is no selective breeding or supplementary feeding. The proximity to the large cities of the Northeast has increased the value of land and created outlets for products. And it has made possible the raising of dairy cattle and the fattening of beef cattle (using *palma* cactus).

This area is not entirely subject to the droughts that periodically devastate the Sertão, since its rainfall regime is determined by the same air masses that determine the regime of the Zona da Mata. On the other hand, in the years of the great droughts, 1777, 1845, 1877, 1915, 1932, 1952, and 1958, the Agreste, as well as the Sertão and even the Zona da Mata suffered the effects. Rainfall was below average and the migrants from the Sertão, seeking refuge in areas less affected by a lack of water, provoked serious housing and foodstuff shortages.

In the Agreste, away from the wet areas, the rainfall averages are relatively low, almost always less than 1,000 millimeters per year and concentrated into a few months, March to June, causing serious problems for the cattle raisers. The pits, depressions dug in the soil, and the pools, depressions excavated in the rock with dynamite, dry out, and the rivers stop running, reducing the number of wells and increasing the distance from one to another. For that reason, the fazendeiros try to construct dams, pits, pools, and water holes so that the livestock can remain on the property for most of the summer. The water holes that Athanassof considered unhygienic and responsible for the transmission of epizootic diseases[24] are dug in the beds of the large rivers to reach the water table in the alluvium. As the dry season progresses and the water table drops, the water holes must be deepened. The livestock that come to drink trample down one side, inasmuch as the other side is protected by a fence, and defecate, urinate, and otherwise pollute the water, making it unsuitable to drink.

When water and food are depleted, the remains of mixed crops of cotton, beans, and maize gone, the fazendeiro resorts to migration, driving his animals to the Zona da Mata, if it is nearby and land is available there, or to the mountains and nearby wet areas where the cattle can gain relief from the heat. In such times, the agricultural areas can accept animals coming from the *caatinga*, because the Zona da Mata, in that season, is crushing sugarcane. The skimmings of the boiling sugarcane juice and the bagasse serve as acceptable rations. In the wet areas, the harvest of maize and bean leaf stubble in the fields is used as supplementary food for livestock. In the region of the lower São Francisco (Propriá and Colégio), the livestock is brought to the banks of the rivers, where they feed on the stubble in the rice fields. There is, consequently, a unique association between agriculture and cattle raising, determined by these seasonal migrations.

Lack of water is, undeniably, the most serious problem the population of the Agreste has confronted since the colonial period, although it does not reach the accentuated proportions of the Sertão.

The Sertão

The Sertão and the Northern Littoral is a more extensive area, occupying approximately 49 percent of the Northeast region. The designated drought polygon does not circumscribe only the

Sertão: it is useful to remember that it covers a high percentage of the states of the Northeast. Some of them, such as Ceará, Paraíba, and Rio Grande do Norte, are almost entirely within the polygon (94.8 percent, 97.6 percent, and 92.0 percent respectively) while in Pernambuco the percentage drops to 88.7 percent, and diminishes considerably in Alagoas (43.7 percent), Sergipe (47.1 percent), and Bahia (56.6 percent.).[25]

The Northern Littoral and the Sertão can be combined because on the North Littoral of the Northeast the Sertão reaches almost to the beach. In São Bento do Norte the *facheiro*, a cactus typical of the Sertão, can be found only 50 meters from the sea. And Mossoró, only 50 kilometers from the coast, is considered a city of the Sertão, the inhabitants consider themselves sertanejos, and the landscape of the area is typical of the Sertão.

The idea that the Sertão reaches to the coast is so rooted in the beliefs of the inhabitants of Rio Grande do Norte and Ceará that, referring to Ceará at the end of the last century, Theophilo affirmed that "the part of the interior that is not made up of mountains is called Sertão."[26] The CNG[27] acknowledges the same concept, designating Sertão areas very near the coast, such as the *municípios* of Massapê and Jaguaruana.

In the Sertão and the Northern Littoral, thanks to its vastness, one can find regional diversity expressed not only by natural conditions but by different types of human activity. The coast, for example, forms a narrow strip following the sea; the beach, over all of its extension, is covered by sand dunes that, carried by the wind, move generally westward. This incessant movement of the dunes causes serious problems for the inhabitants of the coastal strip; sand covers saltworks, scattered houses, and even small urban settlements. The dunes make road construction difficult and silt up the river mouths, restricting use of the estuaries as ports for even small boats. Because of low humidity, the tidal fluctuation of 2 to 3 meters between low and high tide, and the low elevation of the coast, salt producers use the lowlands of Açu, Mossoró, and Jaguaribe rivers: they transform these into a succession of dikes and crystallization tanks in which the salt water evaporates and pyramids of salt pile up. As a result, Rio Grande do Norte is the major salt producer of Brazil, accounting for more than 57 percent of the national total, and Ceará is the third highest producer, with 14 percent of Brazil's production.

In Ceará the sandy coastal strip is covered by typical vegetation, with the cashew the most important economic species. It was the cashew[28] that already in the precolonial period provoked migration of Indians during the fruiting season. During the occupation of Recife and Olinda by the Dutch, cashews constituted a genuinely dangerous attraction to the Dutch soldiers suffering from scurvy, because of ambush by the native Pernambucanos.[29] Today in Ceará this fruit supports a flourishing industry of nuts, cashew-apple juice, preserves, and cashew nut shell oil. In Pernambuco, unfortunately, the cashew trees are being systematically destroyed, to provide fuel for bakery ovens and to clear areas held as land speculation for suburban or urban lots. Coconut groves still cover extensive coastal areas of the Northeast.

Another very characteristic area is that represented by the wide valleys of the Sertão rivers. At times these valleys are up to 10 kilometers in width, with depressions transformed into lakes during flooding, and are covered by genuine gallery forests of carnauba palms. Among these, those of the Açu and Mossoró rivers in Rio Grande do Norte and the Jaguaribe and Acaraú rivers in Ceará stand out. Such rivers, some up to 100 meters in width, meander down the middle of the valleys. In the past, the river would be entirely dry most of the year, but today, with the building of large dams on the upper courses, the rivers have become permanent, and even in summer a ribbon of water is always present in the riverbed. Above that level, between 4 and 5 meters, is lowland covered with carnauba palms, with open places occupied by houses or fields of cotton, maize, sorghum, and other subsistence crops. In such areas, property is held in long, narrow lots beginning at the bank of the river and running to the *caatinga;* they are at times only 8 to 10 meters wide, and several kilometers deep. The road across such an area becomes a genuine, almost settled, street.[30] The carnauba palms are able to survive because of the permanent water table in the alluvium; recently, in all these valleys irrigated agriculture has been developed on a large scale. The property owner generally digs a water hole and with wind- or motor-driven pumps, draws up water that flows through canals to the fields. This irrigated cultivation had a sharp increase when, in 1957, loans were made to large and small property owners to purchase motor-driven pumps and to establish irrigated agriculture. Plantings of bananas, fields of cotton, sorghum, and maize, and orchards sprang up. The few old wind-driven pumps are being abandoned, because of their dependence on irregular wind energy and the fact that they irrigated less area. Since 1960 enthusiasm has cooled, especially along the Rio Apodi: technical maintenance of the machinery was not regular; worn parts had to be replaced (and obtained in Recife more than 500 kilometers away); and high prices for parts and fuel excessively burdened the population.

Still it should be emphasized that the dry valleys have been transformed into human anthills if they are compared to the wide areas of the Chapada do Apodi, almost deserted, or with the broad pediplains that exist in the interior of Ceará, Paraíba, Pernambuco, and Bahia.

The Chapada do Apodi extends east-west from the Rio Ceará-Mirim, in Rio Grande do Norte, to the west of Russas in Ceará, interrupted only by the valleys of the rivers Piranhas-Açu, Apodi-Mossoró, and Jaguaribe. Geologically the Chapada do Apodi consists partly of calcareous rock, which affords a subterranean drainage system, formed, certainly, during an era when the region enjoyed a more humid climate.[31] Rainfall on the Chapada surface drains deep into the rock and supports perennial springs in distant locations. Lack of water on the Chapada do Apodi has impeded development; the settlement of people and cattle raising was delayed until the decade 1951–60, when wells were drilled that brought underground waters to the surface. That led to the establishment of cattle ranches and farms to grow cotton, manioc, vegetables, and carnauba palms. Only now has man begun to settle and economically occupy the area.

The extensive pediplains of the Sertão, formed on crystalline rock, occupy, however, the largest areas of the Northeast, interrupted by calcareous high plateaus and crystalline mountains. They include the northern parts of the states of Piauí, Ceará, Rio Grande do Norte, and Paraíba, where they are drained by the Parnaíba, Jaguaribe, Apodi-Mossoró, and Piranhas-Açu, as well as by other rivers of the northern watershed of the Atlantic. In Pernambuco, Alagoas, Sergipe, and Bahia the pediplain has been eroded to the level of the Rio São Francisco; however, it presents a certain uniformity over its entire area. It is cut by intermittent streams that run only a few days each year, after the cloudbursts of summer, and have, in general, wide, shallow beds, separated by gently sloping interfluves. The soils are very thin, at times almost nonexistent, since large rock outcrops occur. In the lower areas, where the smaller-textured rock material is brought down by the freshets, sandy deposits are formed. Riverbeds are generally very sandy. Since the rains are concentrated in the first months of the year, from January to June, and fall chiefly in the form of great cloudbursts, the climate is considered dry. The region is covered by *caatinga* vegetation, whose density and height vary considerably according to local climatic and edaphic conditions. In conformity with the greater or lesser amounts of rainfall, Bernardes[32] and Guerra[33] classified the climate of this area as tropical with rainfall in the summer-fall period *(Aw)* and as dry, hot steppe, with summer rainfall *(BSHw)*. In this region the most favorable areas are surrounded by fences of rock, wattle and daub, sticks, branches, and at times even barbed wire, and planted with manioc, beans, maize, and cotton. Tree cotton, of several varieties, the most important among them being *mocó* and *verdão*, is widely cultivated in almost all of the Sertão and constitutes the typical cash crop of the large, small, and medium properties. Certain areas, such as the Seridó Valley in Paraíba and Rio Grande do Norte, are, despite being very dry, famous for the quality, long staple, *mocó* cotton produced there.

The largest areas of the pediplain are, however, occupied by open grazing of cattle and goats (which do not benefit from selective breeding or supplementary feeding). The animals are able to move long distances in search of water and pasturage during the summer months. A popular and appropriate adage is that "livestock raises man there, instead of man raising livestock." If the summer is extended and there is a shortage of water, and the livestock has nothing to eat in the *caatinga*, cowboys cut tree branches, burn the spines off certain cacti, such as the *mandacaru*, *facheiro*, and *xiquexique*, and also burn the *macambira* bromeliad and feed them to the livestock. It is also customary, when possible, to drive the livestock to the mountains, to the shores of the large reservoirs, to the banks of the Rio São Francisco, or to other places that have water, in order to await the return of the rains in the usual grazing areas.

In barren areas, where the carrying capacity is very low (at times it is necessary to allow between 5 and 10 hectares per head), open grazing is the practice, with little attention given to the livestock or increased production: sanitary measures, more balanced feed, and selective breeding do not occur. The result is that the animals are small, and weigh less when compared to animals coming from other areas with more favorable natural conditions and with more developed livestock-raising systems.

The mountain areas form scattered blocks within the complex of the Sertão. In terms of area, they represent a modest portion of the entire Northeast, but their importance is great because they function as population and agricultural production centers. In Ceará, which is almost entirely dry, there are certain famous mountains, such as Meruoca and Baturité, where there are centers of agricultural production responsible, according to Caio Prado Júnior,[34] for the development of the port cities of Fortaleza, Camocim, and Acaraú, on a dry coast devoid of natural harbors for shipping.

In the western part of Rio Grande do Norte, there is a series of mountains, including the São Miguel, Luís Gomes, Porta Alegre, Martins, and João do Vale, with elevations above 700 meters, that are separated from the Borborema Plateau by a surface eroded by the Rio Piranhas. Because of a slight difference in the rainfall averages in relation to the surrounding areas and lower temperatures because of the elevation, there is a more intense agricultural activity, in spite of the poor soils and serious erosion, the latter a consequence of cultivating slope areas and using outdated cultivation practices.

In Paraíba and Pernambuco there also are mountains of this type, such as Teixeira, and Baixa Verde, where, at an elevation of 1,010 meters, the city of Triunfo is found. These mountains, because of elevation and exposure, have a more humid climate and represent, thanks to the lush green vegetation, a genuine contrast with the pediplain that surrounds them. Agriculture is intensive and varied, permitting a dense population, but provoking, at the same time, an accelerated destruction of the slope soils. In Pernambuco, if one travels from Flores, on the banks of the Rio Pajeú, to Triunfo, at the summit of the Serra da Baixa Verde, one will be impressed not only by the contrast in vegetation, but also by man's rapid exhaustion of the soils of the humid areas. In order to gain a meager return from agriculture, man wastes soil resources that took centuries to form.

In the late months of summer these mountains are almost always used as refuges from the heat for the cattle. During major droughts they represent a point of convergence of the refugees, which causes serious disruptions to the permanent population of the mountains.

The Cariri, occupying the southern portion of Ceará and bordering Pernambuco, is situated at the base of the northern slope of the Chapada do Araripe and represents a tiny island within the dry expanses. Pinheiro[35] looked upon it as "a narrow strip of Sertão, with springs that never go dry." In fact, the moisture of the Cariri is a gift of the Chapada do Araripe, since the rain that falls over it, encountering a relatively flat and permeable surface, filters downward through the permeable sandstone, until it reaches an impermeable layer. A perched water table forms, and because of the slope of the beds, flows in the direction of Ceará, where the water reaches the surface through a series of permanent springs.[36] The volume of these springs is not all the same. Hence the people of the region classify them into three types: *nascentes*, those with abundant water; *olhos d'água*, those of average volume; and *miradouros*, those of small volume.[37]

The existence of more than one hundred springs, in an area containing eleven *municípios* with a combined area of less than 10,000 square kilometers, has produced a series of small perennial streams. And the existence of more productive soils has made the Cariri an island of agriculture in the midst of the *caatinga*. Formerly in this region there was a forest cover, which, after the eighteenth century, was cut down at a rate proportional to increasing settlement and the development of agriculture. Crops adapted to humid regions, such as sugarcane and coffee, were planted, affording an opportunity for the emergence of a cultural landscape that constitutes a genuine contrast to the Sertão. In the area of Barbalha, for example, sugarcane fields were planted beside imposing babassu palm groves, as if there were a meeting between the landscape of eastern Pernambuco and the palm forests of Maranhão.

Finally, in the Sertão complex there is the riverside of the São Francisco. In fact, the great river of the Northeast crosses the driest areas of the Northeast. Along its right bank, in Bahia, is the famous open country of Catarina, known to be one of the driest and most uninhabited, even hostile, areas to man in the Sertão. The dry *caatinga*, sparse in density, develops on sandy and rocky soils, almost devoid of organic matter, and reaches the bank of the river at Petrolândia and at Jatinã. But the Rio São Francisco has a very irregular regime in spite of being the only permanent stream in the area it crosses. Its water level fluctuates considerably between winter (dry season in its middle and upper courses) and summer (rainy season). Hence its discharge varies from only 900 to 1,000 cubic meters per second in winter, to between 10,000 and 12,000 cubic meters per second in summer. During high water, it floods the riverbanks, considerably broadens its bed and covers old fields, fazendas, and even streets and plazas of the riverine cities. Juàzeiro, Bahia, is one of the cities most affected by the floods, and Cabrobó, Pernambuco, had to be relocated to higher ground after the destruction caused by one of the floods early in this century.

In time of flood, the islands and riverbank land are under water, being fertilized by the river, and, as the waters recede, are cleared by the farmers along the river for fields. These fields benefit not only from the humus deposited by the floodwaters, but from the moisture left in the soil. New areas are being discovered and cultivation continues to expand, constituting what is called *vazante* ("riverbed") agriculture. This guarantees the Sertão dweller maize, beans, peanuts, broad beans, for his food supply, and sugarcane to make brown sugar and sugarcane brandy, as well as onions, generally grown as a cash crop for supplying the cities of southern Brazil.

More recently, the use of water wheels, motor-driven pumps, and, since the installation of an electrical generation plant at Paulo Afonso by the CHESF (São Francisco Hydroelectric Company), electric pumps, have permitted the irrigated cultivation of onions, fruits, and other crops, guaranteeing the riverine property owners a reasonable standard of living.

The success of irrigated cultivation of onions in the São Francisco Valley opened new perspectives on agriculture in the region. Private groups using modern techniques in Pernambuco (Santa Maria da Boa Vista, and Floresta) have undertaken the cultivation of table and wine grapes. SUDENE is establishing the notable Bebedouro project, aimed at the cultivation of pasture to improve beef cattle raising. Regional economic groups project the installation in the São Francisco Valley of a sugar factory that would encourage irrigated cultivation of cane and have a capacity to produce 800,000 sacks of sugar per year. The opening of the Salvador-Brasília highway increased the value of land in western Bahia where, with the assistance resulting from the provisions of Articles 34/18,* financed by SUDENE, entrepreneurs from São Paulo and the Northeast are establishing modern cattle fazendas.

The cattlemen customarily drive their livestock to the river for water, the grasses that grow along the banks, and the salt that is left on the surface of low areas along the river after the floods. This practice permits the cattle to escape the effects of drought; and they gain weight, which increases their value when sent to the slaughterhouses in Recife. Thus the riverbanks constitute a narrow and winding strip of exceptional land in an immense territory that offers man little. The great unifying feature of the Sertão, however, is the climate, and chiefly, the problem of the periodic droughts that scourge the Sertão, and are a constant preoccupation of its inhabitants.

All of the Sertão has a hot climate, with average annual temperatures of about 25 degrees Celsius, and with an annual range of less than 5 degrees Celsius, customary in the low latitudes. As for the rainfall regime, the existence of two well-defined seasons can be observed: one rainy, comprising the months of summer and fall; and another, much longer, that is dry and extends over the months corresponding to winter and spring. Thus, the provident sertanejo stores some of the food crop from the rainy season for the months of summer. For supplementary feeding of livestock, he uses the stubble in the maize and cotton fields, as well as the native cacti, *mandacaru*, *facheiro*, and *xiquexique*, and the *macambira* bromeliad. Everything runs smoothly, with a season of plenty and another of hardships, if no drought occurs. The sertanejo is always worried about the possibility of drought; it has been recurring since colonial times, with greater or lesser intensity, but with an impressive periodicity.

The sertanejo worrying about a possible drought is always busy with tests and predictions about the forecast of rains in the

---

*Translator's note: Article 34 of Decree No. 3395 (December 1961) and the amendments introduced by Article 18 of Decree No. 4239 (June 1963); federal legislation regulating SUDENE's administration of investment incentives in the Northeast.

coming year. For these tests the day of Santa Luzia, December 13, is the most important; it is taken as a reference point for the month of January and the year that follows, and the days that follow correspond to the other months: the fourteenth is February, the fifteenth is March, the sixteenth is April, and so on until the twenty-fourth, which corresponds to December. Each day in which it rains corresponds to a month that will have rain, and those without rain correspond to a month that will be dry. Another test consists of placing six lumps of salt, each representing one of the first six months of the year, on a level surface in the open air, on the night of Santa Luzia. In the morning, the lump of salt that is most dissolved represents the month that will have the most rain in the following rainy season. If these tests give negative results, the sertanejo becomes apprehensive and begins to think of the horrors of the drought and of the possible necessity of migration. Also, the perspectives for the coming year are discouraging if in November or December it does not rain in western Piauí. That is because the rainy winter season in Piauí precedes that of the eastern portion of the Northeast.

Also, if no rain falls up to the day of São José, March 19, the sertanejo totally loses hope and, if he is poor, talks of migrating; if he is rich, he tries to stockpile the necessary food to get through the crisis. Even if it rains after March 19, the rainy season will not be of sufficient duration to permit development of the crops that are planted.

The Middle North

The Middle North includes an extensive area of Piauí and Maranhão, where the woody savannas predominate on the interfluvial plateaus, and the palm forests on the lowlands. It has an area of 422,911 square kilometers and is drained by such large rivers as the Parnaíba, the Itapecuru, and the Mearim with its two large tributaries, the Grajaú and the Pindaré. The Middle North forms a type of circular plain, surrounded by a series of interfluvial plateaus from which flow the rivers. Tertiary period geologic formations are dominant there and, consequently, the soils are sandy and very permeable. In Piauí one can find stretches that are drier, areas in which the *caatingas* infiltrate as genuine bolsons in a westerly direction and the main tributaries of the Parnaíba—the Gurgueia, Piauí, and Poti—are intermittent, becoming, during the prolonged dry season, dry valleys with wells at a few points in the riverbed. The Parnaíba, however, despite a great fluctuation in volume of water between the dry and wet seasons, is a permanent stream, revealing in the period of low waters numerous rapids downstream from Teresina. The Boa Esperança dam, in the middle course, forms a large reservoir and contributes to a greater regularization of the river's regime.

In Maranhão, more humid than Piauí, the rivers are perennial (even the Balsas, a tributary of the Parnaíba), though irregular. Large areas remain under water during the rainy season, giving rise to genuine lakes that make communication and the utilization of land for agriculture difficult. The Baixada Maranhense, for example, is entirely flooded during most of the year, forcing the cattle in the area to make long migrations or to be herded onto small pieces of higher ground during high water. The grasslands that exist there are rich in sedges, and are a good deal like the grasslands of Marajó Island and the lower Amazon. In southern Maranhão, with important cities like Imperatriz (experiencing rapid growth after construction of the Belém-Brasília highway), and Carolina, one finds that the vegetation is typical of Brazil's Central-West region, especially the northern portion of Goiás, where the babassu palm forests alternate with woody savannas of various types and density. It is an area of very extensive, open grazing of livestock. The technical patterns of livestock raising are being modified because of the influence of cattle raisers from Minas Gerais and Bahia who have moved north along the Belém-Brasília highway; they have established fazendas on the unoccupied land, thanks to the greater facility with which the meat can be shipped to the consumer markets in Belém and the Southeast region of the country. These factors lead one to consider the Middle North an area of transition between the Northeast and the North and Central-West regions of Brazil.

Guiana Maranhense is part of the Amazon region, drained by the rivers Gurupi and Turiaçu, in Maranhão. It comprises about 91,000 square kilometers and is situated in the northwestern part of the state, where settlement is beginning to expand, destroying the natural forest and provoking, as a consequence, the expansion of the palm forests. Once the natural forest is destroyed, the babassu palm, having a more rapid growth rate than the other trees, completely dominates the secondary forest. The Amazon rainforest is being replaced by a palm forest. The farmers of the Northeast have moved into this region, following the trails and existing roads as they open up. After destruction of the forest by the traditional slash-and-burn method, they cultivate rice as a cash crop and manioc and maize as subsistence crops. The exhaustion of the soil occurs rapidly and the peasant is always moving westward, seeking virgin lands. The rear guard of businessmen and large property owners transform the abandoned land into grasslands for cattle raising.[38] An identical occurrence was recorded by Velho[39] in Pará, in the area of Marabá, now crossed by the Transamazon highway. The destruction of the forest by burning, without the utilization of the hardwoods and essential oils, and the predatory use of soil for agriculture and extensive grazing, without any concern for conservation, constitute serious problems that threaten the entire country. They lead to the destruction of a tremendous natural heritage, created over millennia. The advance of settlement in the Guiana Maranhense is following a form similar to that of the Middle North, to which it is closely linked; to study the economic evolution and the labor relationships of one region is to study them both. Although physically part of the Amazon Basin, the Guiana Maranhense was, until the construction of the new highway that linked Belém to São Luís, so isolated from the Amazon that its settlement was carried out from Maranhão and the Northeast.

Population and Size of Landholdings

Despite embracing less than 19 percent of the area of Brazil, the Northeast contains about 28 percent of the country's population. Despite underdevelopment and the steady migration to the South, Southeast, and Central-West regions, population continues to increase steadily. From 1950 to 1970, the population increased from 17,973,412 to 28,675,081, an increase of almost 60 percent. The national increase was more than 70 percent. By 1980 the population of the Northeast should reach 36,000,000.

This population is unequally distributed among the four geographic regions into which the Northeast is customarily divided. The Sertão and the Northern Littoral, which occupies half of the area of the Northeast, includes within its wide expanses little more than 35.6 percent of the population (10,057,911 inhabitants); in the Agreste about 18.7 percent of the population of the Northeast (5,273,637 inhabitants) is found; in the Zona da Mata and the Eastern Littoral, which makes up 18 percent of the land mass of the Northeast, about 29.8 percent of the population (8,418,094 inhabitants) lives. The Middle North and the Guiana Maranhense, occupying nearly a fourth of the Northeast, includes about 16.9 percent of its population (4,383,323 inhabitants).

If one excludes the region of the Zona da Mata and the Eastern Littoral, where the urban population is greater than the rural, the other regions have the majority of their population in rural areas. This population is dedicated to agricultural activities: agriculture, livestock raising, and forest extraction. This is well illustrated in Table 1.

TABLE 1
Rural and Urban Population by Regions of the Northeast, 1970

Region	Rural Population	Percent of Total	Urban Population	Percent of Total
Middle North and Guiana Maranhense	3,220,813	71.8	1,162,510	28.2
Sertão and Northern Littoral	6,422,775	63.8	3,635,096	36.2
Agreste	3,320,338	62.9	1,943,298	37.1
Zona da Mata and Eastern Littoral	3,321,654	39.4	5,117,440	60.6

Source: Anuário Estatístico do Brasil, 1970.

The various state capitals of the Zona da Mata and the Eastern Littoral all have populations of more than two hundred thousand. Among them, Recife and Salvador stand out, with a combined population in the urbanized areas of more than three million inhabitants: that is, more than a third of the regional total. The Sertão and Northern Littoral has an urban population percentage that is relatively low (36.2 percent) in spite of the presence of Fortaleza, which, with nine hundred thousand inhabitants (in the urban area), is the third largest city of the

Northeast. The percentage of urban population in the Agreste is low (37.1 percent) because, in that region, only one city, Campina Grande, exceeds one hundred fifty thousand inhabitants. In the Northeast in general, the rural population is considerably greater than the urban population, making up more than 57.9 percent of the total. To understand the solutions to the problems of the Northeast, one must study labor relationships and, consequently, the standard of living of the great numbers of people that live in the rural areas.

It is important to differentiate the economic levels within the rural population. Beside a large mass of rural wage laborers, there is a small group of large and medium property owners with a high standard of living. Between the two groups there is an appreciable percentage of small property owners, who, in conformity with the location and quality of the lands they possess, now have a reasonable standard of living, similar to the foreign colonists in the South and Southeast regions of Brazil. Some toil on land under very precarious conditions; some work as wage laborers on the large and medium holdings nearby and have a standard of living identical or similar to the workers without land. They form, many times, the great peasant mass of the Northeast who, finding in the countryside economic conditions that are genuinely repulsive, migrate to the South (northern Paraná), to the Southeast (Rio de Janeiro and São Paulo), to the Middle North (Maranhão), and to the center of the country (Brasília), seeking better living conditions and work. Likewise, there are those who moved to the cities of the Northeast for the same reasons. They ended up in the state capitals, where they established themselves in shantytowns.[40] These constitute great masses of beggars and underemployed people who live by sporadic odd jobs, who roam and congest the streets and bridges of the large cities of the Northeast. Migration accounts for the spontaneous growth of the population of the northeastern cities between 1940 and 1960, and caused sociologist Gilberto Freyre to refer to Recife as a "swollen city." In truth, the considerable increase of population, without a corresponding increase in possibilities for employment, is much more a swelling than an orderly growth.

I believe one of the causes that most aggravates the problem is the system of land tenure, dominant since colonization. It tends to contribute to the concentration of property and the lack of guarantees, of written and respected contracts, that would give greater stability to the sharecroppers in the Agreste and the Sertão and to the agricultural workers in the Zona da Mata. In reality, those who cultivate, on their own, lands belonging to someone else, regularly pay rent to the owner, but find themselves without guarantees against the interests and, at times, the dominance of the owner. Legislation is inadequate and without authority, and the difference between the economic and political power of the renter and the middle or large landowner is enormous.

On analyzing the data from the agricultural census, one observes the smaller number of landholdings in relation to the number of rural families. It is to be remembered that an establishment is only a producing unit and not a property. Frequently a property possesses more than one establishment. In the Zona da Mata and along the coast the sugar factories possess tens of sugar mills. Also in the Sertão the existence of property owners with numerous fazendas and small farms is common. One can observe, moreover, the existence of properties belonging to, because of inheritance or purchase, professionals, businessmen, and industrialists, based in the cities. This acquisition of land by city dwellers has been intensifying in recent years because of the credit opportunities they are given, opportunities the small- or medium-sized property owner has difficulty obtaining, and to the land speculation that exists as a consequence of insecurity in times of inflation.

It is desirable to make a classification of property into large, medium, and small holdings, but it would not further the purpose of this study. Every time one tries to fit natural and socioeconomic factors into such a scheme difficulties ensue. In accord with Pierre George,[41] the great teacher of French geography, the criterion for the classification of landholdings into large, medium, and small varies considerably from one area to another, as a function of the quality of the land, natural conditions, geographic situation, population density, socioeconomic development, transportation facilities, agricultural and livestock systems, and so on. Thus a property of 100 hectares in the wet area of the Agreste is considered large because it is surrounded by numerous others smaller than 10 hectares and because it supports the owner at a middle-class economic level. In the *caatinga* of the Sertão, however, it would be considered small, having scanty agricultural resources and not being able to sustain more than eight to ten cattle. In the Zona da Mata and the Eastern Littoral, despite a property of this size being able to provide a middle-class standard of living to its owner, it is considered medium or small, in conformity with the greater or lesser area of sugar mills around it. There is a perceptible contrast among the standards of living of such a property owner, the sugar mill owner, and the supplier of sugarcane of the region, not to mention the sugar factory owners, who still represent the most prestigious industrialists in the Northeast.

The concentration of landholdings in the Northeast is a consequence of the essentially commercial character of agriculture there.[42] This character has manifested itself since the start of colonization. Even today, despite the perceptible growth of the middle class and the internal markets (consequences of industrialization), it is predominant. Its control manifests itself in the protection bestowed by the government agencies on the large farms, and in the complete disdain for subsistence farming, or "poor farming," as it is frequently called in the Northeast.[43] The first group has easy access to credit, minimum price guarantees, assistance from the experiment stations, organized commercialization, and so on. The second group is abandoned by commercial credit sources to the tremendous price fluctuations between the harvest and the off-season and the greediness of the middlemen. Hence the constant growth of large-scale agriculture and, consequently, of the large property owners, and the stagnation, perhaps even the decline, of small-scale farming, linked to small properties.

To understand the land tenure problem of the Northeast it is interesting to consider the properties large, medium, or small in accordance with the greater or lesser capacity to absorb manual labor and, consequently, the income generated. These criteria were established by CIDA (Inter-American Committee for Agricultural Development) in its studies of Latin America.

Analyzing the data from the censuses of 1950 and 1960, Figueroa,[44] a technician of the Food and Agricultural Organization of the United Nations, working jointly with SUDENE, organized the information shown in Table 2.

TABLE 2
Evolution of the Concentration of Land in the Northeast, 1950–1960

| | 1950 | | 1960 | |
Category	Families (%)	Area (%)	Families (%)	Area (%)
Large multi-family	1.0	50.6	1.0	42.0
Medium multi-family	9.5	41.9	10.7	47.0
Family	7.1	5.0	9.1	8.0
Sub-family	18.1	2.5	30.4	3.0
Sharecroppers	9.1	—	5.4	—
Laborers	55.2	—	43.4	—
TOTAL	100.0	100.0	100.0	100.0

Source: Manuel Figueiroa, *Cuestones de Política Agrícola Regional no Nordeste,* MINTER/SUDENE, Recife, 1972.

An analysis of Table 2 indicates, at first glance, a very high proportion of workers without land: wage laborers and share-croppers, 64.3 percent in 1950, dropping to 48.8 percent in 1960. Meanwhile, the subfamily holdings, minifundia, 18.1 percent in 1950, increasing to 30.4 percent in 1960, did not have a corresponding increase in area (from 2.5 to 3.0 percent), which indicates that the available lands, insufficient for almost a third of the rural agricultural families became, in a decade, almost twice as small. The family farms, that is, those that have conditions to employ four members of the owner-family for the entire year, became more numerous—from 7.1 to 9.1 percent—and had their area reasonably increased—5.0 to 8.0 percent. The average-sized, multifamily farms that corresponded to 9.5 percent in 1950, became 10.7 percent in 1960, and had their area increased from 41.9 to 47.0 percent. In this category CIDA classified those farms that employed from five to twelve workers during the entire year.[45] Finally, the large multifamily enterprises, that is, those that employ more than twelve workers during the entire year, corresponded to 1.0 percent in the two censuses and controlled, respectively, 50.6 percent of the area in 1950 and 42.0 percent in 1960. This indicates a reduction in the area occupied by the largest establishments, though they still controlled the largest portion of the available land.

If one analyzes the cadastral survey of rural property in the Northeast, done by INCRA in 1972, one sees that the concentration of landholdings in the Northeast continues to be very high (Table 3).

TABLE 3
Distribution of Rural Property in the Northeast, 1972

Size of Holdings in Hectares	Number of Holdings	Total Area in Hectares
1-10	363,376	1,573,150
10-100	478,644	16,593,655
100-500	129,319	26,042,087
500-2,000	23,291	20,268,430
2,000-10,000	3,617	12,911,352
10,000-100,000	286	5,982,468
More than 100,000	15	2,659,135

Source: Instituto Nacional de Colonização e Reforma Agrária

An analysis of Table 3 shows the great concentration of hold-ings, since the owners that have more than 2,000 hectares repre-sent only 0.39 percent of the total population but occupy 25.05 percent of the land. Owners with fewer than 10 hectares corres-pond to 36.39 percent of the total, but own only 1.83 percent of the land. The holdings that can be considered medium, between 100 and 500 hectares, make up to 12.95 percent of the total population, but occupy 30.27 percent of the land. The large properties, from 500 to 2,000 hectares, correspond to only 2.33 percent of the total holdings but occupy about 23.56 percent of the total area. Thus if one considers large all holdings with more than 500 hectares, one finds that they make up about 2.72 per-cent of the total population and occupy about 48.61 percent of the land. This concentration of land is the major reason for the poverty dominant in the rural environment and, consequently, for the underdevelopment of the region.

In times of economic boom, with the rise in demand for a major crop or when an agricultural or agroindustrial enterprise is linked to the large economic groups, there is a constant expan-sion of the large establishments. Thus, in the sugarcane area, during the first half of the twentieth century, the consolidation of the old sugar mills (which had been maintained as individual production units since the sixteenth century) around the small- and medium-sized sugar factories took place. In the same period, the larger factories, tired of assimilating mills, also began to absorb smaller factories. Anyone traveling through the sugar-cane area frequently sees ruins of small factories that have dis-appeared, absorbed by others. The factory owner, with more the mentality of a landowner than an industrialist, always considers a symbol of progress and prosperity in his business, the acquisition of additional adjoining land. Thus, valleys and *municípios* formerly belonging to many owners are today the property of only one.

The concentration of land ownership is each time greater; the constant increase of profits, credit facilities, and the use of capital coming from other economic activities also permits the formation of economic groups that control various sugar factories. Thus the Ribeiro Coutinho group controls five of the eight factories in Paraíba and three of the four in Rio Grande do Norte.[46] At the same time, the Costa Azevedo group, owners of the Catende factory (the largest in the Northeast) acquired and remodeled the small Piranji factory, and today have the capacity to produce more than a million sacks of sugar per year. A group, headed by then Deputy Dias Lins, was dedicated initially to the textile industry and insurance, then entered into sugar production, acquiring in one year two factories of large capacity, União e Indústria in Pernambuco and Serra Grande in Alagoas. More sensational was the Bezerra de Melo group's entry into and development of the agroindustry of sugar. Having its economic base in the textile industry and in hotels, the group initially acquired the Rio Una in Barreiros, and tried to develop the agricultural and industrial practices in order to increase the income of the business. With more of an industrialist's mentality than a landowner's, they gave prestige to the work of the technicians, forming a team that functioned with notable cooperation. The owners prospered in such a way that, in less than twenty-five years, the Bezerra de Melo group acquired in addition the factories of Santo André and Central Barreiros, in Pernambuco, and Santana in Alagoas. They became, in that manner, the largest sugar producer in the Northeast. They have available, therefore, thousands of hectares of land in the *municípios* of Rio Formoso, Água Preta, and Barreiros in Pernambuco, and Jacuípe, Jundiá, Porto Calvo and Maragogi in Alagoas.

The development of heavy metal industries in the Southeast region of Brazil and, afterwards, in the Northeast itself, permitted in the decade 1961–70 the reequipment and expansion of the industrial capacity of the factories. The expansion of cultivated area that followed the reequipment stimulated extraordinary growth. Small factories like Triunfo and Coruripe have multiplied several times their production of ten years ago. With the pattern of mergers and transfer of factories, came a new spatial organization in the sugarcane area. New factories are located in areas more topographically and climatically favorable to sugarcane, while traditional sugarcane areas, confronted by the program put into practice by PROTERRA, could be restructured and transformed into areas of food production.

3

Land Tenure and Labor
in the Zona da Mata and Eastern Littoral

Portuguese Colonization and the Problem of Labor

The coast of the Northeast was, undeniably, the first part of
the extensive Brazilian littoral to be explored. Large ships from
Europe, on their way to the Terra de Santa Cruz, passed by the
Northeast and found, behind the reefs and up the estuaries for 1
or 2 kilometers, shelter from both the forces of nature and
enemies. Here also was Brazilwood, widely used in Europe by
the dye industry.

Even before colonization, from the time of Martim Afonso's
voyage (1530), there were trading posts in Pernambuco, en-
trepôts where valuable native products were traded for trinkets
and sent back to the respective metropolises. If a caravel transporting the products did not encounter enemies en route, the
venture guaranteed great economic success. In these trading
posts the Portuguese got accustomed to indigenous foods, indigenous clothing, and, probably, indigenous women, since it was
difficult for European women (even those disposed to cross the
Atlantic) to live in America in the uncertain early years of the
conquest.

Among the trading posts founded on the Northeast coast, certainly temporary in character,[1] Itamaracá stands out. According
to Varnhagen,[2] sugar was sent from there to Portugal in 1526;
and in the same year, Diogo Leite brought ten slaves to it for

agricultural labor.[3] Luís Ramirez, who visited the place, said thirteen Europeans lived there, and that they had adopted certain indigenous foods, for they had fields of manioc and maize, and raised some parrots. The only European animals they had were chickens.[4]

It was with Duarte Coelho, who arrived in 1535, however, that genuine colonization was initiated. A man of mettle with admirable common sense, and an equally admirable grant of land from the King (it extended from the mouth of the Rio Santa Cruz, on the north, to the mouth of the Rio São Francisco, on the south), he moved in with his wife, brother-in-law, relatives, friends, and companions who desired to seek their fortune in America.

He had numerous tribulations to contend with; he was to grant land to Christians and enslave Indians for labor. He was permitted to export annually to Portugal twenty-four Indian slaves.[5]

Arriving in Pernambuco, Duarte Coelho tried to conquer the land of the Indians; in fifteen years he founded two towns— Igaraçu and Olinda—and five sugar mills, one of them his own. He had an arduous struggle. The Tabajara and Caetés Indians, incited at times by the French, constantly waged war against the donee. Chronicler Rocha Pita[6] said that land awarded by leagues was conquered foot-by-foot. One of the donees, in a letter to the King, complained that he was "worn out, poor, and in debt."[7]

Not being enraptured by the ambition to discover gold or silver, or to be involved in the business of the Brazilwood monopoly of the Crown, Duarte Coelho sought his fortune through the cultivation of sugarcane since that product was in high demand on European markets. The hot climate, with a dry season and a rainy season, predominant in his captaincy, and the heavy clay soils considerably favored this agricultural activity. He tried to take possession of the fertile humid lowlands. He sought to grant land to the people who had accompanied him, to enslave the Indians, and to obtain from the King the credit necessary for the installation of sugar mills and the cultivation of sugarcane.

In fact, during a period of twenty years, he conquered little land around Igaraçu and Olinda and, when he died in 1554, the Caetés still constituted a serious obstacle to the colonization efforts of the Portuguese.

It fell to Jerônimo de Albuquerque, the donee's brother-in-law, to conquer the lowlands of the Capibaribe, considerably increasing the area favorable to sugarcane. And in the 1570s the sons of the donee, Jorge and Duarte de Albuquerque Coelho, conquered the lowlands of the Jaboatão, Pirapama, Ipojuca, Serinhaém, Una, and Manguaba rivers, extending European settlement almost to the mouth of the Rio São Francisco. This southward expansion was the result of the colonizers' inspiration and the need for land and workers for cane fields.

This onslaught through Indian territory was energetically carried out. The lands were taken and the people imprisoned as slaves, their settlements and defenses were destroyed, and the food found was consumed. New crops were planted,[8] often in the same planting mounds in the fields cleared by the Indians.

Having obtained a great expanse of territory, the donee was able to give his companions large parcels of land in forest areas considered favorable to cultivation. These lands were crossed by perennial rivers and streams, and located near the navigable stretches of the rivers that discharge into the Atlantic, permitting shipment of the sugar to Olinda or directly to Portugal. In fact, until the construction of railroads in the last century, the estuaries of the small rivers had a decisive influence on the settlement of the Northeast. Before railroads, cities located some distance from the sea on the estuaries were shipping points for the products of the interior. Thus developed in the last century Mamanguape, Paraíba; Goiana and Rio Formoso, Pernambuco; Porto Calvo and Coruripe, Alagoas; and Maruim and São Cristóvão, Sergipe.

The proximity of a port reduced the transportation costs, not only of sugar, but also of the machinery and tools necessary for the sugar mills. The rivers and streams, numerous but not deep, furnished water for human use, irrigated the cane fields along their banks, and, at times, powered the mills. The forest furnished game, in earliest times, when the number of cattle was insufficient, and provided firewood for the furnaces, and wood for construction of housing and making sugar boxes. Natural conditions favored the development of a civilization that was eminently agrarian, the kind Duarte Coelho and his successors began in Pernambuco.

But the possession of land given in extensive latifundia, at times tens of leagues in extent, was not everything. It was necessary to cut down the forest, to establish the sugar mills, the big house, the slave quarters, and to plant sugarcane and subsistence crops. The landholders needed animals, cattle, and horses imported from Europe, and slaves. The capturing of Indians became, then, a profitable activity looked upon very favorably by the second donee, Duarte de Albuquerque Coelho.

During this donee's administration (1554–78), after the routing of the Indians of Serihaém, the natives became very despondent. Europeans, eager for slaves, ascended the rivers to imprison them, bringing them to the littoral almost without resistance. There they were sold at the price of sheep, 1$000 *mil-réis* per head, according to chronicler Frei Vicente do Salvador.[9]

It was during this period that former Jesuit Antônio de Gouveia became famous. Knowing magic tricks, he went to the interior with some companions and convinced the Indians of his power. He then brought them to Olinda to sell them to property owners always eager for slaves. That resulted in, for the adventurous padre, not only great profit, but the epithet of the Padre of Gold. He was also called to Portugal to respond to charges before the Inquisition[10] despite the fact that these Caetés Indians had been condemned to slavery for devouring Bishop Pero Fernandes Sardinha in 1555.

During this heroic phase of the conquest, each property owner "was required to maintain four regiments of muskets, twenty swords, ten lances and twenty armored doublets or jerkins, besides maintaining a vault; each tenant, for his part, must possess a weapon: lance, musket or sword,"[11] in order to resist any attack by the Indians. From this time, or inspired by it, came the truly fortified big houses that existed in Pernambuco, the structure at Megaípe being a fine example.

The Indians were remote from the littoral. And the importation of African slaves, probably carried on since the administration of the first Duarte Coelho, was costly. So the colonists tried to send raiding parties up the Rio São Francisco to bring slaves from the Sertão. This route freed the raiders from having to enter the forest or climb the Borborema Plateau, where the Indians would have the advantage in fights with the Europeans.

The raids along the São Francisco failed completely. Purveyor Francisco de Caldas, and his helper Gaspar Dias de Taíde, were defeated by Indians, who ate them. In 1578 Captain Francisco Barbosa da Silva headed a raid, but the raiding party returned to Olinda, tired and lame.[12] As a result of these raids, the Tabajara Indians allied with the Potiguares of Paraíba and began to attack the weakened captaincy of Itamaracá. The Luso-Brazilians in turn conquered the regions to the north of Nova Lusitânia. Those from Olinda conquered Paraíba, Rio Grande do Norte, and Ceará, and drove the French out of Maranhão, all in the short period of thirty-five years, between 1580 and 1616.

Sugarcane accompanied the conquerors from Olinda, and the sugar valleys of Paraíba do Norte, Paraíba, and Cunhaú, where Jerônimo de Albuquerque founded the sugar mill of the same name in Rio Grande do Norte, sprang up.

In the places where climatic and edaphic conditions did not permit sugarcane cultivation, for example, on the coastal table-lands that north of Olinda extend to Rio Grande do Norte or the *caatingas* located to the east and north of the Borborema Plateau, the landowners established corrals and raised cattle necessary to supply food and animal labor to the sugarcane area of Olinda.

The number of sugar mills increased steadily; there were five in 1550,[13] thirty in 1570,[14] sixty-six in 1584,[15] and 144 on the occasion of the Dutch conquest[16] of Pernambuco. In addition, there were nineteen in the captaincy of Paraíba and two in Rio Grande do Norte, making a grand total for the Northeast of 165.

It stands to reason that the constant increase in the number of sugar mills required a corresponding increase in the number of workers, of slaves. Population growth made necessary the cultivation of food crops. Since the administration of Duarte Coelho, food had been raised, obviously. But, addressing himself to the King in 1550, Duarte Coelho said that among the inhabitants of his captaincy, the rich set up sugar mills, others planted cane and crushed their cane in the mills of the rich, and others, even poorer, planted cotton and food crops, "the principal and most necessary item for the land."[17]

During the first century of colonization, beside sugarcane, New World products that the Europeans became accustomed to cultivating included cotton, bitter manioc, sweet manioc, maize, various types of broad beans, and vegetables. Plants introduced by the Portuguese, who sailed over the entire world and brought them from Europe, Asia, Africa, and Oceania,[18] included rice, various fruits, some vegetables, and coconuts.

But the principal problem, the most serious, was manual labor; workers were necessary not only for the cultivation of sugarcane—planting, weeding, and harvesting—but also for the making and transporting of the sugar, the cultivation of food crops, and housework. Indians did not satisfy the manual labor requirements; initially they were few in number, and wars and migration to the interior seriously diminished their numbers. Besides, their cultural development had not yet reached the phase of sedentary agriculture; in the epoch of discovery they still subsisted, chiefly, on food from gathering, hunting, and fishing. Even more, knowing the region well, they could easily run away to the forest, where they lived on available food, and knew the dangers and how to avoid them. In favor of the natives— although its application was always ridiculed—was a series of laws regulating those instances in which the Indians could be enslaved. Enslavement, however, would only finally be prohibited by a law dated October 27, 1831.[19]

For these reasons, African slaves were imported to Brazil from the earliest times. Negro and Indian slavery coexisted from the initiation of colonization. In 1542, Duarte Coelho himself asked the King for authorization to import Negroes from Africa. During the following years, Negroes were brought to the Northeast and, in 1559, Queen Catarina herself directed the governor of the Island of São Tomé to permit the departure, for each sugar mill owner in Brazil that presented a certificate from the governor general, of 120 Negroes from the Congo, paying only a third of the fees that were charged.[20] Thus, despite high prices, African slaves were imported to Pernambuco, when the Portuguese still occupied small areas of the captaincy. The expansion to the south, bringing about unrestrained hunting of Indians, did not dispense with the importation of Negroes from Guinea. In Olinda in 1584, Fernão Cardim affirmed that there were large numbers of slaves from Guinea and only a few local Indians.[21] Actually, the Negro, coming from an agrarian civilization and already accustomed to the servile regime in Africa, offered more productive work than the Indian. Thus the landowners preferred Negro slaves over Indians. Two facts, however, made the great investment of capital in African slaves perilous: a very high mortality rate among them because of the poor living conditions of the slave quarters, poor diet, excessive work, and acclimatization; and a high percentage of escapes to the interior, where they united in *quilombos* ("runaway slave settlements"), sufficiently numerous and common in all of Brazil. The Palmares *quilombo*, because of its long duration and the area of influence it embraced, succeeded in breaking the "curtain of silence" that historians spread over the Negro resistance against slavery in Brazil. These Negro revolts, however, in the beginning of the seventeenth century alarmed Governor Diogo de Botelho, who sent military forces to combat them. Diogo de Meneses e Siqueira, governor general, was very concerned about the agriculture in the Northeast. In letters to the King,[22] he wrote that he felt the great number of slaves from Guinea, because of their high price and the risks that resulted from their maintenance, was the cause of ruin of many sugar-mill owners. He became an advocate of Indian slavery.

The mortality and the *quilombos*, however, did not restrain the landowners from continuing to import Negroes from Africa. In the beginning of the seventeenth century, Brandônio would say to Alvino in their dialogues: "In Brazil a new Guinea has been created, with so great a multitude of slaves coming from there that one feels they are there; so much that in some captaincies, there are more Negroes than local Indians, and all of the men who live there have put almost all their property in the same merchandise."[23]

But the production of sugar was not only an agricultural activity; it called for a certain technical level that neither Negroes nor Indians possessed. Thus, Duarte Coelho had already in the earliest times the foresight to import technicians from Europe, almost always Jews.[24] These people, who never dedicated themselves to agriculture, but demonstrated industrial inclinations, took advantage of the occasion to leave the Old World exactly when pressure was exerted by the Inquisition against the Jewish people. So large were the numbers of Jews, and such their importance in Pernambuco toward the end of the sixteenth century, that the captaincy of Duarte Coelho received a visitation from the Holy Office of the Inquisition. The representative lingered in Olinda, trying to punish the "new Christians" who actually retained their faith and Jewish religious practices. Certainly these technicians imported by the first donee were the first sugarmasters, boiler-room workers, sugar purgers, stokers, and box-makers of the colonial mills. They and the small farmers would eventually constitute the central nucleus of a rural middle class. That class, small in number and dominated by the aristocracy of sugar, maintained itself until the almost total proletarization imposed in recent years by the concentration of land and the resultant appearance of the large sugar factory.

The Dutch in Brazil and the Practice of Slavery

The Dutch conquest of Pernambuco and other captaincies of the Northeast was a more diverse undertaking than that of the Portuguese: it represented a different sort of adaptive experience by Europeans to the tropics. All of the Dutch were, chiefly, merchants, coming face to face with the Northeast region and arriving with a craving to expand their business. The Portuguese, however, had confronted an unfamiliar, wild land inhabited by Indians believed to be still in the Stone Age. Profits had to be wrested from the indigenous land and people and transformed for an external market eager for tropical products. Products therefore went through a constant increase in valorization. The Dutch arrived knowing the land and the possibilities for profit. They also saw the great possibilities of placing sugar on the European market. Hence modern historians[25] feel that it was the sugar trade and its potential profits that were the principal cause for the Dutch choice of Pernambuco for the beginning of the conquest of Brazil. (The Dutch had failed in this effort in Bahia in 1624.) They conquered a colony that was economically organized in terms of sugar production, aimed at supplying the external market, had available a sizable white population, possessors of large landholdings on which, utilizing slave labor, a plantation monoculture had developed. Thus, as Freyre explains in a series of books in which he interpreted the social formation of the Northeast,[26] the Portuguese colony that the Dutch conquered had its economy based on a trilogy: latifundium, monoculture, and slavery. From that came the permanent relationship with Africa, which furnished the labor necessary for agriculture, and with Europe, to which were exported sugar and

Brazilwood and from which were imported foods such as wheat flour, cheese, butter, and wine, and clothing, shoes, adornments, and so forth.

The intention of the Dutch was not to destroy this just consolidated civilization, but to take from the Portuguese the position, profits, and privileges that they enjoyed. Defeating the Portuguese, they made modifications in the overall structure of the colony, but maintained intact the most profitable economic institutions of the time. Thus great numbers of Dutch became sugar mill owners, sugarcane farmers, and even owners of corrals shortly after the conquest.[27]

Pernambuco and the neighboring captaincies, which were economically and socially dependent upon it, were in a full phase of development when, in 1630, the Dutch began the invasion. According to Verdonk, who acted as a spy,[28] Olinda was the great center of the colony. It had almost 10,000 inhabitants, among them almost 4,000 slaves, and it was also the point of convergence of the sugar trade, since the port of Recife, then a mere settlement,[29] was 6 kilometers away. The sugarcane areas par excellence, with the richest and most famous sugar mills, were on the lowlands of the nearby Capibaribe. There were thirteen or fourteen mills; following it was the region of Cabo de Santo Agostinho, which had sixteen sugar mills. The lowlands of Ipojuca, and Serinhaém, in Pernambuco; Goiana, in the captaincy of Itamaracá; and Paraíba do Norte, in the captaincy of the same name had ten mills each dedicated entirely to the cultivation of sugarcane. Few cattle were raised and subsistence crops cultivated in terms of self-sufficiency.

Zones of cattle raising and food crops aimed at supplying the captaincy itself with beans, manioc, maize, rice, tobacco, and fruit, included the basin of the Rio Una and the present-day territory of Alagoas; among them were a few sugar mills. Porto Calvo, for example, in spite of the sugar mills established by Cristóvão Lins,[30] was more a zone of livestock raising than of agriculture. Livestock raising grew in importance proportionally to the movement southward; that activity was almost exclusively carried on in the zone of the São Francisco and the territory of Sergipe. It is fitting to remember that in the northern part of Bahia, the Dias d'Ávila family established, and initiated during the administration of Tomé de Sousa a veritable dynasty of cattle raising. As a function of this economic activity, the conquest of wide areas of the Sertão was realized, and the family became the most famous and powerful latifundia owners of colonial and imperial Brazil. The famous Casa da Torre, constituted, undeniably, a symbol of livestock raising latifundium in Brazil.[31] It stands to reason that the penetration and peopling of the interior was limited during the first century of colonization; the cattle raisers would have to occupy the deforested areas of the basin of the Una River, great expanses of the existing tablelands in Alagoas, and the grasslands of Sergipe and Bahia.

To the north of Olinda was Igaraçu, a poor village with a few sugar mills and a small sugar production since it was surrounded by tablelands with sandy infertile soils and by extensive mangrove swamps. To the north of Paraíba there was only one mill in Camaratuba, in Cunhaú, and in Potengi, Rio Grande do Norte. In this area livestock raising, fishing, and the cultivation of food crops dominated the economy, supporting a population never more than a few kilometers from the coastline.

Thus, one can see that sugarcane cultivation was in full expansion, taking over forest lands and subsistence crop land that had cleared the most distant and inhospitable locations. There were extensive areas with soils favorable to but not yet taken up by sugarcane. It was able to extend itself over the fertile valleys to the south and north, as well as toward the interior, where the dense forests were known only to those hunting Indian slaves or individuals involved in the exploitation of Brazilwood. These areas possessed a few sugar mills that did not operate every year, grazing fields, and food-raising plots. They provided the necessary food to the sugarcane area and to the towns and villages of the captaincies of the Northeast. The ocean and the rivers were abundant with fish, the mangrove swamps offered tasty crabs, and the forests ample hunting.

Each sugar mill was an economic unit that brought together a considerable number of people. Generally, besides the owner, white inhabitants included the chaplain, the sugarmaster, the stoker, the master purger, the skimmer,[32] the foreman, and the growers. It is true that, with time, Mulattoes and Negroes were promoted to these positions and there were slaves that even became sugarmasters. Each sugar mill also had, on the average, fifty to sixty slaves belonging to the owner, as well as those belonging to the growers. These were Negroes from Guinea, local Indians, or Indians from Maranhão.

The Dutch conquest was completed after more than five years of intense fighting that caused great destruction in the captaincies. Olinda, the most important urban center, was burned. Several sugar mills had their big house, slave quarters, and mill itself entirely destroyed by fire. Many machines were thrown into the rivers or the sea. The cane fields were destroyed. The livestock was partly killed and partly dispersed. The fazendeiros of Sergipe and the São Francisco Valley moved what animals they could to Bahia, or went upstream along the great river. The slaves, taking advantage of the fighting, escaped to the interior, to the forests, and organized *quilombos*, where they returned to the life they had led in Africa. Bands of outlaws operated in the formerly flourishing area abandoned by most of the property owners, who retreated to Bahia.

It fell to the Dutch to reorganize the economy. In spite of many Dutch initially becoming mill owners and cane growers, they understood that it was necessary to have the support of the Portuguese, who knew the practices of sugarcane cultivation and sugar making, if the conquered captaincies were to flourish. Maurício de Nassau, who arrived in Recife in 1637, was the figure most appropriate to conclude and consolidate the conquest. His great administrative qualities were combined with a great spirit of tolerance and a profound love of the conquered land. The tasks were very arduous. It was necessary to combat the outlaws in the sugarcane areas, win the confidence and collaboration of the Portuguese and their descendants who remained in the conquered captaincies, destroy the *quilombos*, make allies of the Indians (who in general hated the Portuguese), conquer the supply points of slaves from Africa and Maranhão, round up the cattle that had dispersed, reorganize the livestock raising, and take steps in order to normalize the food supply of Recife and the city of Maurícia (established in his name on the island of Antônio Vaz). They were tasks for numerous people to accomplish over many years.

In a survey made in 1639, when many sugar mills had already been repaired, Adrien van der Dussen stated that 27 percent of the mills in the conquered captaincies crushed no sugarcane that year, there even being some the Dutch felt would be difficult to reconstruct. Of the mills discussed, the majority—seventy-eight—were water powered, while thirty-seven were powered by oxen; the report does not indicate the type of power used for the remaining thirty-three. It is interesting to note the great number of mills—twenty-three—acquired by the Dutch West Indies Company. Those were confiscated from the Portuguese, who retreated to Bahia with the forces of Bagnuolo. Previously, the Dutch were uninterested in sugar production and more devoted to trade, as suited the people, generally city dwellers, and by which profits were more easily made. Only a few, such as Servaes Carpentier and Gaspar van der Lay, became really adapted to life on a sugar mill. The latter married a woman from Pernambuco and remained in Brazil after the expulsion of his compatriots.[33]

But sugar production not only depended on the reconstruction of the mills. It was necessary that the property owners and growers have slaves. They were, before the Dutch conquest, made up of three groups: the Indians of the region who, legally, either had been captured in battle or had been acquired from the Tapuyans; the Indians imprisoned in Maranhão and sent to Pernambuco; and the Negroes brought from the coast of Africa, from various countries or originating from various ports from Guinea to the Congo and Angola.[34] The Dutch, to obtain the support of the Indians that belonged to the tribes of the region, freed those belonging to the first group, conceding as legal the enslavement of Negroes and Indians from Maranhão. Also, in order that the sugar industry be reorganized, they occupied certain points on the African coast, such as the ports of Costa da Mina and Luanda and the island of São Tomé, and themselves began to carry on the slave traffic as a company monopoly. The slaves were transported crammed into ships under the most precarious dietary and sanitary conditions and suffered a high mortality rate. Conditions, it is said,[35] were even more precarious than those found aboard Portuguese ships and aggravated, especially, for those coming from the coast of Guinea who, because of the light winds of the doldrums, almost always had to make a much longer voyage.

Arriving in Recife, the Negroes were offered for sale at the slave market and almost always sold on credit, with the balance paid at harvest time, by landowners and growers. The Dutch company would, with this, make great profits, since a slave was purchased in Africa for a modest price—from 12 to 75 florins in Guinea, and from 38 to 55 florins in Angola—and sold in Recife at high prices—from 200 to 300 florins for the average slave.[36] When the Negroes were strong and healthy they would bring, at times, 600 or 800 florins. This commerce was so important that, from the end of 1636 to the summer of 1645, the Dutch brought to Recife 23,163 Negroes, more than 2,500 slaves per month. The profits, however, disappeared because the buyers almost never settled their debts. The company began to sell slaves for cash, but since the property owners and growers did not have available capital for that, the Negroes were sold to Jewish businessmen who resold them on credit for exorbitant prices and at high rates of interest. This created a vexing situation. The price of the sugarcane products did not generate enough income to cover the expenses of reconstructing the sugar mills, acquisition and maintenance of the slaves, maintenance of the family itself, and losses caused by outlaws (Dutch soldiers, who at times were very overbearing, and the guerrilla bands from Bahia, who set fire to the cane fields in areas of Dutch control). Outlaw incursions became more frequent after the return to Holland of the Count of Nassau.

In that period, however, the mill owner was more an industrialist than an agriculturalist; he cultivated only a few cane fields, when he wished, preferring to process the cane provided by the growers. Thus, in the report of van der Dussen, when he mentions the number of sugarcane fields cultivated around sixty-one mills, only some 13 percent belonged to the owners, the large majority (more than 85 percent) of the fields being on lands of the growers.

These growers at times cultivated their own land, taking their cane to the nearest acceptable mill. To the grower fell the planting, cultivation, harvest, and transportation of the cane to the mill, where it would be delivered to the owner; the owner and his employees and slaves would take charge of the crushing, with the sugar produced being divided into equal parts, one part for the owner and one for the grower. Thus the grower needed slaves and oxen and carts in order to take care of the cane cultivation. It stands to reason that the number of slaves and pairs of oxen available would vary with his means and the cane fields he could cultivate. After the crushing, the grower was responsible for the expenses of drying the sugar, packing it, and for the freight charges to market or to a convenient location.

If the grower did not have land of his own, he would rent it from a mill owner, thus obligating himself to crush his cane at the owner's mill. In this case, he received only one-third of the sugar produced if the land was fertile and near the mill, or two-fifths if not. The syrup that drained from the sugar in the purification house was the property of the owner, who used it during the off-season as food for the slaves, horses, and oxen. A grower who cultivated forty *tarefas* of cane (each *tarefa* corresponded to the quantity of cane crushed by a mill in twenty-four hours), would need to have available, approximately, twenty slaves with hoes, scythes, and axes, and from four to eight carts with a quantity of oxen that would fluctuate, according to the number of carts, from twelve to twenty-four. A *tarefa* corresponded, in the oxen-driven mills, to twenty-five or thirty carts of cane and, in those powered by water, from forty to fifty carts.

The number of *tarefas* of each grower would depend as much on the area available as the capacity and the number of growers around the mill. The crushing could be extended only from September to April. Also, it was up to the grower to carry out, by means of his slaves, cultivation of subsistence crops, generally on the less fertile and more distant lands, to feed his family and his slaves. Thus they led a very modest life, since the profits obtained were almost always invested in slaves, animals, and tools. Subsistence crops still were cultivated by free men whom the property owner authorized to live in locations distant from the mill. They paid a small annual rent, always in kind and generally called quitrent.

The owner, who would crush his own and the grower's cane, had to invest great amounts of capital; despite receiving a good share of the cane he crushed, he was almost always trying to amortize his debts. He had a large capital investment in construction (mill, purification house, brick factory, besides the big house, slave quarters, and, at times, a chapel), machinery, the acquisition of Negroes (between forty and seventy individuals, according to the mill's capacity), thirty to forty oxen, about ten or twelve carts, and an enormous series of implements. Also, it fell to the owners to pay the wages of a group of employees, including those who directed the crushing, planting, slaves, and oxen.[37]

The Negroes were obligated to work all day, from sunrise to sunset, assembled and formed into work gangs under the orders of a foreman. There were mills that, owing to their importance, possessed various foremen, the chief of them being called the head foreman. It was customary for the Portuguese owners and growers, being Roman Catholics, to permit the slaves to rest on Sundays and saints' days, whereas the Dutch, being Calvinists, observed only Sundays. The slaves belonging to Jews had more leisure time, inasmuch as they, for religious motives, observed Saturdays and, for the fear of the authorities, also observed Sundays. Hence the slaves would prefer Jewish owners over Catholic, and Catholic over Calvinist.[38] From this discussion one can observe the importance of the Negro in sugar production. The necessity to produce sugar made the Dutch Calvinists put aside their antislavery religious scruples[39] and led Heeren XIV in 1640 to affirm that "without Negroes and without oxen, nothing can be hoped for in Pernambuco."[40] Thus, Pernambuco and Angola had to remain in the hands of a single master to supply sugar to Europe. The treatment received by the Negroes, from their Dutch as well as Portuguese masters, was sufficiently severe, in keeping with that period. The slaves were frequently subject to mistreatment, or to corporal punishment: they were beaten with a horsewhip, switch, or leather strap, placed in irons or in stocks, or even chained by the feet or neck. It was unwise, however, for the owners to kill or mutilate the slaves that had cost so much money; it is possible that some more perverse owners at times mutilated or branded their slaves, but it must have been infrequent. Those who were prudent and aware of the value of their slaves, such as the notable João Fernandes Vieira, recommended against punishing the slaves with either sticks or stones when they deserved it, in order to avoid decreasing their value. But he did recommend that they be put over a cart and whipped, and, after the whipping, the wounds cleaned with a razor or knife that would cut well, putting thereafter, over the wounds, salt, lime juice, or urine. After that, the poor slave still was chained to a wall for some days.[41] The living conditions of the slaves, obviously, were not very humane.[42]

In the Dutch-controlled part of Brazil, however, they did not use slaves alone in agriculture; the free Indians that lived in their villages devoted themselves to gathering, hunting, and modest agriculture of manioc and beans, and agreed, at times, to work for a while, inasmuch as they would be promised sugarcane brandy or some other strong drink. According to seventeenth-century accounts, the Indians had little ambition, lived in hovels in great destitution, and were not disposed to work if it were not for the stimulus mentioned.[43]

The destruction caused by the war and the high price of slaves, made the mill owners and growers use available labor for sugarcane cultivation and neglect the cultivation of food crops. The result was that during Dutch control, a lack of basic foodstuffs (chiefly manioc meal) became frequent. This provoked serious disturbance in the capital. The Count of Nassau resolved to direct that each owner and each cane grower plant food crops and that they be required to cultivate five thousand planting mounds for each slave they possessed. Farmers who devoted themselves to other crops would be obligated to cultivate one thousand planting mounds for each slave.[44]

Thus, trying merely to substitute for the Portuguese, initially, in the sugar business, and later being dedicated more to the trade in the product than in its production, the Dutch, despite the considerable development of the city of Recife and the urban life of the area under their control, did not introduce appreciable modifications either in the techniques of sugar production, or in the rural labor relationships. They militarily and politically dominated a vast area of Brazilian territory. But sugar production remained in Portuguese hands, since the Dutch did not learn well the techniques of its manufacture, or the best methods of dealing with the slaves and making them produce.

Economic Development and the Relationships Between Rural Labor in the Second Half of the Seventeenth Century and in the Eighteenth Century

During the period between the expulsion of the Dutch in 1654 and the opening of Brazilian ports to friendly nations in 1808, sugarcane cultivation in Brazil underwent phases of crises and of grandeur. The first were provoked by the development of the sugarcane industry in the Caribbean, where better soils and more developed agricultural and industrial techniques allowed more economical production. The monopolistic policies of the European powers with regard to the trade of their colonies caused serious upsets to the Brazilian sugarcane industry, because of the small population of Portugal and the serious problems created by the trading companies.

On the other hand, the closely linked wars in Europe in the second half of the eighteenth century, in which the principal colonial powers were involved, and the revolutions that sprang up at the end of that century in the Caribbean—Haiti, chiefly—very much favored the Brazilian sugar industry. It produced a phase of economic euphoria, postponing, until the beginning of the nineteenth century, the emancipationist struggle that occurred with such intensity in Pernambuco. Because Portugal stayed to one side of these conflicts, Brazilian sugar was easily placed on the European markets.[45] Sugar production, despite its ups and downs, gave to Portugal, in all its period of control over Brazil, more income than gold mining.

It is interesting that, despite the fluctuation in the demand for sugar on the European markets and the low levels of agricultural and industrial techniques, the population of the Northeast during this period occupied nearly all of the region. It is true that wide areas continued to be covered with forest and that the sugar mills, towns, and villages were situated some distance from one another. But the land of the Northeast was practically settled; this did not occur in other parts of Brazil, such as the South region and São Paulo until the twentieth century.

A survey made in 1774[46] records almost continuous settlement over the area under study, from Natal, Rio Grande do Norte, to Penedo, in the current state of Alagoas. Sergipe and northern Bahia were also quite populated by 1774. The sugarcane area was almost always located near the littoral, but in Pernambuco it had already moved into the interior, in communities like Tracunhaém, Vitória de Santo Antão, and São Lourenço da Mata. At the end of the sixteenth century, these cities were right in the heart of land devoted to Brazilwood exploitation. Scattered over the region there were 387 large and eighty-five small mills. In Sergipe, at the end of the eighteenth century, there were thirty mills—ten in the Valley of Vaza-Barris and twenty in Cotinguiba—and ten smaller ones devoted to making sugarcane brandy.[47] The large mills are distinguished from the smaller ones (engenhocas) because they were devoted to sugar making and not to the making of raw brown sugar or syrup, materials used to make sugarcane brandy.

The greatest concentration of mills was in the present state of Pernambuco, where they numbered 287, compared to sixty-three in Alagoas, thirty-two in Paraíba, and only three in Rio Grande do Norte. In Pernambuco there were better natural conditions, greater population density, and greater proximity to the port of Recife, which made freight charges cheaper.

Progress during the previous period in the sugar industry was minimal, since animal-powered mills continued to be dominant over water-powered ones, despite the latter offering greater production capacity. The low stream gradients in the littoral area, and the low water levels in summer in more distant places, certainly led the property owners to prefer the mechanical force of animals to hydraulic force in the operation of their mills. One can observe, however, that the oxen, largely used to power the mills before Dutch control, had been almost entirely replaced by horses and mares, which were much faster. They continued, however, to use firewood for the furnaces, while the bagasse was burned where it was dumped. Fertilizer was not used in the cane cultivation; the manure of the animals and the decaying bagasse were thrown away. The planters continued to clear the land by burning the native vegetation after it had been felled. They never tried to obtain new varieties of sugarcane, always cultivating the variety introduced in the sixteenth century, called afterwards "creole." Only beginning with the nineteenth century were other varieties cultivated.

Beside sugarcane raising, other smaller-scale economic activities that did not occupy areas sought after for sugarcane, had some importance. Among the crops cotton stands out, since, thanks to the discovery of the steam engine, the flourishing textile industry in Europe began to consume it liberally. Anyone studying the economic history of the Northeast will see that it can be summed up, in the last two centuries, as a struggle between sugarcane and cotton. In conformity with the external demands and the fluctuation of prices, sugarcane, starting from the most humid areas where it predominated, advanced into less humid areas. These latter were, in turn, sought after by cotton, predominant in the semiarid region, when the prices increased and those of sugar decreased. Cotton still supports an important industry of general textiles widely consumed in Brazil and sold in quantity at the market of Santo Antão. Livestock raising, as essential to the sugar industry as to the supplying of the then flourishing urban centers, occupied not only the Agreste and the Sertão, but even certain parts of the Zona da Mata and the Eastern Littoral, chiefly in Rio Grande do Norte, in the basin of the Mamanguape River, in Paraíba, and to the south in the valleys of the São Miguel, Coruripe, São Francisco, and along the rivers in Sergipe. These cattle permitted the existence of various tanneries and enlivened important open markets in the town of Santo Antão and in the village of Pau d'Alho. According to a document of the period,[48] possibly exaggerated, on Saturdays in Pau d'Alho between ninety and one hundred cattle were slaughtered.

Other crops, including manioc, maize, beans, and native and exotic fruits, were widely cultivated even on the lowlands, usually characterized by sugarcane production, such as the Capibaribe and the Joboatão, guaranteeing the food supply not only of the rural population, but also that of the urban population. Coconut cultivation had just begun in that period, replacing native cashew trees in the beach areas, and molding a landscape very diverse from what previously existed. Many of the cities already were distinguished as towns or villages.

In the Recôncavo of Bahia, sugarcane was limited to occupying the areas of clayey soil, leaving for tobacco the sandy soils; tobacco cultivation expanded greatly because the product came to be used as specie for the acquisition of Negroes in Africa. Thus, the area that produced sugar for the European market and was supplied with Negroes from the coast of Africa, also became the supplier of tobacco to Africa.

Throughout the region a structured aristocratic society divided into classes emerged. At the top appeared the figure of the mill owner, with prestige and power equal to the amount of land he owned, the production of his cane fields, or the number of slaves he possessed. To emphasize his position, he constructed a big house of two stories, or with a high sidewalk, on a hill or a slope, from which he would speak to the farm hands, employees, and slaves. He always went out on horseback,[49] from which he gave orders. Hence the popular passion for good horses.

The development and installation of a sugar mill involved a great amount of capital, not only because of the construction of indispensable buildings (housing for the caldron and settling tanks; the purging house, where the sugar was put into forms on raised platforms over tanks into which the syrup trickled through a hole; a dryer, where, after the draining off of the syrup, the sugar was placed in the sun to dry; a packing house, where the sugar was prepared for export; and complementary buildings like the corral, stable, big house, foreman's house, and the slave quarters). Capital was also used in the acquisition of slaves, oxen, and horses without which the cane could not be planted or crushed. There were always tens of slaves; very large mills had available one hundred fifty to two hundred slaves, a figure than on first sight might appear exaggerated, but that was not, because of the conditions of cultivation and industrialization of the sugarcane.

When the rainy season began, generally in March, even though the crushing of the cane was not concluded, the forest had to be cleared for planting more cane. This clearing, which always required a large number of hands, was done with an ax in the case of forest, or with a scythe, when it was an area previously exploited, and always followed by the earthing up of planting mounds. During this period, this land could be used for growing maize or beans, planted at the end of March and the beginning of April, and harvested in June and July, and used to feed the slaves. In June and July sugarcane was planted. This cane would be crushed the following year; that is, thirteen to eighteen months after planting. The crushing began in September and extended until March or April of the following year. Because of the long vegetative cycle of sugarcane, the mill owner had, and even today has, two crops to deal with, that of the current year and what will be crushed the following year, requiring that the cane fields be kept free of weeds until the cane reaches its full development. Since sugarcane, once cut, resprouts, one distinguishes that of the first and subsequent cuttings. The first cutting requires five annual weedings, while the others can be kept clear and give a good yield, on the average, with three weedings per year.

Because of this overloaded agricultural calendar, the mill owners always needed labor, always needed to acquire slaves (to be
paid for when the sugar was shipped), and, consequently, always
were in debt because of the high price of Negroes and their
frequent loss to sickness, accident, or escape. Escape should be
stressed. Despite the idea that the Negro endured with pa-
tience, without reaction, captivity, the fact is that he was always
fleeing to the forest to organize *quilombos*, committing suicide,
rebelling, in short, in diverse ways against the dominance of his
master.

In second place on the social scale of this sugarcane aristocracy
were the growers who, not being able to build a mill though
they held land, or not even owning land, would cultivate cane
on the land of, or crush his cane in, the mill of the owner. In
conformity with his means, the land available for cultivation, the
number of slaves that he possessed, and the harvests that were
produced, the greater or lesser economic and social standing of
the grower was determined. Many times, sons of mill owners
became growers for their fathers or brothers; large growers
would possess, at times, numerous slaves to tend the cane fields;
others, even poorer, had few slaves and they themselves had to
cultivate the soil or personally oversee the work.

The nerve-racking issue for the growers was their relationship
with the mill owners. Their profit or loss was going to depend
on the behavior of the owner; if there were mill owners who
would respect the rights of the growers, there were also those
overbearing owners who caused much trouble for those dependent upon them. Frequently the owners prohibited the grower
from entering the purging house during the crushing of the latter's cane. It was alleged that the presence of the grower would
connote an inspection and, consequently, a distrust of the
owner. Now, without being able to watch over the crushing of
his cane, the grower would be uncertain of the quantity and
quality of the sugar produced; the owner would be able to give
him a share less than he had a right to, or exchange good quality
for poor quality sugar. Other times, an owner would give a true
accounting of the production but withdraw part of the grower's
sugar as a loan, promising to repay it at the next harvest. This
seriously hurt the grower, who crushed his cane once a year,
and at harvest time needed money to pay his obligations.[50]

Other harmful measures were taken by despotic owners when there was a disagreement with a grower; to harm the grower it was sufficient to prohibit him from cutting cane at the proper time. Once the ripening period passed, the cane began to dry out and diminish in its sugar content, provoking a serious drop in production for the grower. At other times, the owner would permit the cutting, but when the cane arrived at the mill leave it unprocessed for three or four days. The cane thus became acidic and useless. The owner would lose his half share, but he would not go broke. He would have available his own cane and that from the fields of the other growers. But the grower who had only the one cutting available could lose in a week what cost him a year of hard work, leaving him without the necessary means to meet his financial obligations; he could be insolvent and, consequently, ruined.

At other times, after the grower had cut and had his cane crushed, he would undertake to stimulate the just harvested cane fields by burning the straw so that the second cutting would sprout and give a reasonable yield the following year. This practice is still used today, especially in humid areas in order to eliminate rats in the cane fields. At that time the owner would advise the grower that his rental agreement was ended; he would give a short period of time to vacate the place, and turn it over to somebody else. With little or no indemnification, according to the conscience of the owner, the grower lost the parcel of land and the second growth of cane he planted and had to establish himself in another location. From these examples, however, one should not conclude that all of the owners behaved that way; many of them were fair. What should be emphasized is that the then dominant economic structure and the sociopolitical organization emanating from it, permitted these abuses unless the growers had someone to appeal to in defense of their rights. The sociopolitical organization, however, was oriented toward guaranteeing the owner the exercise of full authority over his lands, tenants, and dependents.

The insecurity about renewal of rental contracts would constitute for Tollenare, who visited the Northeast in the second half of the nineteenth century,[51] the principal impediment to the growers who, because of it, would build small crude houses alongside temporary enclosures for animals, since at any moment they could be ousted. Profits were always used for Negroes and cattle because these were movable belongings. Analyzing the problem, the French observer thought that the growers needed to be protected by a law that obligated the owners to rent their vacant land under contracts that lasted nine years. Thus, the grower, guaranteed a longer period of rental, could make better installations in the areas exploited, and also concern himself with soil conservation.

It was a very difficult life for sugarcane growers in the seventeenth and eighteenth centuries. But their problems resulted not only from the relationship with the owner; the slaves that were needed constituted a great investment of capital and, as they had little money available, the growers bought them on credit, to be paid for after the harvest, generally at a high rate of interest. Weather also caused serious trouble: if the summer was very dry, without rain, the cane on the slopes would only grow a little, and if the winter were excessively rainy, flooding would damage the cane on the lowlands. Rivers like the Paraíba, with more irregular regimes, in some years destroyed entire crops and even, at times, mills.

Wild grasses in the fields, always growing and requiring removal in order not to compete with the sugarcane, were a constant and stubborn enemy of the growers. Open grazing of animals such as goats, pigs, and even cattle and horses that escaped from their enclosures, caused great losses of sugarcane, obliging the growers to post guards. Many times the guards killed the plundering animals, causing dissension between the owners of the sugarcane and the owners of the animals. Anyone who knows the sugarcane area of the Northeast knows how the growers hate the robber cattle, that is, the cattle able to break out of their enclosures and invade the planted fields.

Despite all of this, the grower had a better situation than the squatter, who cultivated subsistence crops, and the employees, since they, receiving a wage, were even more closely bound to the mill owner. After them were the slaves, considered objects, who received treatment similar to that given cattle and horses.

The squatters, generally Mestizoes who lived on mill land, constituted a high percentage of the free rural population. They generally got from the owner authorization to clear a small plot of forest and establish a hut and a field for crops. The hut was excessively poor, thatched with leaves, and in which the only belongings were woven mats and clay pots. The women[52] commonly made lace, while the men planted some manioc to furnish food. Hunting, good in the forest, and fishing in the rivers and mangrove swamps, if they were near the beach, contributed enormously to their diet. In rainy years, when production was greater, they were wont to sell the surplus and in that way buy clothes and a few utensils. The land rent they paid was, generally, very low, not necessitating the carrying out of large exploitations.

Insecurity was a constant in the life of the squatters since the landowner, with or without motive, could evict them. This frequently took place because of a clash of interests or personal problems: the owners had a special fondness for the wives of the squatters,[53] something that even provoked murders. There were landowners who scarcely left their property without bodyguards, fearing the aggressive action of evicted squatters. Constituting a good portion of the rural population, these squatters were a reserve of manual labor that could be utilized by the sugar agroindustry, which did not absorb this available mass of labor because of a preference for slave over wage labor. The squatters were forming, slowly, awaiting the extinction of the slave trade, a reserve of manual labor that the landowners would have at their disposal when slaves were lacking.

In the work of the sugar mills there were not, however, only slaves. There were some free men who, because of their qualifications, held various administrative posts and, it is also said, technical posts required by the sugar industry. Although dependent upon the owner, from whom they received their orders and their wages, they held positions of distinction because it was their duty to direct the Negroes in their work and to make and pack the sugar to be sent to the consumer market.

Among the salaried workers, according to Antonil,[54] the chaplain stood out. On the mill, he had many activities to carry out. According to a religious survey done in 1774, many mills had ornate chapels. The chaplain's duties included spiritual guidance and the teaching of Christian doctrine, as much to the owner's family as to the workers and slaves. It was his duty to say mass every Sunday, listen to grievances, settle squabbles, counsel the discontented, and organize religious festivals. The chaplain blessed the cane crusher on the day the harvest began, and he blessed it again at the finish of the harvest, the day crushing was stopped. The chaplain received a salary of 40$000 to 50$000 *mil-réis* around the beginning of the eighteenth century, equivalent to the remuneration of the crushing foreman, but less than that of the head foreman or the sugarmaster.

The head foreman was second in authority, after the owner. He received orders from the owner, at times written, and transmitted them to the foremen of the cane crusher and of the cane fields. When the owner was absent, the overall administration fell to the head foreman. His authority was only limited by the desires of the owner, who could fire him at any moment. Generally it was the duty of the head foreman to punish the slaves, but with care so as not to make them incapable of, or inefficient in, work. It was also his duty to supervise the slaves, counting them every day to see if any had escaped, compelling them to attend mass every Sunday and to make confession every year, and providing medication for those who were ill. It also fell to the foreman to prevent the slaves from fighting among themselves and to see that they not miss work. So that the Negroes might feed themselves, the head foreman required them to work on their fields on saints' days, Saturdays, and during the winter, when the mill was not operating. In this way the owners freed themselves from the financial burden of feeding the slaves. Diégues Júnior[55] asserts that the practice was initiated in Brazil, carried from there to the Caribbean, and became known as the Brazilian system. At first sight it appeared generous on the owner's part that his slaves could cultivate, on their free days, a parcel of land for themselves. But, since the owner required them—as did João Fernandes Vieira,[56] hero of the restoration of Pernambuco—to work on "their fields" on the saints' days, the slaves lost the rest that the church guaranteed them. Likewise, the products of that labor were used to feed the Negroes themselves. Obviously, the so-called Brazilian system was to the advantage of the owner and not the slaves. The head foreman gave more care to the oxen: they were not fenced in, and the animals were allowed whenever possible a day of rest for a day of work.

The tasks and responsibilities of the head foreman were

numerous: he supervised construction projects; rode around the cane fields; protected the forests; thwarted invasions of the property by neighbors; repaired the dams, sluices, and bridges; supervised the brick factory and the distillery, the building where the sugarcane brandy was made; cleaned the pastures; divided up and packed the sugar, and so on. For that much work and that much responsibility the head foreman earned the princely remuneration of 50–60$000 *mil-réis* per year.

Under his orders the foreman of cane crushing, who received about 40–50$000 *mil-réis* per year, took charge of putting to work the Negro women, who carried the cane to the crusher. He tried to prevent accidents, and looked after the daily washing of the crusher so that the juice would not sour, damaging the sugar making.

The foreman of the cane fields, who earned less, about 30$000 *mil-réis* per year, cared for the fields, putting the slaves to work on the planting, weeding, and cutting of the cane, and also supervising the subsistence plots. Among his obligations was to always be alert "so that the cane fields not catch fire because of carelessness of the newly arrived Negroes, who at times left in the wind the embers that they carried with them to light their pipes."[57] There was always the specter of fire to frighten the owner, who could lose, in a day, the result of years of work.

In the cooking of the sugarcane juice and in the sugar making, worked the sugarmaster and the undermaster or night stoker. They remained in the boiling-house during the harvest, the first during the day and the second at night, where there were four or five furnaces designed for the cooking of the sugarcane juice. This cooking, of greater or lesser intensity and duration, had to vary in conformity with the soil and topography of the place where the cane was planted, and on that depended the good or poor quality of the sugar. It fell to them to look after the placement of the sugary syrup in molds on the drying platforms and to see it transferred to the purging house, where it would pass to the jurisdiction of the purger. The sugarmaster drew a wage of 100–120$000 *mil-réis* per year, while the undermaster earned 30–40$000 *mil-réis*.

The purger's duty was to run the purging house and direct the purging process, that is, the whitening of the raw sugar, which was done by sprinkling water and clay on top of the mold. Besides the responsibility of obtaining sugar of good quality and finishing the work of the sugarmaster, he had to watch over the syrup that trickled from the tanks, the raw material for making sugarcane brandy. His wages were much less than those of the sugarmaster; only on the big mills did it reach 40$000 *mil-réis* per year.

The box maker's duty was to pack the sugar after it was purged, separating it according to quality. After the packing he had to determine the placement of clay in the corners of the boxes, withdrawal of the tithe, the portion belonging to the growers, and so forth. For this work he drew a wage of 30–50$000 *mil-réis* per year.

Besides these workers were the slaves, numbering one hundred fifty to two hundred on large mills. Their importance was such that a chronicler of the colonial period referring to them declared:[58] "The slaves are the hands and feet of the mill owner, because without them in Brazil it is not possible to create, maintain and increase the fazenda, nor have the sugar mill running." They were found everywhere, as much in the mills as in the cane fields, subsistence plots, brick yards, saw-mills, and on boats. Every year various numbers, originating from several points on the coast of Africa, were acquired by each mill. Some were weak, especially those from Cabo Verde and São Tomé. Those from Angola had more mechanical skill, while those from the Congo were industrious and good for work with the sugarcane and in the big house. The most expert were, at times, taught new jobs, becoming boiler-room workers, carpenters, calkers, mill workers, boatmen, sailors, etc.

They lived in slave quarters, in small row houses in families or not, but always working. Men and women were used in the arduous tasks in the field and in the mill. But in the field, the women did not work with an ax. In the planting and weeding of the cane fields, the slaves were put to work at sunrise and returned to the slave quarters at night, finishing their work at sunset. At the sugarcane harvest, it was the duty of each Negro to cut daily three hundred and fifty sheafs of twelve stalks; these were bundled by a female slave. Each cane cutter was accompanied in his work by a bundler. That quantity would make one mold of sugar.

Once cut and bundled, the cane was transported to the crushing house and deposited in a large room, the *picadeiro*. This occupied one side of the building, in which the crusher was also located. On the other side was the large wooden mechanism for turning the cane crusher (*almanjarra*) in the animal-driven mill, or a water wheel in water-driven mills. Many slaves worked there: some lifted the cane from the *picadeiro* and placed it close to the crusher; others, with great risk, since through carelessness they could be caught and squeezed between the rollers of the crusher, put the cane into it; a third still, passed the bagasse between the rollers; a fourth tended, fixed, and lighted the oil lamps; finally, another attended the large kettle in which the sugarcane juice accumulated and in which it would be boiled. Since the mill operated twenty-four hours a day, these seven slaves and another group of seven took turns.

Slaves who were ill always worked in the furnace house, since it was believed that the high temperatures there would cure them. Rebellious slaves or criminals, ill-regarded and persecuted by the owners or the foreman, were placed in irons to work in the boiler room or elsewhere in the mill in order to purge their faults. Another slave cleaned and lighted the oil lamps, skimmed the foam off the kettle, and directed it into a caldron. Because the furnaces consumed much wood, a large number of slaves worked in the forest, each one receiving the daily task of cutting and stacking a pile of firewood seven hand-spans high by eight wide, enough to fill an ox cart.

It was the Negro slaves who put the cooked syrup on the drying platform and then after three days transported the clay molds to the purging house. There, working with the purger and box maker, slaves put the purging clay over the molds of sugar; others assisted on the platforms to separate the raw sugar; others brought the molds, removing from them the blocks of sugar, and kneaded the purging clay.[59]

These slaves endured a truly hard life, working over the entire year in the planting, weeding, and harvest of the cane, as well as in the making of the sugar. One day each week, generally, was devoted to the cultivation of subsistence crops. Any complaint was punished, since, as Antonil informs us[60] "in Brazil it is customarily said that for the slaves it is necessary to know three things—bread, wood, and cloth."

Their diet consisted of manioc meal and sun-dried meat, given to each slave in a gourd; besides that they would receive daily a ration of sugar syrup, a food otherwise reserved for cattle and horses.

Living like veritable animals in loathsome quarters, poorly fed, without rights or comforts, the slaves, for more than three centuries, were the mainstay of the Northeast's sugar economy.

Slave and Wage Labor in the Nineteenth Century

The nineteenth century was a period of great economic, political, and social transformation. The old sugar mills, which had, during three centuries, a very slow evolution, were shaken by a series of innovations that improved the agricultural technology and profoundly transformed both the industrial processes and the transportation network. Sugarcane began to experience competition from another export crop also of interest to the large landowner, cotton. Although this competition had been overcome in the humid areas, within a few years it was competing with the sugar economy.

Among the improvements introduced in the sugar agroindustry, there stood out, in the first years of the century, the use of the plow. Introduced in the eighteenth century, the plow was not used widely until the nineteenth. The introduction of a new sugarcane variety, Cayenne, was made from French Guiana during the short period when that territory was occupied by Portuguese troops.[61] The owners who frequented large regional centers like Recife and Salvador noted the existence of other lands where sugarcane could be cultivated. They concerned themselves with the introduction of new techniques and new varieties of sugarcane, noting that, with time, the Cayenne, like the creole variety, would deteriorate and production would fall. For that reason, during the last century, they began to cultivate new varieties, the imperial and crystalline, which emerged from spontaneous variations of the Cayenne variety. These would be supplanted only in the Brazilian republican period by the butter variety, or Flower of Cuba, obtained from selection and crossing done at the Cachoeirinha mill in the *município* of Vitória, Pernambuco, by its owner, Manuel Cavalcanti de Albuquerque.[62]

The new varieties increased productivity. The owners had felt the need to increase production and improve the quality of the product in order to compete with the sugar from the Caribbean and from Europe itself (thanks to the industrialization of the sugar beet), on the European market.

The owners began, then, to sense the handicap of their mills powered by cattle and mares, which not only produced less than the water-powered mills (from 25 to 30 *tarefas* per day against 30 or 40), but also made it necessary to maintain an inordinate number of animals. These animals were easily fed during the harvest when there was a lot of heavy foam and impurities skimmed from the sugarcane juice during its cooking. In the off-season, from April to September, they ate sugarcane buds. But in the winter they had to be removed to other areas. Areas such as the region of Bom Jardim would receive many livestock from the community of Tracunhaém. The livestock grazed on the green fodder that existed there, and were herded by cowboys, poor, free individuals who from that work drew a meager wage.[63] Other properties located in communities near the littoral used to reserve great uncultivated areas to graze horses during the winter, sending cattle to the beaches in order to feed on the grasses that grew in the shade of the coconut palms.[64] The introduction of the steam-driven mills seemed to these landowners a great solution to the livestock burden. Despite the advantages of steam-driven mills, the difficulty in obtaining capital and credit, and the backwardness that dominated the mentality of the property owners of the time, hindered its rapid spread. The first was established in Pernambuco in 1819. By 1854, thirty-five years later, there were five steam-powered, 101 water-driven, and 426 animal-powered mills.[65] In 1857, however, the number of steam-powered mills increased to 18. In 1914, of a total of 2,786 sugar mills in Pernambuco, including the small ones producing raw sugar in the Sertão, those powered by steam numbered only 785, compared to 329 water- and 1,182 animal-powered. Only 490 mills were closed down, supplying their cane to modern factories.[66] As I emphasized in a previous study,[67] these improvements were initially made in the areas with the most favorable conditions of climate, soil, and topography. Only afterwards, did they reach the peripheral areas. Steam-driven mills only appeared in the Ceará-Mirim Valley after 1865,[68] in the sugar valleys of the Paraíba in the last decade of the nineteenth century.[69] Alagoas, with conditions more favorable than in the states farther north, already possessed two in 1851 and five in 1852.[70]

During this same period, lime began to be substituted for potash in the making of sugar, vertical cylinders were replaced by horizontal ones in the crushers, wood and metal replaced clay forms, and the use of bagasse as fuel became generalized as certain modifications were made to the furnaces.[71] These improvements had considerable consequences: they diminished the rampant destruction of the forests for firewood to take care of the insatiable appetite of the boilers, and at the same time resolved for the owners the problem of the disposal of the bagasse.

In the second half of the ninteenth century the sugar mills began to use apparatuses capable of making white sugar, and no longer needed to purge the sugar with clay placed on top of the mold. Central mills were established.

These central mills were powerful, capable of crushing cane from the various small mills and making sugar of better quality. According to the politicians who idealized them, they would separate agricultural from industrial activity. These mills were set up with a governmental guarantee of interest on capital invested by foreign companies that did not cultivate cane. They did not require slave labor. Since they were going to receive the raw material from very extensive areas, they had to build railroads to replace the ox carts formerly used in the transportation of the cane from the fields to the mill. The ox cart was limited to carrying the cane from the fields to the railroad sidings. This was the total modernization of a relatively static landscape three centuries old. The government was involved because it guaranteed the interest on the capital used by the English, French, and Dutch companies; it even determined the location of the central mills so that each nationality had a zone of influence and did not squabble over the cane of another. By the enactment of the Golden Law of May 13, 1888, there were already a series of functioning central mills: São João, founded that year on the lowlands of the Paraíba River;[72] Santo Inácio, Cuiambuca, Firmeza, and Bom Gosto, established in 1884 in Pernambuco; and in Sergipe, also in 1888, in the *município* of Riachuelo.[73] In Alagoas, dating from the last decade of the century were those of Brasileiro in the valley of the Paraíba do Meio, the Utinga Leão in the Mundaú, and the Sinimbu in the small Jiquiá Valley.

These central mills, despite the application of foreign capital, were serious failures; the majority of them did not crush cane for more than a year. The failure afforded the opportunity for the transformation of some central mills into modern sugar factories, thus keeping agricultural and industrial activities in the same hands.

These improvements, however, prompted the government to concern itself with transportation facilities, first roads and then railroads, which ran from Recife toward the interior, to the production zones of sugar and cotton. The first had their routes delineated by the French engineer Vauthier, who was in Brazil for several years working for the province of Pernambuco.[74] Railroads were constructed beginning in 1858.[75]

The roads and railroads would free the inland mills of long trips to the small seaports and the respective transshipment of sugar to the coastline sailing vessels that Recife required. It would also provoke the decline of the cities located on the deepest part of the estuaries, ports that had developed commercial functions, including Mamanguape, Goiana, Rio Formoso, Porto Calvo, Alagoas, Valença, and Camamu.

Cotton constituted serious competition to sugarcane, which had been, up to that time, considered the imperial crop. Cotton took over the lands, conquered the lowlands of clay and the deep valleys of yellow clay, destroyed the forests, drove away the animals, and only permitted peasants' crops to develop in the areas in which cotton would not, under the conditions of the time, flourish.

The coconut groves were confined to the narrow littoral strip. In that area a poor, democratic society, that had no tinge of the sugarcane aristocracy, developed. As Koster observed,[76] in a period of very accentuated class division, it was unique that there were settlements like Gamboa, in which the person of greatest attention and prestige of the community was a poor, black man: Koster emphasized, a black man who did not have at his disposal, as others, the enriched "cards of whiteness" in his favor.

This coconut landscape extended near to Recife, in the communities of Mamanguape and Itamaracá,[77] as well as to more distant places, framing the littoral of Paraíba, Rio Grande do Norte, Alagoas, Sergipe, and Bahia. The coconut, despite taking six to seven years to begin producing, did not require local industrialization or expensive machinery like sugarcane. It allowed the breaking up of already designated properties in the first half of the nineteenth century. The land did not require constant weeding, and upkeep occupied only a few men. Five harvests a year furnished the property owners with an almost permanent income. Beside fruit, the coconut grove provided the trunk and leaves used in the making of thatched huts. The tyranny of sugarcane production arrived even in the coconut groves, since livestock from the mills wintered in the shade of the coconut palms, taking advantage of the grasses that grew there.

Manioc, beans, and fruits, consumed by rich and poor, never competed with sugarcane. They always occupied a vanguard position in remote cleared areas (though awaiting the arrival of sugarcane), and in the most settled regions, were limited to soils that were of no use for sugarcane. They constituted the small farming done by slaves and squatters for their self-sufficiency and for sale of the surplus; and for mill owners and growers, they served to feed families and workers. It is still indicative today, in the region of the Zona da Mata and Eastern Littoral that the making of manioc meal is the same as during the colonial period.[78] Sugar making has evolved from using an animal-powered mill to factories that annually produce more than five hundred thousand sacks of sugar. The production of manioc meal has not changed. Despite its importance, manioc has been relegated to a secondary position, always lacking protection and always neglected. It has never been eminent in the Northeast's history. This made the already deficient diet of the squatters and slaves worse than ever.

The cattle were always in bondage to sugarcane. They occupied pioneer areas until sugarcane arrived, then moved farther from the littoral. Each move placed them that much farther from the centers of consumption. It was cattle that tamed and settled the fluvial valleys remote from Olinda, becoming established, to the south in the São Francisco Valley and the grasslands of Sergipe and, to the north, on the tablelands of Paraíba and Rio Grande do Norte. If not for livestock raising, tablelands would have constituted a genuine demographic and economic vacuum between the humid, fertile areas of the lowlands.

Because sugarcane always pushed livestock toward the interior, the livestock market of Igaraçu, north of Recife, had to be transferred to Goiana, afterwards to Pedras de Fogo, and, finally to Itabaiana, already in the Agreste,[79] where it has remained to the present.

With cotton the problem was different: it confronted sugarcane and was not only a poor man's crop,[80] but also a rich man's crop.[81]

Cotton cultivation, carried on in the Northeast since colonization, had a phase of stagnation during the seventeenth and the first half of the eighteenth centuries. It developed afterwards in keeping with the making of ordinary textiles used in dressing the slaves and, even more, as a consequence of the industrial revolution and the developing English textile industry. Portugal, as the usufructary of Brazil's riches, gained enormous sums as an intermediary between Brazil and England; this stimulated the cultivation of cotton and resulted in 1751 in the creation of a Cotton Inspection Station and, shortly thereafter, a Cotton Customhouse.[82] Cotton cultivation, which began in a humid region, later disseminated to the Agreste and the Sertão, as if repelled by sugarcane and by the climate. But, during the periods of depressed cotton prices it retreated to the Agreste, leaving the Zona da Mata free for sugarcane; when the price increased, or when there was a crisis in the sugar industry, the cultivation of cotton advanced toward the littoral. Cotton eventually won over the rich and poor sugar mill owners and growers.

It was a crop easy to cultivate, cheap, and democratic (allowing itself to be planted with broad beans, beans, and maize); it furnished from the farmer's field, at the same time, cash as well as food crops. Cotton's short vegetative cycle required only a few weedings or hoeings; consequently, it did not occupy the workers during the entire year as did sugarcane. It was not, thus, advantageous to acquire slaves at high prices, have them work for only part of the year, and remain inactive several months without producing anything and consuming food. Cotton cultivation in the second half of the nineteenth century almost never used slave labor. Squatters instead were paid for their agricultural work. When the demand for workers became great and the manual labor insufficient, wages rose to *mil-réis* rates per day. High wages, paid daily, were still more advantageous than the difficult and expensive acquisition of slaves. A lightweight product, cotton was easily harvested by women and children. All in all, cotton, when European markets needed it, held a series of advantages over sugarcane. Koster, in the first decades of the nineteenth century, encountered rich sugar mill owners (such as one from Cunhaú, a representative of one of the most noble ancestors of Pernambuco—Albuquerque Maranhão) cultivating it on his land, alongside sugarcane, and raising livestock.[83] Cotton cultivation expanded greatly when the United States, during its Civil War, could not supply the European market. On that occasion cotton spread over the Paraíba Valley, dividing with sugarcane the lands drained by the Mamanguape. It was cultivated on the interfluves of the Siriji with the Tracunhaém, in northern Pernambuco. In these regions it not only contended with sugarcane for land, it also converted the landholdings into diversified enterprises, since they maintained the cotton gins.[84] Many poor squatters—Mulattoes, Mestizos, and even Negroes—became rich cultivating cotton and rose socially; they were the "cotton whites."

The duel between sugarcane and cotton was also felt in all its intensity in Alagoas and Sergipe. In Alagoas, for example, despite the belief that its cultivation was declining, cotton has an economic importance even today in *municípios* of the Zona da Mata such as São José da Laje and União. In the last century it not only progressed hand in hand with sugar, since the sugar mill owners devoted themselves to one or the other crop, it even, in certain periods, replaced sugarcane, as social historian Diégues Júnior explains.[85] It also was very important in Sergipe, although the principal product was, in 1848, sugar, according to a contemporary statement.[86] Then, in Sergipe about six hundred mills were producing twenty thousand boxes of 50 *arrobas* (750 kilograms) of sugar each year.

Coffee, introduced into the region at the beginning of the century, did not seriously compete with sugarcane in the Zona da Mata, since it occupied only the slopes of the Borborema Plateau. Only in the Agreste, in the wet areas, did it compete with sugarcane. As an export product, as a major crop, it would transform the Agreste landscape, causing this region (settled with the view of supplying the internal market with livestock) to be driven even more toward the external market, to which it had been inclined since the cotton boom.

As for the problem of labor, the period now being considered is that in which slave and wage labor began to compete. In the first half of the century, slave labor still dominated and the slave traffic with the coast of Africa was carried on with great intensity. Tollenare, who was in Recife in 1817,[87] had an opportunity to observe the selling of slaves when Negroes of both sexes, of all ages, and of various physiognomic types were sold wearing only a loin cloth, exposed to the eyes of prospective buyers or of the simply curious. The price of a slave was quite high; one cost about 900 francs. An ox cart, generally, 200 francs and a horse, 70 francs. Thus, on the average, a slave was worth about four oxen or thirteen horses. In those markets slaves were sold to the sugar mill owner, who would take them to his property. In southern Pernambuco and in the Recôncavo of Bahia, despite the existence of much unused land, were the richest sugar mills and the most favorable areas sugarcane cultivation. At the beginning of the century, the large mills possessed, in general, more than one hundred, at times even one hundred and fifty to two hundred slaves. Despite the existence of a large number of . squatters, the owners did not often resort to wage labor; they limited themselves to receiving the low income derived from the rental and the cultivation of each squatter.

To the north of Recife, sugar mill owners who possessed numerous slaves and massive two-story houses were rare; for that reason, along with slaves, it was customary to hire wage labor—partly civilized Indians, Mulattoes, and free Negroes. Koster himself, as a mill owner in Jaguaribe, made long trips to Goiana and Paraíba, with the intent of hiring Indians to work in his fields during the peak work periods of planting or harvesting.[88] There were also lands owned by the religious brotherhoods: these were rented to small farmers who cultivated subsistence crops, and maintained the internal food supply.

It was common, in this region, for the mill owner, not able to acquire slaves on account of their high price, to make up the needed labor by helping squatters settle on their land in return for work on the fazenda. These workers had permission to clear areas of forest, erect huts of clay or straw, make a small cultivated field, and give two or three days of work each week at a low price, or free, to the owner.

What were called "bondage" squatters developed and they

have constituted a large portion of Northeast Brazilian rural workers from the second half of the last century to the present. These squatters attempted to place themselves under the protection of the owner; they did not enjoy any governmental guarantees. The owners received grants of land much smaller than those given in the time of Duarte Coelho (grants began to have a maximum size of four leagues in length by one width in 1695,[89] were reduced to three in length by one in width in 1729, and to one square league in the nineteenth century[90]). They were restrained from having large latifundia, but on their lands they were absolute masters.

Ruffians and livestock rustlers operated openly in the sugarcane region, creating an uncertain situation for the population. Some of them, like Antônio Bernardo and Cabeleira, became famous and still live in folk songs. For this reason the poor squatters tried to place themselves under the protection of these "rulers," receiving from them aid and a place to live. The owners, on the other hand, with available workers for the crops and persons that allied with them in the struggle against neighbors, better occupied their lands. If a squatter was imprisoned, his patron considered his authority diminished, his reputation lost, and tried to free him. Even today, rare is the landowner who does not feel his authority diminished if one of his squatters is detained by the police. To retain the squatters, the owners would customarily lend small amounts of money to them, only permitting the debtors to leave their land when the debt was paid. Koster himself pursued a squatter who tried to leave the Amparo sugar mill, which he owned, without settling his debts.[91] This custom is in generalized use in great areas of the Northeast, despite Brazilian legislation prohibiting imprisonment for debts. It is somewhat justified by Article 1,230 of the Civil Code, which maintains that the leasee of agricultural services is responsible for the payment of debts to the lessor.

The squatters lived in huts, and were very poor. They had only woven mats and clay pots, but always were armed with a knife, locally called a "fish knife," whose use was prohibited by the authorities. (Pasmado, located between Igaraçu and Goiana, was famous for making this type of weapon.) Generally, the squatters watched over the forests, transported the sugar by horse to the ports or to the railroad station, and also worked with the slaves in hoeing.

With the restriction on slave traffic and its subsequent abolition, the law of the free born, and the sale of a large portion of the slave population to the coffee planters in southern Brazil, who were in a spontaneous phase of expansion, the number of slaves diminished and wage laborers increased their contribution to the production of the sugar industry.[92] North of Recife certain jobs (bricklayer, carpenter, brickmaker, barrelmaker, etc.) were filled by free men who many times resided in villages, towns, and cities. This was even more common in Rio Grande do Norte and in Paraíba, where the number of slaves was lower, though less common south of Recife and in Alagoas and Sergipe. Visiting Sergipe in 1859, Avé-Lallemant found the great cane-growing area—Cotinguiba—had declining production because of the lack of labor; this was caused as much by the diminution in the number of slaves as by an outbreak of cholera that raged in the region during 1855 and 1856.[93]

In fact, the percentage of slaves in the population of the states of the Northeast from the middle to the end of the last century was not large. In Rio Grande do Norte the number of slaves never was very high. As Câmara Cascudo points out,[94] Rio Grande do Norte never directly imported African Negroes; the slaves there were acquired in Pernambuco, because sugarcane arrived there late. In 1805, they made up only 16.3 percent of the total number of inhabitants of the then captaincy. The number of slaves climbed in proportion to the increase in sugar production; thus, in 1835, there were in the province 10,240 slaves, and the number continued to climb until 1870. The advance of cotton cultivation and the great drought of 1877 ruined many property owners, and caused the sale of a great number of slaves to southern Brazil. By 1884 only 7,623 slaves remained in all of the province. A comparison with Bahia in 1854 shows that while in Bahia there were 1,200 sugar mills with 70,000 slaves, in Rio Grande do Norte there were only 144 mills and 1,508 slaves: that is, ten slaves for each mill, compared to fifty-eight for each one in Bahia.[95] In the middle of the century it was common for there to be mill owners, of small mills it is true, who maintained their property with four or five slaves and twenty to thirty free workers. These workers, besides remaining rigorously dependent on the owner, earned very low wages, about $400 *réis* per day. On the approval of the Golden Law, there were in Rio Grande do Norte only 482 slaves; the transition to free labor had already been made.

In Paraíba the picture was no different; great was the number of free workers who earned $400–500 *réis* daily; and after abolition the former slaves joined that group.[96]

As a matter of fact, in Paraíba there never was a high percentage of slaves in the population; they represented 16.3 percent (20,000 slaves of 122,407 inhabitants) in 1825 and only 5.7 percent (21,526 slaves of 377,226 inhabitants) in 1872.[97]

Even in Pernambuco, especially in the north in the dry forest, wage laborers were, in the second half of the nineteenth century, in general use. Millet, profoundly engrossed in Brazilian problems, declared that the suppression of the slave traffic did not do any harm, since sugar production increased after 1855.[98] He emphasized that though the cotton crops were cultivated almost entirely by wage labor, more than half of the sugarcane crop was attributable to the sharecropper system. Only certain very heavy jobs, such as cutting, transporting, and handling of the cane, continued to be done solely by slaves.

Millet himself admitted that in 1875, apart from the large mills (which produced more than five thousand loafs of sugar per year, a loaf of sugar weighing an average of 75 kilograms), others (about two thousand in Pernambuco and neighboring captaincies, whose sugar was sold in Recife), had at their disposal on the average from four to twelve slaves each. The free workers received very high wages, from $800 *réis* to 1$000 *mil-réis* per day. If these wages are compared with the price of sugar, which between 1872 and 1874 fluctuated between 1$600 and 2$200 *mil-réis* per fifteen kilograms, it is obvious that the net profits of the mills did not pay the costs of production.[99]

In Alagoas, the situation differed from that of the northern states. In 1871, the slaves constituted less than 16 percent of the total population of the province; according to the calculations of Espíndola,[100] there were 48,816 slaves in a total population of 310,585 inhabitants. This proportion decreased because of the abolition of the slave traffic, the law of the free born, the sale of slaves to southern Brazil, and the measures freeing more and more slaves after 1879. Abolition did not greatly disrupt the sugar economy. Unlike São Paulo, the Northeast did not receive European immigrants. They could not adapt to the subhuman working conditions that existed there. Neither did the Northeast have a crop under expansion, such as coffee. The formidable reserve of labor represented by the squatters was easily absorbed by the sugar agroindustry. The slave who saw himself suddenly liberated, without any help, without any land to cultivate, without government assistance, sensed that the liberty acquired constituted only the right to change masters at the time that pleased him. He became a wage laborer: as a squatter, he continued to live in straw huts or slave quarters, to eat dried meat with manioc meal, and to work at hoeing from sunup to sunset for a wage that varied between $400 and $600 *réis*.[101] The wage of a rural workers suffered a serious reduction after the Civil War, when the United States regained the European cotton market from Brazil. The price of cotton fell, its cultivation was reduced more and more, and thousands of workers found themselves without anything to do. Because of the increase of available labor, the landowner reduced the wages to about 40 or 60 percent of those paid during the cotton rush. The sugar crisis resulted more from the lack of external markets, and from the competition of European beet sugar and Caribbean cane sugar, than from the freeing of the slaves. Economic and social conditions made abolition feasible. The liberated slave did not have any perspective of a good place for his work. The freedom to come and go, not to be the property of anyone, was the only victory the slave attained under the Golden Law.

Development of Sugar Factories and the Proletarization of Workers

The central mills of the 1890s constituted a failure in the effort to modernize the sugar industry, and dashed the dream of Barão de Lucena to separate agricultural from industrial activity. The foreign companies that established the central mills were not compatible with the natural and economic conditions of the Northeast's milieu, machinery was insufficient and of poor quality,[102] and suppliers of raw material did not always fulfill their contractual clauses.

The improvement of the sugar industry was, however, an economic imperative. The raw sugar of inferior quality produced by the smaller, primitive mills could not compete on the international market. After 1870 many landowners were attempting to improve the industrial installations in order to produce sugar of better quality. Thus emerged the sugar factory, to replace the primitive mills. It was installed at the expense of the landowners (almost always the richest property owners) or at times by the enlightened and enterprising owner of various mills. The last two decades of the nineteenth century were a period in which the factory underwent its initial thrust in Pernambuco, the leading sugar-producing state of the Northeast. Between 1885 and 1900, about forty-nine factories were installed.[103] The installations, however, were made without prior study of the existing conditions, without an analysis of the areas of influence belonging to each factory, and, frequently, by individuals or companies who lacked sufficient capital for the running of a large industry. Many of the factories so established ceased their industrial activities after a few years. Also, rare were the founders of factories who continued as their owners. The majority, without capital at their disposal, went into debt, and had to sell the industry to a third party. If one examines the list of factories founded in this period, one observes that twenty-four no longer exist; they are, like the old, primitive mills, shut down, contributing cane to others that had better luck.

This sugar factory boom was looked on with great congeniality by the government of Pernambuco. The administration of Barbosa Lima was very generous in the granting of loans to the new industry. These loans were conditional on public utilization of the railroads, which the government would build, and to other clauses that tried to avoid public funds being used to benefit only the landowners. Contributing to the boom was the large increase in the price of sugar in the decade 1891–1900; the crystalline type reached a price of almost Cr$10.00 old *cruzeiros* per 15 kilograms. This euphoria would exist until 1901, when a crisis hit sugarcane cultivation, and the price dropped to less than Cr$4.00[104] Since the crisis lasted practically until World War I, the factory boom was quite diminished, though not by any means paralyzed.

During this same period, other northeastern states also received their first sugar factories. Founded by former mill owners, these factories resulted from the transformation of the primitive central mills, which had acquired land and cultivated sugarcane. This is how the Central São João in the Paraíba Valley, the only factory in the state of Paraíba in the nineteenth century, came about. In Alagoas, where the ecological conditions of the valleys of the Paraíba do Meio and the Mundaú were almost as favorable as those in southern Pernambuco, the first factory—Brasileiro—appeared in 1890, founded by Barão de Vardesmert. Three years later Leão, in the lower Mundaú Valley, and Sinimbu, in the small Jiquiá Valley,[105] were established. Sergipe also received its first factories in the nineteenth century. Only Rio Grande do Norte began the twentieth century tied to primitive sugar production.

Despite the economic crisis that began in 1901, sugar factories continued to be founded. Internal consumption absorbed more than 70 percent of production. By 1910 there were 130 factories, a majority of them small, in Sergipe. Because of the disorganization of the European beet sugar industry brought on by World War I, prices increased and so did the number of new factories. The production capacity of those already in existence improved and increased. As Table 4 shows, Rio Grande do Norte and Paraíba had, in the 1920s, a decrease in the number of factories, while in Pernambuco, Alagoas, and Sergipe, their number increased.[106]

TABLE 4
Sugar Factories in the Northeast, by State, 1910–1920

State	Number of Usinas	
	1910	1920
Rio Grande do Norte	4	3
Paraíba	5	2
Pernambuco	46	54
Alagoas	6	15
Sergipe	62	70
Bahia	7	22
TOTAL	130	166

Source: Gileno de Carli, *O Açúcar na Formação Econômica do Brasil.*

One must, however, stress that the sugar production was not greater or lesser according to the number of factories. Despite a small number of factories, Pernambuco's production was eight times that of Sergipe. Alagoas, with only fifteen factories, had a production 50 percent higher than Sergipe, which had seventy. The explanation is that in Sergipe, small factories, each one corresponding to an old mill, were established. In the other states the factories were steadily increasing their capacity to crush cane and were proceeding, each year, to absorb additional mills and even other factories. The production of Sergipe's thirty-six factories in the harvest of 1954–55 was 785,613 sacks, and, in the harvest of 1955–56, was 716,765 sacks of 60 kilograms. Catende, the largest factory in Pernambuco, had in those two years, 761,884 and 866,277 sacks. In 1955–56, the Central Barreiros alone had greater production than the thirty-six Sergipe factories combined: 824,390 sacks. In recent years Sergipe has witnessed the concentration of landholdings. Between 1956 and 1961 the number of factories declined from thirty-six to twenty-two. In 1973 they numbered only six. The total sugar production of Sergipe, however, remained relatively stable: it reached 635,900 sacks in the harvest of 1959–60 and climbed to 790,079 sacks in the 1960–61 harvest.

In 1973, analyzing the production quotas established by the IAA (Alcohol and Sugar Institute), the largest factories in Pernambuco were: Central Barreiros (1,200,000 sacks), Catende (983,000 sacks), Central Olho d'Água (703,162 sacks), Cucau, and Santa Teresinha (700,000 sacks each). These five factories produced a total 4,286,000 sacks, or about 30 percent of the total production of the state (17,810,000 sacks).

Besides Pernambuco, only Alagoas is a large producer of sugar in the Northeast: twenty-six factories produced 9,510,000 sacks. The other states possessed small factories and small production quotas. Paraíba had seven factories with a quota of 1,620,000 sacks; Bahia, six factories and a quota of 1,000,000 sacks; Sergipe, six factories for 900,000 sacks; Rio Grande do Norte, two factories for 600,000 sacks; and Ceará, Maranhão, and Piauí, each with a single factory and quotas of 200,000, 100,000, and 60,000 sacks. The government policy being implemented to stimulate the merger of factories and their transfer to better areas, will provoke, naturally, a geographic redistribution of them. Only with difficulty can the small factories producing fewer than 100,000 sacks per year be maintained. The sugar factory became an authentic "king" of the land,[107] always ready to extend its railroad tracks, like veritable tentacles to the areas where cane could be obtained. This hunger for land would make the latifundium problem, which since colonization has plagued the Northeast, worse.

The old colonial land grants, of uncommon size, were broken up by the old property owners in proportion to the number of sons that became adults or that their daughters married, so that new mills were founded. Thus one speaks of mills as "headquarters of the land grants," when one wishes to refer to the original old ones. The old, large latifundia were being divided and creating medium-sized holdings. These latter, with the capacity to maintain one mill, generally had from 200 to 1,000 hectares. With a factory, this process of division, this breaking up of properties was not just delayed. Land concentration began again so that today, factories like Catende, Central Barreiros, and Santa Teresinha, control enormous areas (each one more than 35,000 hectares) and more than fifty old mills. Twenty or thirty mills in the hands of one factory is common in Pernambuco. There are factories that control tens of mills and entire valleys.

When they were established, factories had available machinery with a crushing capacity superior to the production capacity. Thus they tried to acquire more land to supply cane for the crusher. This reversed the imbalance, leaving machinery capacity inferior to agricultural production. Refinery owners perpetuated a cycle, thus, and the concentration of land ownership became more and more accentuated.

Railroads, either private or the old Great Western, now called the Rede Ferroviária do Nordeste, helped increase the expansive powers of the factories by permitting the transportation of sugarcane great distances. The Brasileiro factory, which was one of the more important factories in the country during the decade 1931–40, had mills along the railroad in União and São José da Laje, about 30 kilometers distant. In turn the private railroads of each factory not only ran across their own lands, but often, by means of concessions, crossed those owned by others. These latter almost always dismantled their machinery, the property changing, now without being able to process the cane, from producers of sugar to suppliers of cane. The railroads, radiating in several directions, but almost always climbing or descending a valley, marked the extent of influence of each factory. At times the takeover of a zone where there were good mills was disputed among various factories that wanted to extend their railroad lines into the area. These mills were actually auctioned off by their owners. The right of passage through private sugar mills was purchased at a high price. The economic crisis that began in 1923 and reached its low point in 1930, affected the industry until 1940. Many factories and mills closed their doors, put out the boiler fires, and became contributors to others more powerful.

It is interesting, however, to emphasize the small mill's capacity for resistance. With less capital, outdated techniques, low productivity, and an inferior product, the small mill resisted the factory boom, turning back to the regional consumer market. Despite its economic weakness and the governmental advantage obtained by the factory owners, it was the 1950s before the small mill was practically extinguished. It resisted for more than seventy years the onslaught of the factories. For example, in 1914, exactly thirty years after the establishment of the first central mills in Pernambuco, only 490, or 17.5 percent, of the small mills in Pernambuco were shut down, dominated by the forty-nine factories then in existence. In Alagoas in 1931 there were twenty-seven factories, but 60 percent of the mills, about 618, continued to operate and produced about 31 percent of the sugar in Alagoas.[108] Today, however, the small mill is rare. It may crush part or all of a harvest, but it no longer constitutes a resistant force to the advance of the sugar factory.

Factories, with the new development boom caused by World War II, not only considerably increased production, but because of the use of trucks and the improvement of highways, increased their area of influence, extending it to the upper courses of the rivers, to the most distant brooks, even to the steep slopes of the Borborema Plateau.[109] There are instances of factories situated almost in the Agreste, in actual indentations of forest, and in the *caatingas* of the Borborema: in Santa Helena; in Paraíba, with the Central Olhos d'Água, Petribu, and Nossa Senhora de Lourdes; in Pernambuco; and with Serra Grande itself, in Alagoas. The small Crauatá factory, in Canhotinho, Pernambuco, was located on steep slopes drained by the headwaters of the Rio Canhoto, a tributary of the Mundaú. During favorable periods, when sugar prices are good and the IAA permits, factories are established in topographically unfavorable locations. Both the Laranjeiras factory in the Siriji Valley, and the Nossa Senhora de Lourdes in the basin of the Capibaribe-Mirim, were so constructed during the decade of 1951-60.[110]

Today the number of factories has also diminished. In Rio Grande do Norte, the most important—Estivas—crushes fewer than 340,000 sixty-kilogram sacks of sugar per year; in Paraíba, the Santa Helena and São João factories produce more than that, the first exceeding 400,000 sacks per year. In Alagoas, the principal factories, Central Leão and Coruripe, exceeded one million sacks; there were few factories that produced fewer than 250,000 sacks. In Pernambuco the three largest factories, Catende, Central Barreiros, and Central Olhos d'Água, each produces more than a million sacks. Of the forty active factories in the state, only eleven have a production of fewer than 300,000 sacks and are considered average when they produce at least 400,000 sacks of sugar per year. There the process of industrial concentration has reached the point that there are not only large factories absorbing smaller ones, but private companies acquiring more factories and organizing economic groups that control not one, but several. The Bezzera de Melo group holds the factories Rio Una, Santo André, and Central Barreiros, in Pernambuco, and Santana in Alagoas. They control more than 70,000 hectares in continuous area and produce almost 2,000,000 sacks of sugar per year. The Costa Azevedo group, controlling the Catende and Piranji factories, have amost 45,000 hectares producing about 1,000,000 sacks of sugar per year. The Dias Lins group owns the União e Indústria factory in Pernambuco and Serra Grande in Alagoas, with an annual production of about 1,000,000 sacks. José Ermírio de Morais, who recently began to invest capital in sugar factories in Pernambuco, acquired the São José and Tiúma, formed a small empire of about 40,000 hectares and a production of 1,060,000 sacks of sugar in the 1972–73 harvest. In turn, small factories like Regalia, Santa Inês, and Peri-Peri ceased their activities, and were absorbed in recent years by larger factories. One can see the intense concentration taking place in the industrial sugar sector of Pernambuco, with serious implications in Alagoas.

In Sergipe this concentration was not observed until 1961. There the largest factory, São José in Laranjeiras, produced only

121,655 sacks of sugar. Twenty-two factories produced 790,079 sacks of sugar, which gives an average production per factory of 35,912 sacks. The Sergipe sugar industry is in decline, since the small factories are not able to compete with the large ones. Production costs are high because of conditions inferior to those of the large industry. Sergipe and the historic area of Cotinguiba are dotted with traditional cities, old churches (many of them toppled by history), and of time-honored manor houses. This area is witnessing the retreat of sugarcane before the advance of pasture. With the rising valorization of meat, the small Sergipe factory owners believe it more advantageous to raise and fatten cattle for the slaughterhouse than plant cane and make sugar. They have dismantled the factories, sold the hardware, established pasture where there were canefields, fenced the properties, and raised or fattened mixed-breed Zebu cattle. The steer, like cotton before, was favored by the increase in the internal market, and confronted and overcame sugarcane.

The advance of cattle, however, did not cause a fall in Sergipe sugar production, which had a quota of 900,000 sacks for the harvest of 1972-73. In fact, the major portion of the factories disappeared and sugar production became concentrated in six, with a capacity between 250,000 (Central Riachuelo) and 75,000 (Vassouras and Proveito) sacks annually. These factories are small compared with those of Pernambuco and Alagoas, but exhibit a capacity equivalent to those of the other states of the Northeast.

Land concentration became one of the most serious problems of the Northeast, especially in areas with high population density, like the Zona da Mata and the Agreste. Strong social tension and conflicts between property owners and wage earners took place in the Zona da Mata. SUDENE, thus, in its first Directorate Plan, accepted the responsibility to attack the agrarian problems of the Northeast with a twofold policy: (1) promoting the migration of surplus population of the region to underpopulated areas, southern Bahia and northwestern Maranhão; (2) restructuring the sugar agroindustry to increase agricultural and industrial productivity. The latter was to be brought about by the use of modern methods of irrigation, fertilization, and protection in the form of insecticides and herbicides; the reequipment of the factories; and the release of lands, as payment of government loans by factory owners, for the establishment of family-sized parcels for food production.

The Land Statute promulgated toward the end of 1964 and the creation of the Brazilian Institute of Agrarian Reform made an agrarian reformulation for the region possible. A survey of rural properties made in the area in 1965 showed the domination of latifundia (and exploitation) and, consequently, of indolence in land use. The Zona da Mata and the Agreste in Pernambuco were considered priority areas for agrarian reform. Under this reform the Caxangá factory, with more than 20,000 hectares, was expropriated.

Likewise, under the PROTERRA program, expropriation of excess lands from the large holdings, to establish small and medium properties, was begun. Under this program, large property owners (those who held more than 1,000 hectares) had to convey to the government a portion of their land to be distributed among farmers; these latter would receive financial and technical assistance from the government. This portion was as follows: 20 percent of the area of 1,000 hectares; 30 percent of the properties between 1,000 and 3,000 hectares; 40 percent of the properties that had between 3,000 and 5,000 hectares; and 50 percent of those larger than 5,000 hectares. The resulting released land can be divided into from one to six parcels.

The price per hectare of expropriated land was established by the Ministry of Agriculture, and based on the statements of the landowners in accord with the INCRA surveys. Despite an unfavorable initial reaction by the more conservative landowners, an appreciable number of them delivered projects to PRO-TERRA. At the conclusion of the time period to deliver projects to INCRA, January 26, 1973, the agency received in Pernambuco the concurrence of 119 property owners, among whom were several sugar factory owners. Seventy-seven thousand hectares of land were offered for release,[111] of 130,000 that had to be released to INCRA. In Paraíba 12,478 hectares were released and, in Ceará, an area that exceeded 500,000 hectares. The process of merging factories and programs of reforestation coexisted with this program.

In Sergipe the advance of cattle raising had more serious consequences. The sugar agroindustry employed more men than livestock raising; thus high unemployment in the rural sector resulted. The factory owner turned cattleman needed few laborers; he dispensed with and made most of the squatters leave his lands. They flocked, then, to nearby small cities—Maruim, Divina Pastora, Riachuelo, etc.—to the villages and towns in the area, and to Aracaju. These unindustrialized urban areas could not employ the recent migrants. The people, then, without prospects of a better future, either emigrated to Bahia (a great number of people from Sergipe live in Salvador), to the Southeast region of Brazil (Rio de Janeiro and São Paulo), or even to northern Paraná. Livestock raising resolved the economic situation of tens of property owners, but led to unemployment, misery, and the emigration of a large percentage of Sergipe's population.

Bahia, formerly a state of great sugar production, had its cane fields greatly reduced, since the Recôncavo was, in large part, occupied by tobacco (Cruz das Almas, São Felix, Cachoeira), by manioc (Nazaré and Maragogipe), and by cacao in its southern portion. Today it possesses six factories, the largest with quotas of 260,000 sacks (Aliança and Cinco Rios) and the smallest with quotas of 20,000 sacks (Altamira). The state's production total of 1,000,000 sacks has little importance in the Northeast region.

The factory afforded an opportunity for the apperance of a new figure in the sugarcane landscape of the Northeast, that of the supplier of cane, successor to the owner of the small mill. The old owner, on dismantling his mill became a supplier himself. His position as a producer of raw material for the factory of another is reminiscent of the figure of the cane grower of the colonial period. The current factory owner is the equivalent of the old mill owner. Actually, the cane supplier is dependent upon the factory owner, just as the grower was on the mill owner. Until 1930 the factory owner was not obligated to crush the cane of the supplier. The suppliers remained, thus, at the mercy of the factory owners. Squabbles were frequent, friction constant, but the capacity of the suppliers to fight was great. A few of them succeeded in getting the right to possess a supplier's quota, which was part of the overall quota of the factory. They also obtained credit facilities and financing, for the conversion into cash of their harvest, at moderate rates with a rebate during the cane-crushing period. Thanks to their capacity to struggle, the suppliers were able to survive and they account for, even today, the production of a high percentage of the cane crushed in all of the Northeast. In the 1960-61 harvest in Pernambuco, they contributed 49 percent of the cane crushed; in Alagoàs in the harvest of 1958-59, the percentage of cane from suppliers was almost 58 percent.

Not all of the suppliers, however, cultivate their own land. Many times they rent lands from the factory to plant cane. The landowning suppliers have, many times, quotas at several factories. The suppliers who rent land are tied to the factory that owns the land they till, and they can only send to that factory the cane they cultivate. They pay a rent equal to 15 or 20 percent of their production. There are still factories that have growers, small planters of cane who cultivate a few hectares and till the land with their household members and employees. Santa Rita in the Paraíba Valley reserved one of their mills—Gargaú—for such small growers. These growers almost always are employees of the factory—machinists, mechanics, etc.—who work in their specialty during the harvest and till the soil in the off-season. Monte Alegre, in the Mamanguape Valley, had more than sixty growers established on an old nearby mill belonging to the state of Pernambuco. Other factories there, like São João, possessed about one thousand growers; Santa Helena received from growers and suppliers about 70 percent of the cane crushed.[112]

There are factories in Pernambuco, exceptions to be sure, that do not cultivate a stalk of sugarcane. All raw material is purchased from suppliers. These include Laranjeiras, Matari, Muçurepe, and Central Nossa Senhora de Lourdes. The same thing occurs in Alagoas with the Boa Sorte, Santa Clotilde, and Taquara factories. It is fitting to emphasize that, in the struggle against absorption by factories, the cane planters did not organize themselves into cooperatives, though they did establish their own factories. Only one cooperative movement occurred in Alagoas; this took place in the São Miguel Valley and resulted in the establishment of the Caeté factory, in 1946. This factory crushed cane until 1957 (with an interruption in the period 1952–56) when the cooperative collapsed, and was sold to a corporation. Two other Alagoas factories legally organized in the form of cooperatives: Boa Sorte and Santa Clotilde. These, in fact, are partnerships organized by families, Brandão Vilela and Oiticica, old mill owners who, being related, joined to set up a factory. The associates are, then, linked more by bonds of kinship than by cooperativist ideas and convictions.

The tendency of the large factories, however, is to cultivate their own lands, eliminating the cane suppliers. They desire, besides the industrial, the agricultural profit. They acquire a large number of mills, linking them by railroads and roads to the factory, and divide all the lands they own into zones. These are then divided into captaincies, and in turn divided into administrative units that almost always correspond to the primitive mill of 400 or 500 hectares. They have, then, supervisors of the zone, field chiefs, and administrators to manage each of these districts. The area is cultivated with modern methods: with mechanization, fertilizer, and, for those located in drier areas, irrigation. Serra Grande, for example, invested a great deal of capital in reservoirs in order to irrigate cane located in their largest area, on higher lands.

To have an idea of concentration, it is enough to remember that only 18 percent of the cane crushed at Catende comes from suppliers; the percentage is also low at Santa Teresinha (32 percent) and Salgado (6 percent). Because of that there are those who affirm that the tendency is for the mill owner to become a supplier owning his land, next a supplier renting land, and, finally, to have to leave the land he possessed and tilled during almost all of his life.[113]

The selection of more recent and more productive cane varieties is today a problem that concerns the factory owner. The Co 333 variety has dominated the Northeast's cane fields. The victory of Co 333 over the other varieties (Coimbatore, POJ, CB, etc.) is chiefly because of its hardiness and drought resistance, and its reasonable yield. It is a sugarcane with a long vegetative cycle (eighteen months) and fast ripening; therefore, it is always crushed green or dry, provoking as a consequence a drop in industrial yield of the factories. Partial substitution of other varieties of cane with a shorter vegetative cycle, so that the factories can always crush mature cane, is imperative for the sugar industry of the Northeast.

The sugar mill administrator, an employee of the factory, manages the cultivation, and receives a weekly wage and, at the

year's end, a bonus in proportion to the production of the area
he administers. He does not have a private income, does not
direct his own business, and, as an agent of the factory, can be
fired at any time. He does not have therefore either the au-
tonomy of the supplier, or the classic independence and pride of
the mill owner.

In the sugarcane area there is still an economic group that the
factory is eliminating, but that in the first half of the twentieth
century had relative importance and, in certain areas, even great
importance: these are the peasants, or *foreiros*. They existed in
the slavery period and lived in areas away from the mills, cultivating subsistence food crops and paying the landowners a
small annual rent. During the peak work periods of planting and
harvest, it was customary for the peasants to give to the landowner a few days of work each week, at times gratis, at times for
very low wages; it was a bondage which, according to Lacerda
de Melo, resembled the medieval unpaid labor.[114] For that
reason the peasants are at times called "conditional squatters."
Their importance increased with the development of cotton cultivation, in the areas favorable to that agricultural activity. Cotton was a commercial crop par excellence, easily marketed, and
it gave the peasant a reasonable monetary income. Many mill
owners began to install on their land cotton gins, in order to
process the production of the peasants and of the small property
owners in the vicinity. This was common in Paraíba and Alagoas
by the first half of this century.

The sugar crisis and the consequent low prices made many
mill owners terminate their industrial activities. When there
were factories nearby, the owners became suppliers; when there
were not, they were in the habit of dividing the mill lands into
small farms to rent to peasants. This took place chiefly in areas
that, besides being distant from the factories, were also distant
from the main roads. It also occurred on the mills near the slope
of the Borborema Plateau, where there were fertile soils for the
cultivation of fruit and subsistence crops. *Municípios* such as
Vitória de Santo Antão, Amaraji, and Bonito in Pernambuco,
were very suitable for this type of leasing. Those mills were divided into a large number of small establishments; before long
they became the source of food for the cities, which, continually
growing, consumed the production and encouraged the de-

velopment of a small middle class in the countryside. But the end of World War II brought a valorization of sugar, and it began to have good standing on the international market; the modernized factories sought to expand their areas of influence and many mill owners living in the cities off rents decided to return to agricultural activities or make more rent by leasing their lands to the factories. They sought to evict the peasants, at times indemnifying them for the improvements, at others without giving any indemnification, allowing only a few months to harvest their temporary crops. Some factories permitted the peasants to remain on the land, locally called *sítios*, with the condition that they destroy the orchards, harvest the crops, and become sugarcane planters. Thus, in various ways and by various processes, the peasants were attacked and defeated in the first encounters. They sought, afterwards, to become organized. It was this struggle of the tenants, of the small renters against the landowners who wished to oust them from the land they had occupied (often for decades), that gave rise to the case of the Galiléia mill in Vitória de Santo Antão; this in turn gave rise to the famous Peasant Leagues led by then Deputy Francisco Julião. The consequences of the early victories of the large property owners over the peasants were felt by the inhabitants of the surrounding cities. Suddenly they saw a decrease in the quantity of fruit being sold in the open markets, and an alarming increase in prices. The nutritional conditions, always precarious in the humid region of the Northeast, became more and more difficult.

Unfortunately, there are no statistical data available on the subject, but from direct field observations, I can affirm that between 1945 and 1955 there was a large area, formerly occupied by peasants, that was taken over by sugarcane. A large number of peasants had to withdraw from the activity to which they had dedicated themselves.

The wage laborers (also called, in certain areas, field laborers) constituted an immense majority of the rural labor in the sugarcane areas. According to their greater or lesser degree of settlement on the land and their dependence upon the owner, they can be grouped into three categories: squatters, who lived on the land they worked; outside laborers, who lived in cities, towns, and villages of the zone; and the migrant workers (*corumbas*), who lived in the Agreste and the Sertão, but every year traveled to the sugarcane zone to participate in the harvest. With the first rains they returned to their land.

The first are the squatters who reside on mills or fazendas and receive a house to live in and a parcel of land on which to grow subsistence crops. The house, always small and humble, varies considerably in comfort and construction from one region to another. Some factories and mills, chiefly in Paraíba and Pernambuco, are in the habit of constructing houses of masonry, since it makes a comfortable house that lasts longer. The majority, however, are of wattle and daub. Supports are fastened one to another by an interlacing of sticks tied with lianas. Over this interwoven surface the clay is packed. In the past wattle and daub was used even to construct the big house of the sugar mills, like Teitanduba in the Siriji Valley. In Alagoas, however, in the sugarcane zone, one frequently finds houses thatched with straw, with roofs of four slopes, that by their form suggest African dwellings. The better houses of the squatters almost always include a front room, hallway, one or two bedrooms, and a kitchen. The majority, however, are made up of three rooms, one behind the other, from the front room to the kitchen. Never, or almost never, do they have wood floors, the surface being of packed earth. They do not have indoor plumbing, the streams being used for bathing and dense clumps of trees for attention to physiological necessities. This lack of sanitary facilities considerably worsens the regional health conditions. The house and the surrounding area for cultivation are generally called a *sítio*.

The squatter settled on such a *sítio* has a series of obligations to the owner, the principal one being to give him a certain number of days of work each week. On the other days he can, with the help of his family, cultivate in the area around his house any temporary crop; permanent crops such as bananas or coffee are categorically prohibited so that if the squatter moves he cannot seek indemnification. Generally the most cultivated crop is manioc; in Alagoas a lot of maize is cultivated and in Paraíba and in Rio Grande do Norte cotton has great importance in these plots. This system is even generalized in areas where factories are under development and the landowner requires only a bondage of three or four days per week during the rainy season. As the factories evolve, the area under cane cultivation increases. Subsequently, the landowners are not only limiting the plots of land of the squatters, removing them from the most favorable areas, but also requiring that they work five or six days per week on the cane fields. This precludes their tending subsistence crops. It then is contributing to the gradual proletarization of the peasant masses.

In the 1930s, when this system was at its peak, economist Humberto Bastos[115] and agronomist Gileno de Carli made studies of the living conditions of rural workers. In Alagoas, during 1936 and 1937, these workers earned a daily wage of Cr$3.00 old cruzeiros and cultivated fields chiefly of cotton. They ate dried codfish, manioc meal, inferior grade coffee, beans, and sun-dried meat.[116] At Christmas they sometimes ate beef.

The wages, however, fluctuated over the year in conformity with the greater or lesser labor requirements of the mills and factories. In 1940 Carli still found in Pernambuco laborers in the countryside earning Cr$2.00-3.00 per day. Even men who drove the horses and mules carrying the cane during the harvest earned only Cr$2.00-3.00 per day, and the oxcart drivers, with all the prestige they had in the rural environment, drew wages of Cr.$3.30 per day.[117] Living conditions were difficult, wages low, and the provisions, for the value of money at that time, were expensive. There were, however, the subsistence plots, which in winter, if there were not further work, could be planted with beans and cotton. The wife and small children helped tend the plots; at times they raised goats, pigs, chickens, and even, rarely, had a milk cow or a horse. The crops and animals complemented their diet and provided some money, used for buying clothes.

In the period 1956–65 one sees this system of living completely transformed. Chiefly in Paraíba and northern Pernambuco, the mills and factories still gave rights to cultivate crops, but the plots were small and located on worn-out lands. The squatters, furthermore, had to provide five or six days of work per week, which kept them from working on their food crops.

In Ceará-Mirim, the most fertile valley in Rio Grande do Norte, the topographic and soil conditions had a great influence on the population distribution; the settlements were always distributed linearly between the sandy, humic, lowland soils and those of the slopes, steeper in the northern part than in the south.[118] The squatters, who live clustered almost together, do not have land available to cultivate near their dwellings. The owners permit the squatters to cultivate a thousand planting mounds, that is, a third of a hectare, on the sandy slopes or on the tablelands, also sandy, of the level interfluves. Never or almost never do they use this right; the areas are some distance from the houses they reside in, the soil is of low productivity, the area is small, guarantees of harvesting the crops do not exist since the squatters can be evicted at any moment, and the time they have at their disposal to tend the crops is little because the planting period (August to September) coincides with the planting and harvest of sugarcane, when they have to give six days of work per week to the landowners. Anyone visiting the Ceará-Mirim region would be impressed by the close proximity that exists between the sites of the mills. These, besides being small (between 100 and 200 hectares), are long and narrow, all forming parcels with frontage in the bed of the Rio Ceará-Mirim. Thus, they comprise areas of dry lowlands, fertile sandy soil, and part of the tableland. A frontage some meters in width, on the riverbank, corresponds to at times a length in kilometers.

In southern Pernambuco and northern Alagoas, a zone with many large factories, the proletarization of the workers has already reached its pinnacle. The majority of them live in houses reminiscent of old slave quarters of the mills and have no right to cultivate food crops. Even those factories that theoretically give lands for that purpose, in practice prevent the cultivation of the land, since they require of the workers six days of labor per week. This accounts for the growing proletarization of the rural workers. In proportion to the increase in sugar production and the use of more advanced agricultural and industrial techniques, the rural worker is of necessity poorer, with fewer rights, a fact emphasized by Prado Júnior in a recent study.[119] In these areas, the workers are no longer settled; possessing nothing, they live like vagabonds, today on one mill, tomorrow on another. A bundle of clothing is the only possession transported in their successive moves, contrary to what still occurs in the zone of less proletarization. There it is common for the squatter to spend several years, at times even decades, on the same mill, even on the same plot of land. Proletarization results, consequently, from the growing impoverishment of the rural worker, which leads to discontent and dissatisfaction. The property owners, understanding this, carry out small relief efforts that serve as mere palliatives, without positive consequences; or they carry out drastic, violent measures to restrain the prevailing troubles.

Preoccupation with the maintenance of resident workers in the proximity led the factory and mill owners to grant them some social assistance, although in 1941 there was in Pernambuco a large factory that offered only religious guidance. This social assistance, however, is much less than that granted to industrial workers, who contribute to the welfare institutes, are unionized, and have a series of rights guaranteed by the Consolidation of Labor Laws. To the rural workers, not even the rights to vacation and the drawing of the minimum wage have been granted, despite the referred to Consolidation extending those rights in Articles 76 and 129, since 1943. Frequently, however, they receive from the property owners medical, pharmaceutical, dental (read tooth extraction), and social assistance. This is an effort to bind the worker to the company; it is carried out with greater or lesser intensity, according to the economic conditions and the more or less progressive thinking of the landowners. But it was not only with social assistance that many were wont to hold the workers; in some areas a custom prevailed that was very appropriately called "worker purchase." It consisted of the following: the property owner facilitated small loans to the worker; the latter, earning little, with a large family, and buying provisions in the owner's store that always charged high prices, would go on a weekly basis to make new loans, new debts. When the debt had climbed, the property owner began to deny additional loans, alleging that the balance was high. He threatened to make a weekly deduction from the worker's wages in order to amortize the debt. The desperate worker would try to leave for another place but the creditor would not permit him to move without settling his account. Then the worker would ask for a loan equal to the debt from the owner of the mill where he was going to move and, if he obtained it, would pay the former debt and move. He was not free, however, because if he were "sold" to a new property owner, he could only leave when he paid the sum of money owed. When the squatter could not find someone to "buy" him, he would sneak off at night from the property of the creditor. The property owner often obtained the support of the authorities, who would apprehend the fugitive so that he work for the creditor and pay off the debt. At times, the worker who had fled and been returned would work on the property of the creditor during the day and spend the night locked in a guarded room, in private jails. Although today it has become sporadic, infliction of corporal punishment on workers does still occur.

A large portion of the rural workers live, however, in cities, towns, and villages of the sugarcane zone. These are generally small settlements where, besides the rural worker, government authorities, a few government employees, businessmen, land-owners, and artisans reside. The worker lives in a settlement generally called a street, has the freedom to work whichever day he wishes, attend regularly the religious worship he desires, vote for the candidate he prefers or who pays the most for his vote, have a more active social life (dances are organized, gener-ally, on Saturdays), be able to frequent the taverns and drink sugarcane brandy, and receive a slightly higher wage. He does not receive, however, any medical, dental, pharmaceutical, or social assistance, and only with difficulty obtains loans.

In 1963 the Rural Labor Statute guaranteed the wage earner: the right to draw a minimum wage; vacations; a paid weekly day off; and an annual bonus equal to a thirteenth month of wages. The landowners opposed the application of the law but the workers organized in unions and resisted. This created an at-mosphere of tension in the region and the law began to be applied, more or less. With the application of the law the prop-erty owners preferred to decrease the number of squatters, of permanent employees, generally using idle workers engaged by labor contractors living in the cities and towns. Medical and so-cial assistance became available from the rural labor unions. All of this accentuated the process of proletarization of the rural workers. Beginning in 1971, with Complementary Law Number 11, social welfare was extended to rural workers; they began to enjoy the right of retirement for age and disability, and for families, a pension and funeral-expense subsidy. The rights en-joyed by urban workers since the 1940s were awarded thus to the rural worker.

The migrant workers, rustics, or *caatinga*-dwellers are inhabi-tants of the Agreste, and at times the Sertão, who spend the winter or rainy season in their region. There, as owners of small plots or as renters, they cultivate subsistence crops with the start of the rains, remaining until the harvest period. When summer arrives, and the factories begin to crush cane (and the dry conditions do not permit agricultural work in the Agreste), the migrants proceed in groups in the direction of the sugarcane area, at times on foot, at times in trucks, and offer their services to the factories and growers. There they remain until the first rains occur in the Agreste in March or April, when they return to their home in order to plant their fields.

The migrants distinguish themselves by their great capacity for work, by their gregarious spirit, which unites them and keeps them aloof from other workers of the sugarcane region, and by their appetite to suck sugarcane and drink the juice. They, in fact, use the sugarcane juice as a food in order to save the wages they receive and return to the Agreste or to the Sertão, at the end of the harvest, with some savings. Formerly, when there were transportation difficulties and they had to move about on foot, they used to visit their family only on the holidays—the period from Christmas to New Year's Day. Today with the constant movement of trucks, they go at times every fifteen days or every three weeks to spend Saturday and Sunday with their families. Without the labor from the Agreste, the factories of the Northeast would have difficulty accomplishing the cane crushing with the large harvest these days. In research carried out in the last five years at more than five hundred factories, from Rio Grande do Norte to Alagoas, I found not a single one that did without the cooperation of the migrants.

In the Ceará-Mirim Valley, for example, when the lowland remains flooded in winter and the planting of sugarcane can only be done during the crushing operation, there is, in that period, a great need for labor. At the old Ilha Bela factory there is a difference of 50 percent between the number of workers during harvest and off-season; at the São Francisco factory, which does not exploit carnauba palms, differences increase to 70 and 80 percent. The additional labor comes from the neighboring Agreste.[120]

In Paraíba these seasonal migrations are less intense because planting and harvest do not coincide. The increase in number of harvest workers over those of the off-season does not exceed 20 percent. The same phenomenon, with an intensity similar to that in Paraíba, also occurs in Pernambuco, Alagoas, and Sergipe.

The major source of migrants are the *municípios* of the Agreste, such as Taipu in Rio Grande do Norte; Guarabira, Sapé, Ingá, and Itabaiana in Paraíba; Bom Jardim, Limoeiro, Gravatá, Bezerros, Caruaru, Cupira, Panelas, São Bento do Una, and Bom Conselho in Pernambuco; and Palmeira dos Índios, Arapiraca, Junqueiro, Anadia, and Limoeiro de Anadia in Alagoas.

It is interesting that these seasonal migrations, because of the direction of the roads and trails, are made, generally, in a northwest-southeast direction, especially in Pernambuco. Thus the migrants from Taquaritinga do Norte, Surubim, and Vertentes always shift to Vicência, Aliança, and Nazaré da Mata; those from Limoeiro and João Alfredo to Vitória de Santo Antão and Moreno; those from Gravatá, Bezerros, and Caruaru to Amaraji, Gameleira, and Riberão; those of Cupira and Panelas to Catende, Palmares, and Barreiros; and those from Garanhuns and Bom Conselho to Viçosa, União, and São José da Lage, in Alagoas. Those of Palmeira dos Índios and Arapiraca go to the valleys of the São Miguel, Jiquiá, and Coruripe.

The factories farthest from the littoral and nearest the Agreste, such as Roçadinho, Pedrosa, Catende, Serra Grande, etc., receive migrants more easily and in greater numbers. Those located farther away, need, at times, to send trucks to the Agreste cities on holidays to arrange for workers. The Santa Teresinha, Santo André, and Central Barreiros factories, located far to the east, near the littoral, have frequently seized upon this resource to obtain the laborers that they need.

I have been informed that today in some factories—Catende, Roçadinho, and Santa Teresinha, chiefly—workers originating from the Agreste and their families have been settled. This is advantageous for the factories since they are considerably increasing their harvests and always need labor.

The proportion of area cultivated by agricultural machinery is small; the sugarcane cultivation processes are still traditional. Beside that, the lands of the interior are very irregular and even some lowlands are not suitable for mechanization, either being flooded for most of the year, as in Coruripe, for example, or very cut up by canals and drainage ditches, as in the Ceará-Mirim. Because of that there is great use even today of the hoe. In the Coruripe Valley the lowland floods so much that not even the hoe is used, being substituted for by the *furão* ("digging stick"), an implement of Indian origin.

The work regime has undergone considerable modifications in recent years; up to the decade of 1930 pay was daily. The day began at sunrise and ended at sunset. The workers were gathered into crews which worked together, in lines, under the supervision of a foreman. This was the hoeing work crew. At 10:00 A.M. and 3:00 P.M. the families would bring the workers lunch and dinner.

Today the work is done under contract. Weeding is paid for on the basis of area by *tarefas*, which vary from one area to another. In Paraíba and northern Pernambuco a *tarefa* can measure from 10 to 13 meters on each side, according to whether the brush is high or low. In southern Pernambuco the *tarefa* corresponds to a third of a hectare, and in Alagoas to 625 square *braças* (2.2 meters). In the morning the squatter goes to work where the work chief indicates the area he is reponsible for clearing. When the worker finishes, at whatever hour of the day, the chief inspects to see if the work was done as it ought to have been, and the worker leaves, free for the rest of the day. Depending on the vegetation growth, he generally works from daybreak until 2:00 or 4:00 P.M. Women are used in the planting and fertilizing of the cane fields. This is also paid for daily.

During the period of cane crushing, an activity of great importance, it is the cutting of the cane that is the harvest proper. It is hard work that only the best workers, the most willing, carry out. This work is paid for according to the rate of bundles of cane cut and tied. Each bundle must have twelve stalks and an average worker cuts from one hundred to two hundred bundles per day, with an exceptional one being able to cut up to three hundred bundles. The payment per bundle varies a little from one area to another and even in the same area during the harvest, depending on whether the crushing is behind or ahead of schedule.

The wages vary according to the law of supply and demand and with the specialization and capacity of the worker. It was kept, however, at the approximate level of the minimum wage, in a region in which the cost of living is very expensive. In 1977 dried codfish sold for Cr$89.00 per kilogram and sun-dried meat varied between Cr$22.00 and Cr$32.00. Manioc meal sold for

Cr$6.00 per kilogram, beans for Cr$15.00, sugar for Cr$7.00 if crystalline and Cr$9.00 if refined, and eggs, with a price that always varies, were sold at prices up to Cr$1.00 each. These are the prices of the commodities in the cities. The squatters supply themselves many times through consumer cooperatives that more or less comply with these prices, but on many mills and factories there still reigns the trading post system, where the products are of inferior quality and the prices even higher. There are even places where payment is not made with money, but with vouchers that only circulate in the trading post and that create conditions for imposing prices. The markets are supply points, although in the Zona da Mata they are more for the sale of textiles, clothing, shoes, and utensils than for grains, meats, and other foods, as in the Agreste.

By and large, one observes the growing impoverishment of the rural worker in the countryside. In interviews and inquiries carried out, I have had an opportunity to ascertain that their diet consists of manioc meal and dried or salted fish, coming from the ocean and the São Francisco River; among the fish, sand smelt and piranha are commercial commodities. A small shrimp fished for in the littoral lagoons is widely sold dried, in Alagoas, to the poor rural people. At times they purchase what is called "tender-loin," shreads of dried meat of inferior quality. Beans, sweet manioc, and squash are only eaten when cultivated. The sun-dried meat and dried codfish, the everyday meal since the slavery period, has risen so much in price that today it appears only on the table of rich and moderately well-fixed families.

Sanitary conditions are distressing and schistosomiasis endemic, infecting in some *municípios* more than 80 percent of the population. Depending on the area, other diseases such as yaws, Chagas' disease, various types of worms, and anemia occur, consequences of the standard of living of the population of the sugarcane region.

Labor Systems in Areas of Coconut, Rice, and Cacao Cultivation

In the region of the Zona da Mata and the Eastern Littoral sugarcane did not succeed in dominating large continuous areas. It took over the coastal strip (formed by the accretion terraces some 2–3 meters above sea level), some parts of the slope of the Borborema Plateau, the banks of the São Francisco, the Sergipe grasslands that almost reach to the beach, and southern Bahia.

On the coastal strips, away from the accretion terraces, the coconut dominates. In fact, despite being, like sugarcane, an exotic plant introduced by the Portuguese colonizers, the coconut before long spread over the littoral, occupying all of the area under study. Its penetration into the interior depended upon the width of the sandy terrace, which can stretch kilometers, as sometimes occurs in Pernambuco and frequently in Sergipe, or narrow to the point of disappearance, as occurs in Paraíba, to the south of João Pessoa, and in Alagoas, in the area between Santo Antônio and Maragogi. Sometimes the terrace is divided into sections by the mouth of some river, such as the Paraíba do Norte, Goiana, Serinhaém Formoso, etc.

On the beach the coconut groves entirely dominate the landscape and are visible from great distances. They cast their shadows over the dwellings of the fishermen, the gear and nets spread to dry, the shelters where the vacationers relax and the fishermen repair their nets, and the low vegetation itself that grows there. The small settlements and cities of the littoral (Muriu, in Rio Grande do Norte; Pitimbu, in Paraíba; São José de Coroa Grande and Jaguaribe in Pernambuco; Maragogi and Barra de Santo Antônio, in Alagoas; Porto das Cabras and Atalaia Velho, in Sergipe; and Barra do Itariri and Conde, in Bahia) developed in the midst of the coconut groves in such a way that the houses and palms form an indiscriminate mixture. Away from the sandy terrace, because of its importance the coconut is cultivated on a minor scale on the tablelands between the planted fields. This occurs on the Ubu sugar mill in Goiana.

A large area is given over to coconut cultivation, especially in the Northeast states of Bahia, Alagoas, and Sergipe. Coconut cultivation does not require great attention from large or small property owners, produces continuously for decades, and does not need costly industrialization. Production begins several years after planting—five to six years in the beach areas, and fifteen to twenty on the tablelands. The dwarf coconut, however, introduced into the Northeast in the last thirty years, has not been a commercial success even though it bears fruit two to three years after planting and is easily harvested because of its short stature.

This is because its fruit deteriorates more rapidly than the common coconut, making its sale more precarious. As a backyard plant for domestic use, chiefly to furnish coconut milk, it has had great acceptance. Many times, the coconut is cultivated on small properties 20-30 meters across the front, facing the ocean, and extending for hundreds of meters toward the interior; other times properties form genuine latifundia exploited by large property owners. The Central Barreiros factory, for example, whose lands extend to the beach, has a department to supervise and manage the coconut groves on the property, which contain about a hundred thousand trees. Little labor is used in the coconut groves; weeding is annual, almost always being carried out by workers who live in the cities and towns of the littoral, with payment being made by the day or by *tarefa*. This tarefa corresponds to 25 *braças* (a *braça* is equal to 2.20 meters) and requires two and one-half to three days for a man to complete it. When the property owner has sufficient resources, he will fertilize with castor bean cake and mineral salts, chiefly nitrogen, potassium, and calcium. With fertilizer, production of a coconut tree is greater, reaching, on the average, forty to sixty nuts per year. The majority of the small property owners do not fertilize the coconut groves and have, because of that, a production much lower than that of the large landowners.

The principal worker of the coconut grove is the coconut picker. Supplied with a leather strap device and a curved knife, he climbs the palm and cuts loose the ripe fruit and dried leaves. He draws a wage for each palm that he climbs, gathering the fruit, on the average, of eighty palms per day. The coconut palm gives four or five harvests each year, one every two or three months.

The beach population not only enjoys the shade of the palm, but acquires from the owner the leaves to thatch their houses and trunk logs to facilitate the launching of their sailing rafts into the ocean and their beaching on land. They live on the coconut fruits, but almost never own or work in the groves. This multiple use of the coconut vividly impressed Evangelical Daniel P. Kidder, who in the last century visited Itamaracá Island. Concerning its multiple applications, the North American visitor affirmed: "The coconut is in fact the principal vegetable of the region, and, although there are not known on the island all its applications, nevertheless, it provides to the population food, drink, fuel, shelter, and income. Beside the sale of coconuts, its pulp is converted into oil, the shell into vessels, and the fiber into rope. The value of the coconut milk as a drink is recognized by everyone. The leaf furnishes, in addition, the material necessary for the construction of an entire house. It can also be used to make baskets, fences, and when dried can be used to write, since its ash contains potash. The growing tip of the stem constitutes an excellent appetizing food."[121] Famous regional dishes using coconut are made, including beans and coconut, coconut sweet, fish and coconut, and coconut candy. It is also eaten with bread as a substitute for butter by the littoral population.

The processing of coconuts is done in a simple way; one sets up in the middle of the grove sheds made of coconut leaves. Here the nuts are husked and stacked awaiting shipment to the ports, to the processing factory, and the regional consumption centers, in barges and trucks. In the husking the workers are paid per thousand coconuts husked, the most ambitious being able to husk up to thirteen hundred coconuts per day. A good average is a thousand per day. As only the large- and medium-sized nuts enjoy good acceptance on the consumer market, there exist factories, chiefly in Sergipe and Alagoas, that process the small nuts, producing coconut oil and coconut meal. The oil can be of two types: with or without sugar.

Although the coconut is a plant of great economic value, to the point that one calculates the value of beach property not by area but by the number of bearing palms it has, it did not mold a civilization, as sugarcane did, and it does not permanently employ a large number of workers. The beach dweller almost always applies himself to fishing, although by procedures still quite traditional, with sailing rafts or using fish traps or garths.[122] The fisherman is considered in the entire region lazy, a man who likes work very little; this is obviously an exaggeration since the work of a fisherman is very hard. In fact, if the work regime does not have the continuity of the work of other areas, it is because it greatly depends on the weather. Also, food is easily found in the mangrove swamps behind the sand bar. There are great quantities of crabs, crustaceans that make excellent dishes.

In the strips of land more toward the interior, on soils which the coconut groves do not reach because of unfavorable conditions, there exist small *sítios* where fruits are cultivated: mangoes and jackfruits in Itamaracá; bananas in the Ceará-Mirim Valley; and arrowroot—a tuber whose flour is suitable for making biscuits, gruel, and porridge—in Cabo de Santo Agostinho. Small-scale farming is done on holdings in which the owner himself, with the help of his family and one or two employees, takes charge of the agricultural work. The area, however, is small, because just beyond it is the tableland, which is almost sterile, or cane fields on soils derived from the decomposition of crystalline rock.

In the lower São Francisco basin, downstream from Propriá, the principal crop is rice; this gives the best income and is of interest to most of the landowners. Cotton has some importance; the other crops are manioc, winged yams, and sweet manioc, only for local consumption. Onions do not have, there, the importance that they have gained in the middle São Francisco basin.

The influence of the river on the economic life of the region is decisive. As in the Amazon, it is the river's regime, not rainfall, that controls the agricultural calendar. The great difference of volume of water of the São Francisco between the flood, when its volume reaches 13,000 cubic meters of water per second, and the low-water mark, when the volume becomes less than 900 cubic meters per second, means that on the margins there are depressions that are transformed into lagoons during the period of high water, and the mouths of its tributaries are submerged. The floods of the São Francisco, determined by the summer rains of its upper and middle course, do not coincide with those of its small tributaries of the lower course, where the rains of autumn-winter predominate. The Merituba, a fluvial valley of more than 7,500 hectares, is flooded the entire year. Only with drainage can such valleys be used for agriculture.

The flood guarantees the natural fertilization of the inundated area, since the river deposits about 2–3 centimeters of silt and builds a small marginal dike that holds back the water for some time in the depressions. These depressions are locally called rice ponds. The areas located on the windward side receive a greater quantity of silt build-up than those located on the leeward side, and are thus better for rice production. The productivity of the riverbank lands of the São Francisco is high; one can obtain, on the average, 1,800 kilograms of rice per hectare.

Planting and harvest times differ, depending on location. Near the river mouth, Piaçabuçu, or upstream from Penedo, the rice fields can be naturally irrigated, owing to the major influence of the dynamic tide, and the harvest is initiated before August. In that month the volume of the São Francisco is greatly reduced, causing, consequently, the salt water of the ocean to invade the river.

Rice cultivation has been carried on in the region since the last century. A red-grained variety is used. It has little importance on the urban consumer market, but is easily propagated and is very hardy. The CVSF (São Francisco Valley Commission), today CODEVASF (Development Company of the São Francisco Valley), resolved to revolutionize the regional rice cultivation, and introduced a new rice variety called purple stem, which today is dominant. They also cultivate another strain originating from Sete Lagoas, Minas Gerais.

The CVSF gave assistance to landowners and farmers, teaching them cultivation and pest, chiefly caterpillar, control, selling insecticides, agricultural machinery, and threshing machines for the processing of rice at modest costs, and facilitating loan repayment on installments at bank interest rates. Also, they have a mechanization plan, and charge the farmer an hourly rate for the use of a tractor.

The landowner almost always has a lot of land, but does not directly cultivate it since he would not have work during all the year for his squatters unlike in the sugarcane area. Work is begun when the level of the river drops. Fields where rice will be cultivated are cleared by wage labor paid for by the owner. Wages vary with the quantity of workers available and with the type of vegetation to be cleared. The clearing completed, these wage laborers are released, moving on to support themselves with other activities—fishing, hunting, cultivating fields—that sporadically appear. There is, thus, underemployment and misery. The rice then is planted in seedbeds in the Piaçabuçu region, in February or March, in accordance with the distance from the river mouth. It is given to the sharecroppers in the period for transplanting, April and May. The harvest begins in July and lasts until October, when, because of the diminution of the volume of the river, the salty oceanic tide ascends the river beyond Piaçabuçu. Between Penedo and Propriá the seedbed planting takes place in May and the transplanting is carried out when there is a drop in the water level of the river. The harvest extends from September to December.

The seedbed is made by the landowner, who pays the wages of the laborers. The sharecroppers begin their annual activities when they then leave the cities in which they live, accompanied by their families, and establish themselves in thatched huts near the rice fields. The owner distributes seedlings to them. Generally, each family takes charge of four or five *tarefas*, at times, up to ten. In that region, a *tarefa* comprises 25 square *braças* or 3,025 square meters, almost a third of a hectare. The large families can care for greater areas, but the number of families is large and the landowner needs to take care of them all. These areas can be enlarged when the clearing and drainage of certain valleys like the Marituba open more land to rice cultivation. Rice ponds are divided into rectangles measuring 50 by 60 *braças*, and with a slope of 30–40 centimeters. Since the harvest lasts upstream from Penedo until October and November, water gates are installed. These not only impede the invasion of water coming from the first floods, but also control the outflow of water, in proportion to the rice field's location in the pond.

Since the sharecroppers need to obtain food and do not receive wages, it is the custom of the landowner to finance them, charging interest of 6–10 percent per month, to be repaid at the harvest. It is the obligation of the sharecropper to care for the rice field from the transplanting until the harvest, for an interval, on the average, of three months. Once the harvest is over, he threshes the rice so that it can be dehulled in the factories. This threshing can be done manually, with a stick, which damages the product, or by means of a thresher or beater, which is much in use in the valley, thanks to CODEVASF.

To use the thresher, the sharecropper has to pay the owner of it a rental for each *alqueire* processed (the Alagoas *alqueire* is equivalent to 240 kilograms); he even pays the operator who runs the machine by *alqueire*. Besides the operator, working on the thresher are the measurer, employed by the machine owner and paid by him, and from eight to ten helpers, sharecroppers themselves under a collective work arrangement. A thresher can process about 40 *alqueires* per day. It should be emphasized that the machines are sold by CODEVASF on installments, with a down payment of 25 percent and payment of the balance in three years at an interest rate of 7 percent per year. As can be seen, the acquisition of a thresher is an excellent use of capital for the landowners.

At the first processing, the rice is divided, 50 percent for the sharecropper and 50 percent for the landowner. Many times a contract obligates the sharecropper to sell his portion to the landowner at a price equal to two-thirds of the current market price. At times, however, the sharecropper can sell his portion of the crop to anyone he pleases. Property owners protest this, and allege that their profits are small. Recently some property owners in Penedo gave land to rice farmers, and charged only 25 percent of the production. At the same time, they guided and guaranteed the financing of them. It is a measure that, followed by other property owners (chiefly when rice lands are expanded and the offering of labor is diminished), could revolutionize the work regime of the region.

The rice sold to the rice processing plants established in the cities—Penedo and Propriá, chiefly—is dried and dehulled, and sent to the consumer markets in the Northeast by truck, and to Rio de Janeiro and Santos by ship. A company in Penedo— Peixoto, Gonçalves and Company—owns two steamships employed in this transport.

Rice harvested in the Piaçabuçu area is dried in heated chambers because the rains are still frequent in July, August, and September. Until 1962 rice harvested in the summer was dried on the surface of the streets of the more important cities. This still occurs in Penedo, in the part of the city near the docks. The rice sharecroppers do not limit themselves to rice growing activities, which employ them during only four to five months per year. Some also rent land in the Igreja Nova zone to cultivate beans and maize, paying 20 percent of the harvest to the property owner. In any case, they have a low standard of living and spend several months of the year without work.

The property owners are in the habit of cultivating, on the higher lands, with irrigation, herbaceous long staple cotton (Sakaa 4) and on the sedimentary, siliceous strips of land, cotton, maize, bananas, and mangoes. They raise cattle, if there is good pasture in the region, and during the summer use the rice straw as supplementary feed. This complementarity, an association between rice cultivation and livestock raising, occurs in an area where it tends to become ever more important, because the carrying capacity is one head per hectare.

Southern Bahia is practically a new area that is being opened to agriculture and livestock exploitation in the second half of the twentieth century. This is despite the fact that the first towns of the littoral—São Jorge dos Ilhéus and Porto Seguro—were founded in the sixteenth century. These towns, however, prospered little and their captaincies were absorbed by that of Bahia. Beginning about the end of the eighteenth century, forest areas west of Ilhéus were opened and cacao, a crop originating in the Amazon, was successfully cultivated thanks to favorable soils and a hot, humid climate with rainfall distributed over the entire year. Cacao created the wealth of the region, directed entirely toward the external market, since more than 90 percent of its production is destined for export. Its cultivation, and the wealth channeled by it to the region, brought on migrations of workers from other regions of Bahia and from Sergipe. An agricultural system and a society different from any other in Brazil resulted. The cacao tree, requiring shade in order to grow, did not bring about destruction of the forest and, being a permanent crop, created a great necessity for labor only during the harvest period. For that reason the number of permanent workers on the fazendas is small, most of them residing in the cities and towns and rendering service to the property owners as wage earners. In the off-season, the workers stay in the urban centers—Ilhéus and Itabuna, chiefly—living by occasional work, or migrating to other regions. On the fazendas, cacao occupies all of the tillable land. The manioc meal, maize, beans, fruits, and vegetables consumed in the area are imported from other regions and sold, consequently, at high prices.

In modern times, the sandy areas near the coast, unsuitable for the cultivation of cacao, are being occupied by crops that are developing as a function of the industrial growth of the country; these include the oil palm and rubber tree. Large companies, with capital and modern techniques, plant these crops and use wage labor. Livestock raising and forest exploitation are also economically important activities in southern Bahia.

The recent opening of Highway BR-101, which gives easier access between Salvador and Rio de Janeiro, will stimulate the development of tourism, especially if one takes into account that in the area is found Porto Seguro—a historic city linked to the discovery of Brazil—and Ilhéus, popularized in the entire country by the famous novels of Jorge Amado.

Property, Polyculture, and Labor
in the Agreste

Cattle Raising and the Settlement of the Agreste

Since earliest colonial times, cattle raising has been a sub-
sidiary economic activity to sugarcane cultivation. Sugar mills
were almost always run by animal power, and transportation of
the cane from the fields to the mill, and of the sugar from the
mill to the embarkation ports, was always to require a great
number of cattle and horses. In the off-season these animals
were placed in beach areas, or, in more favorable areas on the
large landholdings themselves. They thus spent the winter without disturbing planted fields, or creating trouble for the agricultural activities. Not having barbed wire to make fences, the mill
owners were in the habit of reserving strictly for cattle raising
areas at a distance from the cane fields, as far away as Olinda
and Recife, the great sugar emporiums. On the occasion of the
Dutch invasion, sugarcane agriculture was already concentrated
in the Paraíba do Norte, Capibaribe, Jaboatão, Ipojuca, and
Serinhaém valleys, while extensive cattle raising occupied the
wide tablelands of Alagoas: those areas drained by the São Francisco and Cururipe rivers; to the north, in the valleys of the
Mamanguape and Camaratuba; and in Rio Grande do Norte.

In the earliest times cattle raising was an activity to which
those independent types who wanted no part of the sugar civilization's rigid social hierarchy dedicated themselves. They lacked

the capital to establish mills, acquire slaves, and plant sugarcane. They always tried to establish themselves near the coast or navigable rivers, since water transportation was the only type used for long trips. The war with the Dutch and the fear of losing animals requisitioned by the invaders, made the cattle breeders of Alagoas and Sergipe go up the Rio São Francisco toward the Sertão.

Rich mill owners, like João Fernandes Vieira, André Vidal de Negreiros, and Duarte Gomes da Silveira, customarily founded in the drier and more distant areas fazendas and corrals where they grazed cattle to supply their mills.

The Agreste, located almost entirely on the Borborema Plateau, was near the sugarcane area and enjoyed climatic conditions and favorable grazing lands for the development of cattle raising. But the area was settled late. Only the lower portion, at the base of the plateau and extending to the middle course of the Paraíba do Norte and the Mamanguape rivers, was occupied by cattle breeders before the war with the Dutch. That occupation, which extended almost to the Cupaoba Mountains where Duarte Gomes da Silveira owned scattered corrals,[1] resulted in the invasion of the middle Mamanguape region by the French. With the support of the Potiguare Indians, they dominated the region for several decades in the sixteenth century, and developed an intense commerce in Brazilwood, a typical product of the dry forests.[2]

The more elevated, level surface of the Borborema Plateau remained unexplored. Cattle breeders avoided it when they ascended the São Francisco, and when they reached and ascended the valleys of the Açu and Apodi rivers. To the west when the Bahia cattle breeders crossed over the Rio São Francisco and ascended its tributaries on the left bank—the Moxotó and the Pajeú—they bypassed it. The Ipanema River would be the route of penetration to the Agreste.[3] Only after the war with the Dutch, however, would this region be conquered and economically integrated into the Northeast.

The invasion of the Agreste, however, began during the Dutch occupation. Ambush parties and plunderers linked to the Portuguese government in Bahia attempted to destroy the canefields in the areas under Dutch domination. Knowledge of the Agreste would become more systematic after the expulsion of the Dutch, when the Pernambucanos had to destroy the Palmares *quilombo* and liquidate the Confederation of Cariris.

The Palmares *quilombo*, with a series of satellites, exercised influence during the second half of the seventeenth century over areas that extended from Atalaia in Alagoas to Garanhuns in Pernambuco: large portions of the Zona da Mata and the Agreste. Its destruction afforded opportunity for innumerable land grants to be awarded in these areas previously outside the control of the Portuguese government.

The battle against the rebelling Cariri Indians made possible the continued invasion of the Agreste and of part of the Sertão. Livestock raisers took the Indians' land and enslaved them by pretext of "just war." The remaining powerful Indian tribes withdrew to the mountains, to the high wet areas less accessible to the Europeans and less coveted by the cattle raisers.

After the liquidation of the Negro state and the indigenous tribes, the governors approved land grants on the riverbanks of the Paraíba do Norte, Capibaribe, Ipojuca, and Una. Large fazendas were established since the land given under a land grant was almost always three leagues in length by one league in breadth, an area of more than 10,000 hectares. The Agreste has steep relief and the wet areas are frequent, so the property owners almost always had ample level areas suitable for raising livestock. There they grew panic grass, bluestem grass, and mimosa. In humid areas they produced subsistence crops. They had sufficient water—in the riverbeds during the rainy season, in wells during the dry season. They formed, thus, establishments with self-sufficient economy because they were in an area where, because of the relief, it was difficult to obtain foodstuffs from another region. The cattle, which could move on their own, were the commodity destined for the supply of the city of Olinda and the sugar mills of the humid zone.

Extensive cattle raising, with open grazing, did not require much attention or labor. For that reason, the number of slaves in the region was small. The fazenda was administered by a cowboy who watched over the cattle to keep them from going astray and from disseminating epizootic diseases. The landowner generally lived in the city or on a sugar mill in the Zona da Mata. The cowboy took care of digging water holes during the drought and driving the cattle to the watering troughs, as well as

cutting the "branches" of the cacti and bromeliads, feed that
mitigated the hunger of the animals in the dry months when
there was no pasturage. He kept count of the cattle in the country, branded, earmarked, and prayed over them in case of ill-
ness, and broke in oxen and burros. At times, on the larger
fazendas, there was a veritable team of cowboys, each one with
his specialty. Thus evolved the wrangler, blacksmith, and horse-
breaker.[4]

So that the animals of one owner not be confused with those
of another, they received a mark or brand. The mark was generally made on goats and sheep and consisted of a differentiating
cut on the ear. Cattle were branded with the initials of the
owner on the right side; on the left side was a brand indicating
the river basin in which the fazenda was located. Thus, animals
of different fazendas and river basins grazed together at the most
favorable spots, without having any difficulty in being identified.
When the winter ended, and the fattened animals were ready
for slaughter, cowboys from various land grants would gather to
sort out the cattle and brand the young ones. These gatherings
became authentic festivals, for they brought together the cowboys from diverse locations.[5]

Not uncommonly, some wild animal would escape the cowboy's lasso, and spend years in the *caatinga* without being
caught. It was these wild animals that soon earned fame by at-
tracting the most famous cowboys in their pursuit. Cowboys of
the various areas would chase the wild animal. Whoever caught
the animal, besides earning fame, would receive a prize, the
captured animal or a sum of money. Even today in the Sertão
they have these hunt festivals, preceded by circulars in which
the date, location, characteristics of the animal, and the value of
the prize are announced. The round-up itself,[6] a popular festival
in all the livestock area of the Northeast, consists of a group of
cowboys racing after a wild steer, in a long, narrow enclosure;
certainly its origin was in the former sorting out of cattle.

The cowboy, who was responsible for the fazenda, did not receive cash wages. His remuneration corresponded to a fourth of
the production of the fazenda. Of every four calves born, one
belonged to him and the other three to the owner. At the dividing up of the calves, the cowboy could sell his to the owner. On
large fazendas, because of high production, the cowboy occasion-

ally ended up a fazendeiro. Generally each fazenda, besides the cowboy, employed some free Mestizoes,[7] who did auxiliary work and received a small cash wage, a house, and meals. Those who drove the herd great distances on foot to the humid areas were called cattle drovers. For these long drives, as well as for entire days spent in pursuit of wild cattle in the *caatinga*, the inhabitant of the Agreste or the Sertão carried his own food. In a leather valise, he carried dried meat mixed with manioc meal, *(paçoca)* and raw sugar. Also it was customary to carry a leather bag, which kept water cool and clean.[8]

To provide their food, it was customary for the cowboys and agricultural workers to clear stretches of forest in the wet areas (the Indians no longer offered serious resistance) and cultivate fields of basic foods, chiefly maize, beans, and manioc. It was also customary to cultivate the dry riverbeds, taking advantage of the moisture furnished by the alluvial water table. This agricultural activity is even today called *vazante* ("riverbed") agriculture, since it moves onto the riverbed in proportion to the drop in the water level. Generally farmers did not settle permanently in the wet areas. They made clearings in the forest, where they planted crops and built a hut that would serve as shelter on the days of most intense work and provide a place to store utensils. Generally these huts were thatched with leaves of pindova or sheelea palms and at times with sape grass.[9] Transhumant agriculture of this type was unexpectedly found in 1952 by Lacerda de Melo[10] in the Serra Negra in the Pernambuco Sertão, and by me in 1961, along the lower São Francisco in Alagoas and Sergipe.

The structures of the fazenda headquarters were very poor compared with those of the sugar mills in the Zona da Mata. When the landowner resided in it, the house was roofed with tile. Beside it were the houses of the cowboys and agricultural workers, almost always thatched with straw, the corrals of wattle and daub, and in front, the patio (that is, a large field where all the trees had been cut down and where the cattle from the corrals were kept).

In the middle of the seventeenth century, when the population of the Agreste had grown, even extensive livestock raising operations could not absorb the labor that existed there. Indians seeking refuge in the elevated wet areas were being settled in villages. Droughts were making the inhabitants of the *caatinga* seek refuge in the humid areas. These last adapted to the new environment, to the gathering of forest products and to agriculture. In this way the elevated wet areas came to be densely settled. Concentrated groups of people devoted themselves to growing food crops and to the cultivation of sugarcane. The cane was transformed by the mills into raw sugar and sugarcane brandy. *Sítios* and small villages developed. Agricultural workers on fazendas of the *caatinga* many times became peasants and renters, who supplied the Agreste with food items and, when cultivation and sale of cotton created preconditions, began to furnish them also to the Zona da Mata and the Sertão.

Thus, in the second half of the eighteenth century, in the Agreste region, there were six parishes with a total population of 14,086 inhabitants,[11] distributed as shown in Table 5.

TABLE 5
Parish Populations of the Agreste in the Second Half
of the Eighteenth Century

Parish	Population
Campina Grande	2,480
Cumbres	1,140
Bom Jardim	4,687
Limoeiro	272
Bezerros	1,838
Garanhuns	3,669
TOTAL	14,086

Source: "Idéia Geral da Capitania de Pernambuco e suas anexas, etc.," in *Anais da Biblioteca Nacional do Rio de Janeiro,* vol. 40, 1918.

By 1774, population was growing in the humid area, where Cimbres, Bom Jardim, and Garanhuns were founded. The population devoted itself in general to subsistence agriculture. Three other towns grew up along the penetration routes to the interior: Campina Grande, a livestock commerce center, was the gateway of penetration to the Paraíba Sertão, in the Cariri region; Limoeiro and Bezerros, located in the Capibaribe and Ipojuca valleys, were resting places for the drovers moving from the Agreste or the Sertão toward Recife.

The Agreste population was generally poor, cultivating only cotton and subsistence crops. Cotton cultivation has expanded since the middle of the eighteenth century, but it would be the beginning of the nineteenth before it would bring about a revolution in the Agreste and the Sertão. Maize, beans, and manioc were the subsistence crops, and sugarcane was raised for syrup and raw sugar. These crops produced low profits.

Cattle destined for the internal market did not result in great expense, or in great profits. The poor population earned a living, in conformity with the area in which they lived. In Campina Grande they sold cattle. In Bom Jardim they herded cattle for the sugar mill owners of the Zona da Mata who went to spend the winter in the Agreste. In Garanhuns, Cimbres, and Bezerros they hired themselves out as drovers for cattle going to Recife or Salvador. It is interesting that the influence of Recife and Salvador was so great in the region. Cattle came from Garanhuns and Cimbres to Recife at the same time that they went from Bezerros, located much closer to that city, to Salvador. The influence of the capital of Bahia reached, thus, almost to the sugarcane zone, although the Pernambuco influence penetrated this economically contested area to the westernmost portion of the Agreste.

The Revolution of Cotton Cultivation in the Agreste and The Development of Wage Labor

Cotton cultivation created a veritable agricultural revolution in the Agreste after the middle of the eighteenth century. As an autochthonous crop it was relatively important in the first century of Portuguese colonization, was practically overshadowed by sugarcane in the next, but regained prominence in the eighteenth century, and became and remained one of the principal crops of the Northeast. Various factors contributed to this development: the increase of population and the consequent increase in consumption of cotton cloth, like calico; invention of the steam engine, its use in the textile industry in Britain, and the consequent Industrial Revolution; the opening of Brazil's ports to friendly nations by King João VI in 1808; and international political events such as the United States Civil War, which removed from the international market, for a relatively long period, competitors that used more advanced processing techniques and produced better-quality cotton than Northeast

Brazil. From 1750 to 1940, cotton was one of the principal products of the Northeast, and the only crop to successfully challenge sugarcane in the competition for land and labor.

It was about 1750 that cotton began to influence the economy of the Northeast, according to the writings of Pereira da Costa.[12] The government created an Inspectorate of Cotton, later transformed into the Cotton Custom House, and charged it with the responsibility to inspect and classify cotton products destined for export. Initially cotton cultivation was concentrated in the Zona da Mata, but penetrated steadily into the interior, finding more favorable natural conditions for cultivation farther from the coast. Expansion of cotton cultivation was aided by the stagnation affecting the sugarcane sector, as well as by the low agricultural productivity of the creole variety of sugarcane, and the low industrial productivity of the animal-driven sugar mills. Economist Celso Furtado[13] is of the opinion that this phase made possible the liberation of labor the sugar industry could not absorb, and led to the migration of that excess population to the Agreste and other areas near the Zona da Mata.

Cotton was by nature a more democratic crop than sugarcane. Cultivating it were not only the large landowners, using slave and wage labor, but small landowners, renters, and sharecroppers. Cotton processing was cheaper and less urgent than sugarcane processing and it fell into the hands of businessmen who, first with cotton mills and later with cotton gins, established themselves in cities, towns, and villages, and began to buy raw cotton from the farmers to sell it, after processing, to the exporters. This contributed to the development of urban life, as sugarcane cultivation never did. Even today the cities located in the Agreste are larger and have more commerce than those of the Zona da Mata.

Originally native varieties of tree cotton were cultivated: these produced for about three to four years. Koster,[14] in his travels through the Northeast, found it being cultivated on poorer soils in association with maize. That was one of its greatest advantages. It could share the same fields with subsistence crops, permitting the small farmer to produce, in the same area and with only one land clearing and weeding, both food and commercial crops. Beside this, after the harvest had been carried out during the driest period of the year, the cotton branches and maize stubble could serve as feed for cattle, which were allowed to browse for two to three months in the harvested fields. That advantage was a stimulus to the large landowners of the region, since they could increase their profits without modifying their traditional economic activities, and without forsaking cattle raising. Even today one can see that in the Agreste and Sertão cattle raising is the economic activity most associated with the latifundia. The large landowners are always principally cattle raisers and only secondarily farmers. This pattern is broken in the wet areas where climatic conditions are less favorable to cattle raising and where land is almost always in small holdings.

The development of cotton cultivation increased in the beginning of the nineteenth century when, thanks to the studies of the naturalist Arruda Câmara, extraction of cotton seed oil began. It developed further after the opening of Brazilian ports, when Recife was linked directly to British and later to French markets, and export prices increased considerably.

In the decade 1841–50, seedlings of herbaceous cotton from North America[15] were introduced into Pernambuco and soon spread through the Agreste and Sertão. They adapted to very diverse climatic conditions in the *municípios* of Garanhuns, Brejo da Madre de Deus, Cimbres, and Flores in Pernambuco. The base for a veritable cotton boom took place in this manner, reaching its climax during the United States Civil War when the secessionist southern states, under naval blockade, found themselves cut off from British consumer markets. Not only in the Agreste and Sertão were men drawn into the cotton whirlpool; the same thing happened in the sugarcane valleys of Paraíba do Norte, Capibaribe Mirim, Tracunhaém, Siriji, Mundaú, and Paraíba do Meio in Pernambuco. In those areas forests were devastated and sugarcane lands replaced by cotton fields. Numerous cotton mills functioned on the sites of former sugar mills. People made fortunes, rose in social status, and became equals of and on intimate terms with the proud sugarcane planters. Negroes, who achieved a tremendous boost in social status over a few years were called in some areas "cotton whites."

Cotton even had great importance in the present century; if it had not been for the economic crisis of 1929–30, the scourge of the pink bollworm, and the expansion of cotton growing in São Paulo, perhaps cotton would today still be the great competitor of sugarcane in those subhumid areas of the Northeast.

Chroniclers like Tollenare and Koster, who visited the Northeast in the early years of the nineteenth century, affirmed, chiefly, that the large landowners, euphoric with the high prices of cotton after the opening of the ports, organized cotton plantations. They cultivated it as aristocratically as they had sugarcane. Tollenare, the shrewd French businessman who was in the Northeast in 1816–17, observed cotton cultivation taking place on lands some 10 or 15 leagues from Recife, by landowners who made use of one hundred to one hundred and fifty Negro slaves. In Ceará, there were landowners who had up to three hundred Negro slaves.

There were only minimal expenses involved in supporting slaves, since they were not given meat to eat, but fed a diet of manioc meal and maize mush; and they were obligated to cultivate both manioc and maize in association with cotton. It is possible that there was considerable hunting in the Agreste and that the slave himself would attempt, during slack work periods, to supplement his diet. Allowing that each Negro produced 20 *arrobas* (15 kilograms equals one arroba) of cotton per year and that an *arroba* would be worth between Cr$6.00 and 11.00, the Negro generated an income far superior to that derived from work in the sugar mills. It does not, however, take into account the hidden cost of greater physical wear and tear on the slaves in the sugarcane areas, where the owner would have to require of them harder and heavier work.[16]

The price of cotton was increased significantly by the expense of transporting it to the port of Recife over wretched roads on the backs of animals. Nevertheless, the limited production of the plantings made near the coast resulted in the crop being taken toward the interior to the Sertão, a distance of several leagues from the port of shipment.

Even persons of nobility, owners of dozens of slaves and many leagues of land, were enraptured by the prospect of cultivating cotton. Koster, in his travels in the northern part of the region observed that, faced with the uncertainty of cotton production because of climatic variations, sugarcane planters cultivated sugarcane *and* cotton.[17] They attempted to diversify their economy with two crops so as not to be dependent on the price of only one.

In the Agreste large cotton plantings arose: in Bom Jardim, Pernambuco, for example, a British observer had an opportunity to visit the Pindoba fazenda, whose owner was rich, owned many slaves, received his guests in luxury, and fed them appetizing food.[18] Another planter had recently constructed, certainly with profits earned from cotton, a large two-story house for his residence, and dwellings with "an air of comfort" to house his slaves.

In the humid area of Paraíba, the initial phase of subsistence cultivation—manioc and grains, and sugarcane, on a small scale, to be crushed in vertical wooden mills powered by oxen—had in 1815 been replaced by cotton. And in the town of Areia, Pernambuco, in the first half of the nineteenth century, there were four cotton mills. In that area cotton, despite having against it "the inconvenience of excessive rain, cold spells, and pests" that damaged the standing crops, was more profitable than sugarcane until the middle of the century.[19] Only then was a third economic cycle initiated in the humid area of Paraíba—that of sugarcane—coming after cotton in the same way that it had followed subsistence crops.

In Paraíba in the *caatinga* of the Agreste, cotton also expanded in such a way that local rural landowners "came to compete with the sugar mills, not only in the number of slaves they owned, and in the buildings constructed, but in the advantages and profits that gave the industry its position."[20]

But it was not only the large landowners who threw themselves into cotton cultivation; small landowners and squatters soon began to plant it on the plots of land they occupied, growing it in association with maize and beans, in order to harvest a subsistence and cash crop from the same field. For them, cotton production was small, but the expense was minimal because they invested little labor. Cotton became a crop of the rich and the poor, because it could be planted in association with other crops, on the same short vegetative cycle, and did not need to be processed.

Landowners also realized that cotton branches and maize stubble could serve as supplementary feed for livestock during the driest months, January and February. They granted land "for the stubble" to squatters already on their land and to those of nearby villages and settlements. In March, with the first rains, landowners released plots of land to the squatters, who planted maize, beans, broad beans, and in May, cotton. During the year the squatter could harvest the subsistence products and cotton for himself as long as he finished the harvest in December and returned the land to the owner, whose livestock were then moved there to browse on the stubble of the crops during the period before the first rains. No rent was charged, since there was an abundance of land, few squatters, and the land was given for the stubble. That system remained in effect until the beginning of this century; even today it is, at times, still found in force in the most remote areas and on the least productive lands.

Slave labor was not very profitable for cotton cultivation. Cotton has a short vegetative cycle, and provided work for the Negro slaves only from May to December. Its harvest was largely done by women. It did not require year-round care like sugarcane. For that reason landowners felt that it was a disadvantage to support slaves for the entire year, if they were occupied for only eight to nine months; in drought years maintaining them was especially a problem. Also, the price of slaves increased considerably beginning in 1854, after the slave trade was banned. Hence the large landowners of the Agreste gradually proceeded to substitute free labor for slave labor, paying high wages for the period when cotton prices increased and landowners wished to expand their cotton hectarage. In 1863 in the Sertão of Ceará, they came to pay 1$280 *mil-réis* for a day's work,[21] and in 1875 in Pernambuco wages varied between $800 *réis* and 1$000 *mil-réis* per day.[22] According to statements of a knowledgeable witness of rural problems in the Northeast,[23] in 1875 slave labor disappeared from cotton and vegetable crop cultivation; small-scale exploitation was dominant. Slaves continued, however, to make up nearly 50 percent of the labor force on sugarcane mills.

In the second half of the nineteenth century, almost a century after the cotton revolution, a new crop, coffee, began to transform the Agreste. Large areas of forests in the wet areas were devastated and the contribution of agriculture to the economy of the Northeast increased. Coffee developed as much in the wet areas, hillsides, crests, and uplands about 500 meters, as it did on the edges of the Borborema Plateau, in the area where the Zona da Mata ends and the Agreste begins.

Coffee was introduced into the Northeast in the closing years of the eighteenth[24] and early part of the nineteenth century,[25] but was for dozens of years only a backyard tree, cultivated for domestic use. By the middle of the nineteenth century, however, coffee was introduced into the elevated humid areas of the Agreste and developed considerably, at a time when sugarcane cultivation was giving low profits. Coffee stopped the primitive sugar mills, drove the small and traditional growers of manioc and maize to the poorer sandier soils, destroyed existing forests, and enriched the large landowners.

In the wet area of Paraíba coffee's trajectory was brilliant but rapid. Introduced into the area of Bananeiras, Paraíba, in about 1840, coffee became the "king" of the crops from the last decades of the last century until 1925, when it was wiped out by the pest *Cerococus parahibensis*. Bananeiras enjoyed great days during that period; a coffee aristocracy was formed, with colonels, commanders, and even barons, like the Baron of Araruana. Although only a small city, Bananeiras had a well-constructed church, secondary schools, newspapers, and active commerce. But it suffered a swift decline brought about by an insect pest that technical knowledge of the time could not combat.[26]

In its golden age, coffee extended throughout the wet regions of Paraíba, taking advantage of the destruction of the Cayenne variety of sugarcane by gummosis disease, which reached its climax in 1884. Coffee, thus, had its high point of development in the last decade of the nineteenth and the first two decades of the present century. The destruction of coffee fazendas, from 1921 and 1925, brought about a return to sugarcane cultivation in Areia and neighboring *municípios* in Paraíba. Steam-powered sugar mills for the production of raw sugar were introduced and sugar factories (Santa Maria in 1931 and São Francisco in 1948) were built.[27] Tobacco cultivation developed in Bananeiras and sisal in Areia.[28]

In most of the wet area of the Agreste there was a succession of economic cycles in just a few centuries of agricultural land use. These cycles were determined by the appearance of crops to replace others devastated by pests and disease. Sugarcane, coffee, and, recently, sisal dominated, forcing other crops to areas with poorer soils. These crops gave greater or lesser profits to the large and middle landowner, leaving the majority of the population in a miserable situation.

Slavery did not have much importance in the wet area compared to southern Pernambuco. In 1880 there were only 3,630 slaves, 14 percent of the total slaves of Paraíba.[29] The rural workers endured, and still endure, living in the condition of slaves. Horácio de Almeida, the astute writer from Areia, discussed the squatters of the sugar mills and fazendas of the wet area of Paraíba and declared:

> The wage laborers lived in shacks of straw that looked more like pigpens than houses. And in these dunghills they raised a family, sleeping together on a raised platform of small sticks or on the damp ground, with absolutely no privacy. When it rained, the water would pour like a faucet into the hovel onto the crouched inhabitants. In the cleared space in front of the shack, potbellied children with twisted limbs showed their abdomens filled with roundworms. The young daughters had only a single set of clothes to cover their bodies, and ten-year-old boys were already trying to help their parents. They did not have plots to cultivate food crops because they worked six days a week and also because the owner did not give them land on which to plant. Their only cheer was to drink a few cents worth of sugarcane brandy at the market on Saturdays. The remaining balance of their salary, paid at the end of the week, hardly covered the cost of manioc meal, a drink of sugarcane brandy, and at times a liter of broad beans for the following week. Their unchanged plight was always there, even though they might take a few drinks of sugarcane brandy. Although sad, with little reason to be happy, they were gentle, respectful, and servile. Living on a diet of manioc mush made with water and salt fish, or a mixture of broad beans and manioc meal, they endured the heavy work from day to day with unaccountable physical energy. Those who had a milk goat to help feed the infants were considered rich. Five-year-old children were allowed to smoke by their parents to prevent possible toothaches. Tobacco and alcohol served to deceive the stomach and console them for the degrading social conditions under which they lived.[30]

In Pernambuco and Alagoas coffee cultivation became important in the middle of the nineteenth century. Cultivation expanded in the Zona da Mata in *municípios* located at the base of the slope of the Borborema Plateau, and in the Agreste in the higher exposed wet areas. In Pernambuco it occupied the Serra de Taquaritinga; the localized crests of the interfluves between the Capibaribe and Ipojuca, and the Ipojuca and the Una rivers; and the Garanhuns Plateau. It extended in Alagoas through the *municípios* of Palmeira dos Índios, Quebrângulo, and Viçosa located at the southern edge of the Borborema Plateau. In Bahia it occupied areas of the Diamantina Plateau.

In the Sertão of Pernambuco, mountains, including Triunfo, were soon covered with coffee trees. The ecological conditions were sufficiently favorable in these wet areas if coffee was planted on relatively high slopes that had good soil drainage and aeration; the deep soils conserved moisture and facilitated root penetration. Planting coffee under shade trees, a general practice throughout the region, helped maintain a reasonable soil pH and reduce erosion.[31]

Under favorable conditions and with cheap wage labor available since slavery was about to end, coffee became a commercial crop of major importance in Bahia and in the humid regions of the Agreste in Pernambuco and Alagoas.

Beginning in 1965, coffee production in the Northeast began to decrease considerably. The federal government, through the IBC (Brazilian Coffee Institute), carried out a policy of removing coffee trees of low productivity. The owners were reimbursed for trees removed, and were able to allot the land to other crops or to cattle raising. This policy furthered the trend toward cattle raising in the Agreste, led to unemployment in the rural areas, and stimulated migration to the cities. In the areas of shade-grown coffee, deforestation accelerated soil erosion. Production fell considerably: to 43,282 tons in Bahia in 1970; 14,152 tons in Pernambuco; and 10,082 tons in Ceará. Paraíba produced 1,183 tons, leaving the other states of the region with production of less than 700 tons. Today, in the face of declining Brazilian coffee production and growing demand, the IBC is stimulating the planting of new coffee trees in the traditional coffee-producing *municípios* of the region.

Coffee became a crop of the rich and poor. Since it was a tree crop, however, squatters and renters were forbidden to plant it, so that they could not claim reimbursement for the coffee trees when they left the land. Coffee, once planted, does not begin to bear until the third year; it represents a major investment of capital. It would be a crop only of the rich if, when young, it were not possible to plant intercalary crops of manioc, maize, and beans, subsistence crops for the small landowners. The small landowner could, if he needed, work weeding the coffee fazendas for the large landowner, generally in July and December. During these months the large landowners required a lot of help; weeding was done by hand. During the harvest, from August to December, women and children were chiefly employed for the light harvest work, thus supplementing the meager family income.[32] The situation was similar with regular families on the coffee fazendas and with rural families in other parts of the Northeast.

The Agreste, essentially characterized by cattle raising in the eighteenth century, became predominantly agricultural in the nineteenth and twentieth centuries. Each economic cycle brought further diversification to the Agreste, as did the improvement of technical conditions in agriculture, the increase of population density, the construction of good roads linking the region to the state capitals, and the progressively greater division of land. The Agreste increased its contribution to the food supplies of the large cities of the Northeast, surpassing the Zona da Mata and the Sertão. Cattle raising has steadily lost area and been changed from an extensive to an intensive enterprise; at the same time it has been transformed into a highly profitable activity by such policies as intensifying the fattening of animals. Cattle raising in the Agreste is relatively more important than it is in the Sertão, in spite of the fact that it occupies considerably less area.

Current Labor Systems in the Agreste

The Agreste, as the region of transition that it is, has much more accentuated ecological conditions than the Zona da Mata and the Sertão. Great diversification in the type of land use results in diversification of the labor relationships of the countryside. In this section I shall try to dissect the mosaic that is the

Agreste. After making clear the regional importance of the small property owner and the socioeconomic patterns of the small property owners, I shall study the labor relationships dominant in the sugarcane and sisal areas, in the area of livestock raising associated with the cultivation of cotton and cereals, in the coffee zone, and in the area of tobacco cultivation. Excluded is a discussion of the labor relationships in the rice-growing area of the São Francisco Valley, because they are the same as in the just discussed Zona da Mata.

The first reality with which one is confronted in studying the agrarian problems of the Agreste is the importance of the small farmer, contrary to what occurs in the Zona da Mata and the Sertão. Indeed, more than 85 percent of the agricultural establishments of the Agreste are made up of properties or occupied areas of fewer than 20 hectares, though these cover only 14 percent of the total area of the region. These small property owners make up, undeniably, a rural middle class that has a standard of living much lower than the large and medium property owners, but an economic and social condition far superior to the landless workers. Among them, however, there is an accentuated economic distinction determined not only by the size of one's property, but also by its location and soil fertility. The people, in their empirical wisdom, called larger parcels of land "*sítios*," but called small lots of less than 1 hectare a "house lot." Land use and the standard of living of the small property owner vary greatly from one area to another. In Brejo de Areia, in Paraíba, for example, the small property owners customarily, imitating the mill owners, cultivate sugarcane and sisal, and also at times, between the rows of sisal, the traditional subsistence crops. They have, generally, an occupation (bricklayer, cabinetmaker, carpenter, mechanic, and so on) that guarantees them a definite income.[33] They are artisans, called "artists" in the region; to have an "art" guarantees economic security.

In the wet areas of Pernambuco, the land is very subdivided. There are small *sítios* in the wet areas of the Serra do Vento in Belo Jardim, the Serra Vermelha in Caruaru, and in Bezerros and Camocim de São Félix. The small property owners raise a little coffee, cashew nuts (the cashew tree is used to shade the coffee trees), a little black pepper (planted alongside the cashew trees, which provide support), and some fruits—oranges, mangoes, avocadoes, jackfruits, and so on—planted within the coffee area. All that, however, is insufficient to support a family.[34] There is a veritable confusion of cultivated vegetation since the owner, having available only a small area, tries to use it to the maximum, though the income is trivial. They do not know the technical processes for soil conservation and lack money to buy fertilizer. As a result, production is minimal, and the income is insufficient to support a family. The *sítio* owners supplement their income by working as hired hands for the nearby large and medium property owners, or migrate in summer to the sugar-cane area. There they work in the factories crushing cane, leaving their wives behind to tend their plot of land. They join the great army of landless workers who, beginning in September, migrate to the Zona da Mata, and they return to their *sítios* in March, when the rains begin.

The small property owner is also concerned with food self-sufficiency, trying in the scanty areas available to him to plant some sweet manioc, bitter manioc, and some maize, always in association with beans and broad beans, and to raise a few animals. These last include a milk cow or a young bull, raised on a tether. The cow is to provide milk for the family and to bear calves that, on being weaned, are sold in order to buy clothing. A young bull is almost always acquired in one of the cattle markets, at one or two years of age, and is fattened to be sold when sufficiently large. The cattle market of João Alfredo, for example, is characterized by the absolute domination of young bulls. These, fattened, bring a better price for slaughter than the common cattle fattened in enclosures. They are the major source of sun-dried meat, a food much appreciated in the Agreste and Sertão of the Northeast. It is very common, also, for each family to raise two or three castrated hogs, seeking through their sale at the end of the year to cover the extraordinary expenditures of Christmas and New Year's. Smaller domestic animals (goats, chiefly) are found on all of the small holdings. When there are no cows, these supply milk.

In certain stretches of *caatinga* in the Agreste, where the semiarid climate predominates but the soils are sandy and deep (in Lajedo, Surubim, Vertentes, and Capoeiras in Pernambuco), the land is divided up and the small property owners devote themselves to growing tubers, chiefly manioc, yams, and potatoes. Manioc mills powered by animal traction are found with frequency. Manioc meal constitutes a commercial product par excellence for these small property owners. They have a modest standard of living, though it is superior to that of the wage laborers. Their houses dot the landscape, one near the other, always constructed of masonry with a terrace in front. To move about and transport the agricultural products to the city, they almost always have a horse, mule, burro, or, at times, a small ox cart pulled by two young animals. These last are numerous chiefly in the districts near Capoeiras, São Bento do Una, Caetés, and Garanhuns. On market days, the narrow roads, lined with living fences of *avelós* trees, remain practically obstructed by these snail-paced, deliberate vehicles going to town. Driven by the small property owners, the carts are loaded with saleable products from the *sítio*. In the afternoon the owners return with the week's provisions. The carts are reminiscent of the German and Polish colonists' wagons, pulled by horses, and found often in the states of Santa Catarina and Paraná; they also remind one of the rubber-tired wagons, pulled by animals, widely used in the Apodi Valley in Rio Grande do Norte. There is, thus, a correlation between the small property owners and animal-drawn vehicles, since the small property owner does not ✓ have the means to acquire a jeep or truck. The animal-drawn vehicle—wagon or ox cart—serves to transport the family and produce of the *sítio*, without being very burdensome to scanty finances. These towns, as well as the cities of the Agreste near the wet areas, have large markets. Land division permits a great income division: it also increases the number of middle-income people. Markets like Camocim de São Félix, Cupira, Cachoeirinha, and Capoeiras are much more important than Goiana, Nazaré, or Palmares, large cities of the Zona da Mata. At times the market stalls and panniers have a wide variety of products, and occupy all of the streets of the town. Even larger markets—Campina Grande, Feira de Santana, or Caruaru—are well-known throughout Brazil. In the piedmont humid areas of the Agreste of Sergipe, near Itabaiana, there are small areas in which the land is extremely fragmented. There the farmers grow manioc, onions, and tomatoes to supply the markets in Aracaju and Salvador. The property owners have little land and need to receive the maximum return, so they buy organic fertilizer (from the cattle raising area) and carry on cultivation that is really gardening. Their greatest problem is the wide variation of prices for their products; the government does not guarantee a minimum price. The comparison between the standard of living of the small property owner and the wage laborer now is a strong argument in favor of a greater democratization of land, of a policy that strives for great division of land.

The standard of living can be increased when the small property owners, renters, and sharecroppers receive more efficient technical assistance, an education that induces them to use better the resources that the environment offers, have ample access to bank credit, and have the marketing of their production organized. This would eliminate the activity of the loan speculators during the off-season and of the middlemen in the sale of their products.

In fact, efforts have been made in the last thirty years to bring to the small farmer cheap and easy credit, technical assistance, and a minimum price guarantee for his production. The lack of organization among the farmers, their low cultural level, absence of cooperative spirit, the opposition of the large property owners and businessmen, the static character of the structures of the banking institutions all have retarded the application of laws that attempt to benefit the small property owner.

The creation of the Bank of Northeast Brazil and the expansion of ABCAR (Brazilian Association of Credit and Rural Assistance) services by the states of the Northeast opened new perspectives in the decade 1951–60 by assisting the small farmer with supervised agricultural credit. The Bank of Brazil, beginning in 1960, tried to provide credit to the small farmers, without waiting for them to come to the local branch of the bank. Its action was curtailed by the incapacity to take care of the great increase in contracts. In Pernambuco in 1963–64, the GEPA (Executive Group for Food Production) increased the number of loans considerably with state-supported allotments.

As executor of the program of minimum prices for agricultural products, the Bank of Brazil has been buying a portion of the cotton production (already ginned), maize, beans, and other products of the small farmer, using the facilities of CIBRAZEM (Brazil Warehousing Company) to store them. Still, the middlemen, despite losing a portion of their clientele, continue to control the production of the small farmers located in areas distant from the cities with Bank of Brazil branches and CIBRAZEM warehouses and silos. The renters and sharecroppers, without written contracts, remain dependent upon the owners of the land on which they work, and to whom many times they are required to sell their crops. I believe necessary a cooperativist policy that brings together a larger number of small farmers, to complement the actions of the official entities and effect the measures of protection and assistance to the small farmer.

The labor relationships that involve the landless workers, who occupy greater areas and are typical of the Agreste, are those that characterize the regions where livestock raising dominates, in conjunction with the cultivation of cotton and cereals.

Cattle raising in the Agreste is done on much less extensive fazendas than those of the Sertão. The fazendeiro generally divides the land into fenced areas, some devoted to the keeping of cattle during the rainy season. During most of the year they are divided into small lots and rented to peasants who receive the land in March with the obligation to return it in December or January. The fazendeiros do not need, like owners of properties that are essentially agricultural, many workers, or great numbers of squatters. The cattle-raising practices, despite being more developed than those of the Sertão, cannot be considered intensive, except in certain areas specializing in milk production or in the selection of Zebu breeding stock for sale to breeders. To compensate for climatic conditions, the cattle migrate seasonally, and are given supplementary feeding or the stubble of certain crops—chiefly maize, cotton, and rice.

The seasonal migrations, carried on since the eighteenth century, are made between the Zona da Mata and the Agreste, when the landowner has land available in both regions, or between the *caatinga* and the elevated wet areas in the Agreste itself. In the first case, the cattle are driven to the Zona da Mata in September, when the sugarcane harvest begins; at that time the pasture lands of the Agreste are dry and in the Zona da Mata there is an abundance of cane straw. With the first rains, in March, the cattle are returned to the *caatinga*, where they remain during the period in which the pasturage becomes more abundant, thanks to the growth of panic and finger grass. In the past the sugar mill owner frequently had a fazenda in the

Agreste and there at times he would spend the "winter." Today
that custom is disappearing. Certainly the high price of land and
the intensification of the agricultural work of the mills account
for this in part. Also responsible is the recent expansion of cane
fields because of the steady increase in production capacity of
the factories.

A similar movement is occurring between the *caatinga* of the
Agreste and the elevated wet areas. The mountains, very wet in
winter, do not lend themselves to livestock raising and are used by
farmers who cultivate cereal grains, plants with a short vegetative
cycle. During the dry season, after the harvesting of beans, maize,
and cotton, the cattle are driven to the mountains and high wet
areas, where they subsist on the stubble in the fields. The wet
areas of the Jacarará, Moça, and Ororobá mountains in Pernambuco, and the Mar Vermelho and Quebrângulo mountains in Alagoas are well-known refuges for the cattle. In the wet areas of Paraíba the sugar mill owners generally have cattle fazendas to the
west, in the basin of the Curimataú, and make similar seasonal migrations of their livestock from one region to the other.

When the property owners do not have land in different regions for seasonal migrations, they give the cattle supplementary
feed in the summer. In the past, as well as today, in the Sertão
and some stretches of the Agreste, native plants were and are
used in this feeding: *macambira* bromeliads and the *facheiro* and
mandacaru cacti. The bromeliads, cooked and chopped up, and
the cacti, burned to remove the spines, are fed to the animals
when there is a lack of pasturage.

The improvement in the quality of the cattle and an increase
in technical practices have led the fazendeiros to cultivate plants
that would serve as feed for the animals; during the last two
decades, the planting of *palma* cactus and grasses intensified.
Palma is widespread in the semiarid areas of less rigorous climate, the Agreste of Paraíba and Pernambuco and in the Sertão
of Alagoas in the *municípios* of Jacaré dos Homens, Major Isidoro and Batalha. In the Agreste of Sergipe, which has a subhumid climate, grasses are dominant.

The fazendeiros need to mobilize squatters to plant *palma*.[35]
The cultivation of hundreds of hectares of *palma* requires little
capital because it is a permanent crop that continues to grow for
twelve to fifteen years. The squatters cultivate the *palma* in

cleared areas that the owner turns over to them. They are re- quired to plant the "ears" of the cactus and to keep the fields weeded; they can plant for themselves, between the rows of *palma*, maize, broad beans, beans, and cotton. For a period of three to four years, when the *palma* is not yet large enough to be cut and only needs for its development two or three weed- ings per year, the squatter can care for it and his crops without any capital investment on the part of the property owner. When the *palma* is of sufficient size for harvest, it shades the ground and precludes the intercalary cropping. The squatter withdraws, then, from the field, leaving the land and the *palma* to the owner. From then on the owner limits himself to paying daily wages to workers who once a year clear the weeds and brush that grow in the *palma* fields.

Direct care of the cattle requires few people. The cowboy today is simply an employee adapted to caring for animals, knowing how to lasso them, give them urgent treatment, milk cows, and so forth. He does not much resemble the cowboy of earlier times, though even today those of the Sertão dress in leather and dash through the *caatinga* in search of the wildest cattle. The animals, raised in enclosures of a small size, are brought to the corral to be vaccinated, branded, milked, treated for sores or sickness, and fed. They are always gentle and easily herded by the cowboys. For that reason, the cowboy administers or assists the owner in administration, inspects and fixes fences, drives the animals to be sold to the markets, drives the herd in the seasonal migrations, milks and supervises the delivery of milk intended for sale, and receives cash wages, a house to live in, and the right to cultivate a plot of land. The custom of paying the cowboy with a fourth of the calves born was abolished en- tirely in the Agreste, since the cattle of the region, cross-bred with Zebu and Holstein, have increased in value, and would have considerably raised the wages of the cowboy. Payment in currency, substituting for the "fourth" (which is still in general- ized use in the Sertão, where the creole cattle predominate), does not represent a better situation for the cowboy. He no longer has the opportunity to become a fazenda owner.

Besides the cowboy there are on each fazenda some squatters who live in wattle-and-daub houses and clear the enclosures, clean the corrals, and feed rations to the animals. These and other necessary tasks take three or four days of work per week; the remaining days are used to cultivate cotton and cereals on a plot of one or two hectares, provided them by the fazendeiro. These squatters, whose number is small, receive an extremely low wage for the days of work for the fazenda. The minimum wage is not always respected; and since they do not work six days per week, they lose the right to a paid day off each week and have their annual vacation reduced. Beside that, they receive a house to live in and a plot of land to cultivate. This constitutes a part of their wages. Many times the property owner does not respect the law, contriving to minimize the effect of its application, and the squatters dependent upon him do not enjoy conditions that allow recourse to the labor court.

The use of crop stubble in the feeding of animals induces the fazendeiro to maintain economic relationships with a large number of peasants. These peasants are renters, who hardly ever live on the property of the fazendeiro, but in nearby cities, towns, and villages or even on their own small property. Many of these peasants cultivate remote lands and even own a piece of land, a minifundium where they live with their families. Today, it is rare for the property owner to grant land for the stubble; the number of farmers who want land is great and the areas are small. The plots are almost always rented, the price per *quadra* (1.21 hectares) varying according to the quality of the land and the distance from consumer centers and more traveled roads. The payment of rent is at times made in cash and at times in cotton. The renter does not have any guarantee of renewal of his contract, no document that legalizes the transaction, and remains at the mercy of the property owner in any emergency. Generally the land is turned over to the peasant in March, with the first rains. Once the land is prepared, he cultivates maize and beans; in May he cultivates herbaceous cotton; in June he harvests the beans and some of the still green maize for the June festival days. The harvest of dry maize begins in September, and contributes to the diet of both man and beast. The cotton harvest, begun in December, generally extends until January, when the land is restored to the owner so that cattle can be moved into the fields and permitted to graze on the stalks of cotton and maize. In March the land once again is returned to the peasant for the beginning of the annual cropping cycle (Fig. 3). In Sep-

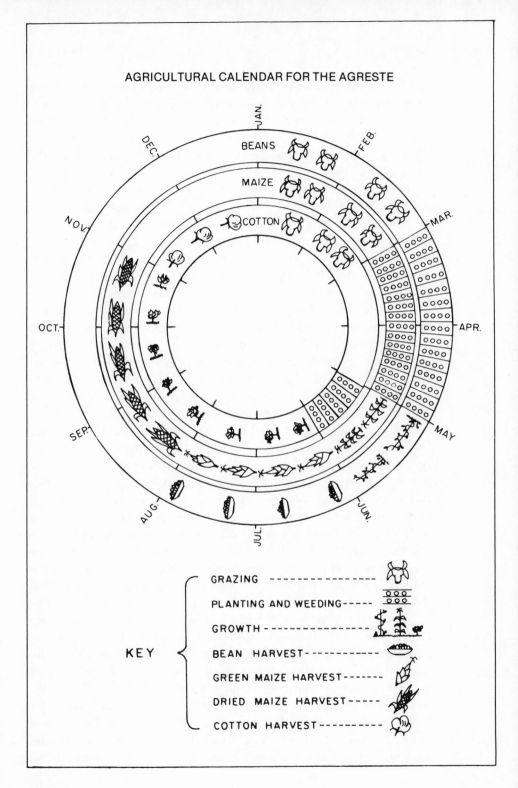

Figure 3.

tember, these peasants have almost no work to do in the Agreste, and migrate to the sugarcane area to work in the factories. This is the typical seasonal migration of the Northeast, which occurs in states from Rio Grande do Norte to Sergipe. The family is able to tend the fields, harvesting the cotton and using the dry maize as food.

In some cases, the landowners reserve areas of the poorest soils to grant, for the stubble, with the condition that the land be returned in October or November. This precludes the planting of cotton, which is always harvested beginning in December.

This system is in decline. The amount of land offered to the peasants by the cattle raisers is less each time. Two reasons have led the large property owners to this policy of restricting land: (1) apprehension about the agrarian reform, which will benefit the sharecroppers and renters, and may mean expropriation of part of their lands; (2) the development of the cultivation of grasses like pangola grass, which permits the reduction of the use of maize and cotton stubble. For the planting of these grasses the owner depends on credit and modest interest rates, furnished by the government and private banks.

The migrant workers are known in the Zona da Mata for not fraternizing with others, by liking to suck sugarcane, and for being extremely frugal, so that they return to their remote houses with a nest egg. These men are so necessary to the factories and mills of the Zona da Mata that at the headquarters of each sugarcane growing property there is always a group of rooms used to house them. Also frequently used are the illustrious houses of the shut-down mills, which have been absorbed by the factories. These are disdainfully called "sheds." Many two-storied houses of barons, commanders, and colonels, which in the golden period of the small mill were rich and opulent, have been transformed into "sheds," where migrant workers are lodged during the harvest. Their stay in the humid zone is determined only by the weather; if it rains in their home area, the migrant worker of the *caatinga* packs his bundle of clothing and returns to cultivate his subsistence plot.

The high population density of the Agreste and the precarious living conditions there have transformed the region into one of out-migration. Many of those born there have abandoned the land and settled in the larger cities, in the state capitals of the littoral—Recife and Salvador chiefly—or traveled in trucks to Rio de Janeiro, São Paulo, northern Paraná, and Brasília. The builders of Brasília are no longer the migrant workers. These workers decided to stay a longer time in the South and Central-West regions of Brazil.[36] This migration to the Central-West, South, and Southeast regions worries the mill and factory owners, who feel the lack of workers more each time in their cane fields and crushing mills.

In the Paraíba wet areas, chiefly in the region that contains the *municípios* of Areia, Serraria, Pirpirituba, and Alagoa Grande, rural labor relationships have taken on very diverse aspects. There the cultivation of sugarcane and sisal dominate. For that reason, although in proportion much more modest than in the Zona da Mata, a type of plantation agriculture, occupying large and medium properties, is developing. The numerous wage laborers are concerned with two export products, both subject to price fluctuation and the whim of the external market. The old mills at times operate, at times are shut-down; much of the cane is crushed in the small factories that have been built since 1930, Santa Maria and Tanque. These and the São Francisco crushed in the harvest of 1955-56 a little more than one hundred thousand sacks of sugar. This is considered a small harvest for one factory in Pernambuco.

The São Francisco factory crushed cane for only a few years, and closed in 1963. In 1973, the Santa Maria and Tanque factories together had a production quota fixed by the IAA of 360,000 sacks of 60 kilograms—180,000 sacks each—production that corresponds to that of an average factory in Pernambuco or Alagoas.

The sugar mill owner, despite not being the prestigious figure of the Zona da Mata, occupies a position of distinction in the social hierarchy of the region, being inferior only to the factory owner. In the countryside are the cane growers and the bondage squatters. The cane growers, traditional figures in the sugarcane region, are today almost gone. They receive from the property owner a plot of land, almost always smaller than 10 hectares, and cultivate it with the help of their family. If the work load is heavy, they will hire a wage laborer to help them. When the harvest begins, they cut the cane and crush it in the mill of the property owners, with the raw sugar produced being divided equally between the grower and the owner. Beside the cane, the grower can cultivate for the sustenance of his family various subsistence crops.

The bondage workers receive a plot of land, an area of about one hectare, and a hut to live in; they cultivate subsistence crops and cotton. The chief product, however, is manioc, which is made into meal. At times, the use of the rudimentary grinding facility is free, but sometimes the owner is paid a share corresponding to one in ten of the gourdsful of meal produced. These individuals are obligated to work for the owner for two or three days per week during the rainy season and five or six days during the harvest. The remaining days can be devoted to cultivating their own crops, or they can work for the owner, thus receiving a better wage. Wages are, however, very low. The daily rate was between 1952 and 1955, between Cr$20.00 and 36.00 for workers from outside on their days off, and from Cr$10.00 to 12.00 for the days of obligation.[37] In 1957, these wages, despite the devaluation of the currency, still fluctuated between Cr$35.00 and Cr$50.00.[38] Except in uncommon cases, in 1965 they did not exceed Cr$100.00 per day. Today owners do not always pay the minimum wage. With the expansion of the area of sugarcane cultivation and the pressure on the property owners to follow the Rural Labor Statute and pay the minimum wage, the squatter system is in complete decline, in actual disintegration. Even more miserable than the squatters are the men of the Sertão who in the dry season migrate to the wet areas to work in the sugarcane harvest. These migrations to the humid areas are equivalent to those made by the migrant workers to the Zona da Mata. The migrants from the Sertão are more numerous when the drought is more intense in the Agreste and the Sertão.

Another important crop that until 1965 created work was coffee. When planted on a small *sítio*, the property owner himself and his family tended the coffee trees and harvested the beans. The large and medium property owners had squatters who, as in the Paraíba wet areas, received a house to live in and a small plot to grow subsistence crops. It was rare to rent land because the property owner never had cattle to take advantage of the stubble. Recently, however, due to the high price of tomatoes, the property owners in Camocim de São Félix began renting, at a high price, small parcels of land (of less than a *tarefa*) for the crop.[39] In general the squatters give three days of work per week to the fazenda, and draw less than the prevailing wage. These days of obligation can be increased or decreased according to the need for labor. In Alagoas it is the custom, when the worker does not live on the property, to receive besides a wage, rations: that is, a meal consisting of beans with sun-dried meat or salt fish, at noon.[40] The coffee harvest begins in August and extends until November or December. It is done slowly, harvesting only the beans that are ripe, leaving on the tree for the next picking those that were still green. There are, thus, two or three pickings per harvest.

In the tobacco-growing regions there is yet another type of labor system. These regions, with important patches of sandy soils in the Agreste, include the *municípios* of Bananeiras in Paraíba, Gravatá in Pernambuco, Arapiraca in Alagoas, and Lagarto in Sergipe. In Bahia, the Recôncavo is the area of tobacco production. Together these four states produce about 10.3 percent of Brazil's tobacco. The largest area, where cultivation is most intense, however, is that of Arapiraca. Situated on a plain at an elevation above 100 meters, the city is surrounded by tobacco fields that extend for 10 or 15 kilometers in all directions. Tobacco fields are denser than those of Cruz das Almas in Bahia and Ubá in Minas Gerais.

Tobacco, an extremely labor intensive crop, but remunerative, is cultivated by renters or sharecroppers and small and medium property owners who have areas that hardly ever exceed 200 hectares.

Planting is done in the rainy season, beginning in March, since the plants undergo two transplants before harvest in August. Thirty days after the first cutting, the tobacco plant can produce a second crop. The laborers are paid to make ridges in the *tarefas* (corresponding to more than 3,000 square meters). It takes four to five days to prepare the ridges of a *tarefa*. Sharecroppers are also used. The sharecropper works with the help of his family. The work is paid for at a daily rate, decided on in relation to that paid in the neighboring areas. The wage earners of the neighboring regions, usually day laborers, flock to the tobacco area during the harvest. To lodge these migratory workers, the property owners customarily build (adjoining or near their house) rooms that are reminiscent of those on the sugar mills of the Zona da Mata.

Once the tobacco leaves are harvested, they are dried on racks made of sticks set up in the field for twenty-five days. Or they are rolled up for curing, which lasts ninety days. Tobacco requires special care, fertilizer, and slow processing before it can be sold on the market. Thus it is cultivated in areas where the population density and the wages of the laborers are very high.

Being a crop of short vegetative cycle, tobacco permits the practice of crop rotation, benefiting through the fertilizer used on it, the crop that follows. Whereas in Ubá the crop that is rotated with tobacco is maize,[41] in Arapiraca it is herbaceous cotton, planted beginning in July within the tobacco fields, to be harvested in January. The property owner and the sharecropper, then, extract from the same piece of land, profit corresponding to two crops. They also cultivate, on a small scale for self-sufficiency, maize, beans, and broad beans.

5

Latifundia, Division of Land, and Labor Systems in the Sertão and Northern Littoral

Cattle Raising and Latifundia in the Settlement of the Sertão and Northern Littoral

The Sertão of the Northeast was integrated into the Portuguese colonization thanks to the movement of peoples from Salvador and Olinda. These two cities, developed as focal points in the areas of fertile clay soils and, consequently, as sugar centers, directed the thrust toward the Sertão in search of land. There one could raise work animals—oxen and horses—for the sugar mills and to supply the developing urban centers.

Exploration of the interior of Bahia was initiated by parties ascending the Jequitinhonha, Paraguaçu, Itapecuru, and Real rivers of the Atlantic slope. They sought mines that would bring them riches and reward. Espinosa, João Coelho de Sousa, chronicler Gabriel Soares, and the famous grandson of Caramuru, Belchior Dias Moréia, whose secret of the silver mines even today has not been disclosed, all followed this route.

Garcia d'Ávila and his descendants, however, established in their fortified house on Tatuapera Bay—the notable Casa da Torre—did not spurn the possibilities of mineral riches, but gave greater importance to cattle. Beginning with the rule of Tomé de Sousa, Garcia d'Ávila sought to obtain land grants that each time penetrated farther into the Sertão, ascending the Itapicuru and Real rivers, and finally reaching the São Francisco.[1] Not even

that great river restrained the men of the Casa da Torre's hunger
for land. Through their cowboys and agents, they established
corrals on the Pernambuco side of the São Francisco, and settled
a large part of the Pernambuco and Piauí Sertão. They went as
far north as the Cariri region of Ceará, pleading for land grants.[2]
They owned the largest landholdings of Brazil, and became
feudal lords of areas larger than many European kingdoms. By
1710 they possessed in the Sertão, more than 340 square leagues
of land on the banks of the Rio São Francisco and its tributaries.
Competing with the Casa da Torre for landholdings was the family of Antônio Guedes de Brito, which possessed land that
stretched from the Morro do Chapéu to the headwaters of the
Rio das Velhas, more than 160 square leagues.[3] These were not,
however, the only large landholders; there were others,
throughout the Sertão whose holdings were much smaller, but
who nonetheless lived like great lords. Researcher-historian Barbosa Lima Sobrinho[4] mentions, among others, Domingos Afonso
Mafrense, João Peixoto Viegas, Lourenço de Brito Correia,
Manuel de Abreu Soares, and Manuel de Oliveira Porto.[5] These
were not the strong men who conquered the Sertão. They did
not confront the heat and thirst of the scorched *caatinga,* or the
arrows of the Indians who, attacked by the white men and having no place to retreat, came to defend foot by foot that arid
land where they hunted and fished for food. The difficult struggle in a hostile environment against warlike Indians, as well as
the protection of the cattle in the corrals, were made by the
cowboys, slaves, and sharecroppers (who had neither prestige nor
land). These last were obligated to place themselves under the
protection of the great lords, not because of fear of Indian attack,
but in order to avoid being harassed by the powerful men of
Salvador. They established themselves, their corrals, and their
cattle in what were called *"sítios,"* paying an annual rent that
reached, in 1710, 10$000 *mil-réis* in Bahia.[6] These *sítios* did not
have the dimensions of the land grants, but were almost always
made up of a parcel of land measuring 1 square league.

These sharecroppers were the authentic heroes who dominated the Indians and established fazendas in the remote Sertão.
They had to struggle—unlike powerful landowners who received
grants of land as reward for favors rendered or through friend-
ship and influence of those close to the governor general. No

historian has yet described the epic dimensions of their accomplishments, as they have for the large property owners of the Casa da Torre.

During the sixteenth century, Francisco Caldas and Francisco Barbosa da Silva led the advance from Pernambuco, toward the great Rio São Francisco. Soon thereafter, expeditions were diverted to the north along the coastline, since there the Sertão reaches almost to the coast and offers good pasturage for cattle. At this time the French on the Northern Littoral constituted a constant threat to the young Portuguese colony. The Pernambucanos turned north, founded Paraíba, expelled the French from the valleys of the Mamanguape and the Camaratuba, and in 1598 founded Natal, on the Rio Potengi. From there the colonists went northwest, conquered the valleys of the Açu, Apodi, Jaguaribe, and Acaraú and, finally, expelled the French from Maranhão. They thus assured Portuguese America possession of the mouth of the Amazon.[7]

In the dry lands of Rio Grande do Norte and Ceará, the Pernambucanos developed livestock raising, and they have continued it to this day. Upon reaching Ceará, Martim Soares Moreno, the romanticized white warrior of José de Alencar's novel *Iracema*, founded the São Sebastião fort and the chapel of Nossa Senhora do Amparo and released horses, swine, goats, and domesticated fowl.[8] In the second half of the seventeenth century the Paraíba Sertão would be invaded and land grants awarded. Some expeditions, like that led by Teodósio de Oliveira Ledo, came from the east, others from the south, to settle the upper course of the Rio Piranhas and the basin of the Rio Peixe.[9] The Paraíba influence penetrated the lands of the Cariri to Boqueirão and from there to Taperoá; the influence of Bahia and São Paulo reached the area drained by the Piancó and the Piranhas rivers.

The various indigenous groups that dominated the *caatinga* of the Sertão did not look favorably on the arrival of the white men who came with cattle, slaves, and agricultural workers and established themselves on the most fertile riverbanks. They built houses, erected corrals of wattle and daub, and loosed the cattle in the pasture, driving the Indians into the mountains, or to the *caatingas* of the interfluves where there was no water during almost the entire year. Living at a Stone Age material culture level, and having lost their principal subsistence activities of hunting and fishing, the Indians considered it their right to kill the cattle and horses of the colonists, as they would any other game animal. This provoked revenge, and the response of the Indians, and finally war. The war caused many deaths and a great deal of destruction, attracted the São Paulo *bandeirantes* accustomed to fighting aginst Indians, provoked the invasion of the interior, and concluded with the annihilation of the powerful tribes and the settlement of the survivors into villages. The war made possible the occupation by cattle raisers of Ceará, Rio Grande do Norte, and almost all of Paraíba. Various new areas were incorporated economically into the Portuguese colony; they began to supply work animals and meat to the more populated areas of the Zona da Mata of Pernambuco, and to the Recôncavo of Bahia.

The livestock raising system was the same as that in the Agreste; but in the Sertão the areas were larger and the fazendas more important, some of them possessing more than five thousand head of cattle. The droughts were more rigorous, causing great losses to the cattle raisers, and communication with the coast more difficult because of the long distances.

At the beginning of the eighteenth century the corrals in Bahia extended along the right bank of the Rio São Francisco and the banks of the Rio das Velhas (today part of Minas Gerais), the Rãs, Verde, Paramirim, Jacuípe, Itapecuru, Real, Vaza-Barris and Sergipe rivers. The area contained about five hundred thousand head of cattle. The corrals in Pernambuco, which must have held nearly eight hundred thousand cattle, occupied the left bank of the Rio São Francisco and the valleys of the rivers Preto, Guaraíra, Corrente, Pajeú, and Moxotó; they extended along the rivers São Miguel in Alagoas, the Paraíba do Norte, Piranhas-Açu, Apodi, Jaguaribe, Acaraú, Piauí, and even the Parnaíba. The entire realm extended from Olinda, on the east, to the border of Maranhão on the west.

The area of influence of the states was not determined by their political limits. The Bahian influence extended considerably into the Pernambuco Sertão, which led historian Capistrano de Abreu[10] to assert that the influence of Pernambuco stopped very near the coast, at the current city of Bezerros.

In the Sertão a civilization sui generis developed. Holders of land grants maintained corrals at the best places on their property. These were almost always managed by a cowboy, either a trusted slave or an agricultural worker, who received as wages one-fourth of the calves and colts that were born. Sharecroppers were given *sítios*, which corresponded to a square league and were rented for 10$000 *mil-réis* per year. Because of long distances and the difficulties of communication in the Sertão, a civilization developed that attempted to extract the maximum from the environment, in order to take care of necessities. Thus, the diet consisted primarily of meat and milk, the latter abundant only in the winter, wild fruits, and some products of the incipient subsistence agriculture carried on in the wet areas, on the riverbeds, or, in good winters, in the *caatinga* itself. Crops of a short vegetative cycle—beans, broad beans, maize, etc.— were surrounded by stick or rock fences in order to prevent damage by the domestic animals.

A variety of domestic articles and furniture were made of leather. Capistrano de Abreu, analyzing the cultural complex that dominated the region, and to which he gave the appropriate designation "leather civilization," said:

> From leather was made the door of the hut, the crude cot resting on the ground, and later the bed for childbirth; leather was used to make ropes, bags for carrying water, the sack to carry meals, the suitcases for clothing, the feedbag for the horses, the fetters to tie them while traveling, the knife sheaths, the saddlebags, the clothing for riding on horseback in the forest, the litters for the tannery or for collecting salt; to make dams the material for the embankments was carried in leather by a pair of oxen, which beat down the earth with their weight; in leather, tobacco was crushed for sniffing.[11]

This system was dominant in the Sertão for centuries. When Spix and Martius traveled over the Northeast, and arrived in Piauí, they still found, even on the fazendas belonging to the imperial government, the system of extensive cattle raising described by Antonil. There, according to Spix and Martius,[12] the tens of royal fazendas were divided into three inspectorates, each one directed by an inspector who earned 300$000 *mil-réis* per year. Each fazenda was managed by a cowboy who owed allegiance to the inspector, serving at times for years in order to obtain what was due him, to receive a fourth of the cattle and horses raised on the fazenda. The cowboy was permitted to raise goats, pigs, and sheep and had the right to their production of milk and cheese. There were on the fazendas "king's slaves," who received only clothing and meat, having to provide the rest of their sustenance from their own plots and livestock.

Since the rains began in December and continued until April, it was customary in that period to round up the cows at nightfall and milk them in the morning. Cheese was made from the milk. After May, when the drought began, the cows no longer produced milk and were allowed to graze in the pasture all of the time. I found an identical system, but naturally without slaves, in 1960 on the Chapada do Apodi, in Rio Grande do Norte. It is still dominant in the higher areas of the Sertão in Pernambuco, Piauí, and Bahia.

Cattle had to be driven to the consumer market, and there were individuals who specialized in driving them. Antonil, with the characteristic precision of his observations,[13] said that the herds were made up of from one hundred to three hundred head, and were driven by Negroes, whites, and Mulattoes.

It was customary for them to be moved with a man riding at the front of the herd, singing the "chant of the Sertão," while others accompanied the cattle, driving and keeping watch over them so they would not scatter. They moved from 4 to 6 leagues per day if water were easily obtained on the trail, but would extend the day's travel to 15 or 20 leagues, continuing day and night, in areas where there was no water. At the river crossings, a cowboy put the skull of a steer over his head, and swam in front of the herd to that the animals would follow.

When the journey extended for fifteen to twenty days, it was customary for the property owners to pay the person in charge of the drive $400 réis per head; this was a period when a head of cattle was worth, on the average, in Bahia, from 4$000 to 7$000 mil-réis. From that amount, the driver had to pay the expenses of the cattle drovers and guides. If cattle ran away on the trail, deduction equivalent to the amount paid to transport them was made.

The cattle drives were very long, occupying a large number of the squatters of the Sertão. Because of the weight loss, the animals were driven to Bahia from Piauí, Ceará, Rio Grande do

Norte, Paraíba, and Pernambuco, to spend some time being fattened on the grasslands of Jacobina. Only after fattening were they driven to Capoame, in the vicinity of Salvador.

Cattle were also driven from Olinda and, later, Recife. A cattle trail left from Olinda, went north, and passed through Goiana, Espírito Santo (Paraíba), Mamanguape, Canguaretema, Papari, São José do Mipibu, Natal, Açu, Mossoró, Praia do Tibau, Aracati, and Fortaleza (Fig. 4). Another trail from Olinda, going through Goiana, També, Vale do Espinharas, Taperoá, Patos, Pombal, Sousa, São João do Rio do Peixe, Icó, and Tauá, reached Crateús, where it linked up with the trail from Piauí to bring cattle from that state to the sugarcane area.[14]

Later, to counterbalance the Bahian influence in the Pernambuco Sertão, the government of Olinda constructed two roads that "reclaimed" the São Francisco. They reached Cabrobó, which, together with Pilão Arcado, were the two Pernambucan parishes of the middle São Francisco in the second half of the eighteenth century (1774). These roads, having to cross the Borborema Plateau, took advantage of the valleys of the Capibaribe and Ipojuca. Thus, the first, left Recife, went toward Limoeiro through the Capibaribe Valley, and ascended the river to its source. Crossing interfluves, it reached the course of the Pajeú at São Pedro, descended the valley of that river, passed through Serra Talhada, and continued to follow the river to Floresta, from whence it turned west to reach Cabrobó. The second road ascended the Ipojuca Valley to the Serra de Ororobá (current route of the railroad and central highway of Pernambuco), and from there descended toward the south to the current city of Inajá. Then it turned westward to reach Tacaratu, Jatinã, and finally, Cabrobó.[15]

Cattle from Ceará, however, arrived in Olinda very thin. Because of the distance they traveled, they accrued higher transportation costs than those from Paraíba or Rio Grande do Norte. This prompted cattle raisers from Ceará in 1740 to ship their cattle already slaughtered, processed into sun-dried and salted meat and hides. The natural saltworks of Aracati, at the mouth of the Rio Jaguaribe made salting of cattle from the coast and the lower and middle courses of the river possible. Shops sprang up that made sun-dried meat, known in the Northeast as "Ceará meat." In this way the region was able to compete with Paraíba and Rio Grande do Norte in the supplying of Pernambuco. The

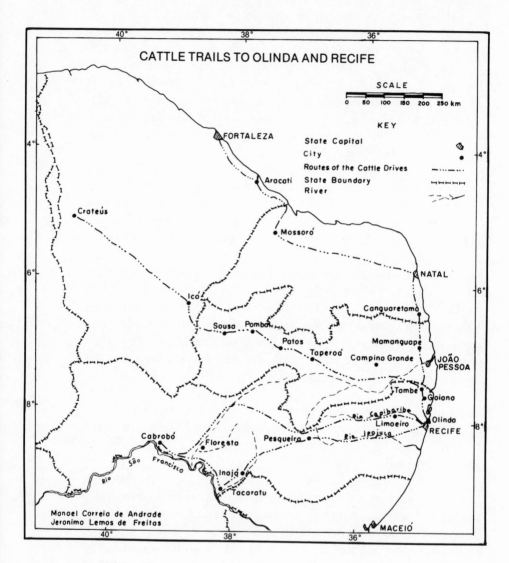

CATTLE TRAILS TO OLINDA AND RECIFE

SCALE

0   50   100   150   200   250 km

KEY

State Capital
City
Routes of the Cattle Drives
State Boundary
River

FORTALEZA

Aracati

Crateús

Mossoró

NATAL

Icó

Canguaretamá

Sousa   Pombal

Patos

Mamanguape

Taperoá   Campina Grande

JOÃO PESSOA

També   Goiana

Rio Capibaribe   Olinda
Limoeiro   RECIFE

Cabrobó

Floresta

Pesqueira   Rio Ipojuca

Rio São Francisco

Inajá

Tacaratu

Manoel Correia de Andrade
Jeronimo Lemos de Freitas

MACEIÓ

Figure 4.

shops in Aracati for making sun-dried meat soon had counterparts at the mouth of the Parnaíba, Acaraú, Camocim, Mossoró, and Açu rivers. The demand of these establishments for animals cut the number available to the sugar mills in Pernambuco. Those shops located in Rio Grande do Norte were prohibited. The others continued in active service until the great drought of 1790–92 practically decimated the Ceará herd, and put an end to the flourishing industry.[16] The collapse of that industry first benefited the producers of the Parnaíba Valley and, shortly thereafter, those in southern Brazil. For a long time these latter completely dominated the market of the Northeast. Only in recent years has there been serious competition from the producers of the Central-West region of the country.

It was cattle raising that settled the major portion of the Northeast. It complemented the humid agricultural area with an economic activity indispensable to the development of both the sugar agroindustry and the cities. Excess population, in the periods of stagnation in the sugar industry, went to the Sertão: those who, for economic and psychological reasons, could not be integrated into the famous civilization of the mansions and the shanties. It permitted, thus, the formation of what Djacir Meneses called *The Other Northeast,* of *caatinga* and cattle, which simultaneously thwarted and complemented the Northeast of clay soils and sugarcane.

The Development of Agriculture in the Sertão

The beginning of agricultural activities in the Sertão must have been contemporaneous with the settlement of the interior and the raising of cattle. But agriculture was not the principal activity; it developed moderately in the shadow of the corrals, because of the long distances that separated the Sertão from the coast and the high price of foodstuffs after shipment for tens or hundreds of leagues. Agriculture was carried on under difficult conditions. The small cultivated fields were bounded by a fence or trench that prevented entry of not only cattle and horses, but also smaller domestic animals, such as goats and sheep.

Agriculture occupied small, more humid, favorable areas, since it was carried out with the aim of supplying the population of èach corral. These areas, where the soils were heavier, included the riverbeds and dry lagoons. The bed of the Rio São Francisco and its tributaries was cultivated, in proportion to the drop of water level that exposed the banks and sandbars; they were, therefore, riverbed crops. Mountain areas also were cultivated, as Girão has written.[17]

Agriculture was restricted to manioc, maize, beans, cotton, and, at times, watermelons and other melons. In the cooler mountains, however, sugarcane and fruit trees soon appeared. The agricultural areas constituted small islands isolated in the vastness of the *caatinga*.

At first the small fields were cleared by the cowboy and his family or by agricultural workers since the property owner did not worry about supplying his managers. They had to provide their own food under the conditions that the natural environment offered.

Salt was not brought from the coast to the interior, but in certain central locations was collected from alluvial deposits of the São Francisco and some of its tributaries (such as the Rio Salitre). Even today earth-salt is collected on the banks of the São Francisco. In the Northern Littoral, from the Açu to Acaraú rivers, the hot dry climate, the low-lying coast, and the presence of tides of reasonable amplitude permitted the development of natural saltworks that date from the first period of settlement. Today the northern coast of Rio Grande do Norte and Ceará is the most important area of saltworks in Brazil.

The preoccupation with cattle was so great that forested areas, such as the Cariri in Ceará, were requested in land grants for cattle raising.[18] Only later, in proportion to the increase of population density, were these humid areas enclosed by large divides that served as a barrier between the areas of agriculture and cattle raising. These areas included the mountains of Ibiapaba, Meruoca, Baturité, and Cariri in Ceará; the João do Vale, Martins, and Portalegre in Rio Grande do Norte; the Teixeira in Paraíba; the Araripe and Baixa Verde in Pernambuco; the Água Branca and Mata Grande in Alagoas; the Itiubá in Bahia; and many others. Within the divide, agriculture was freely pursued and cattle could remain there only if fenced or tethered; outside, the cultivated fields were fenced and the cattle grazed freely on grasslands, since such areas were reserved for livestock. Today valleys like the Açu are fenced laterally to indicate the boundary between one area and another. The fence itself (*travessão*) consisted of either a trench, or stone, branches, or cactus. Sometimes the fence was permanently fixed, but at times it was moveable. It was, in fact, moved forward or backward according to the season of the year or the wishes of a powerful fazendeiro or an influential political figure. During the past fifty years, barbed wire has been used and it is common for the large property owners to fence areas of better pasture with it, reserving them for their own cattle. This has restricted the possibility of cowboys and poor people raising animals in the area of open fields, on "common lands." The importance of these fences extended to the present century. In 1928, the governor of Pernambuco, Estácio Coimbra, was concerned with the construction of a fence 86 kilometers long that would protect the cultivation of manioc on the Chapada do Araripe. Great amounts of money were invested, and that work (considered one of the marks of his administration) created zoning between agriculture and livestock raising.[19] Even today the state of Pernambuco maintains this fence.

The first crops were joined shortly by sugarcane. By the eighteenth century, the first mills were producing syrup and raw sugar. Small mills, with wooden cane crushers driven by oxen or horses, or, exceptionally, by water, produced raw sugar or sugarcane brandy instead of sugar. In 1731,[20] mills of that type were crushing creole cane in the Cariri of Ceará. These increased to thirty-seven by 1765;[21] they produced syrup and raw sugar. Areas that excelled in this kind of raw sugar production included almost all the Sertão mountain areas—Baixa Verde in Pernambuco, and Água Branca in Alagoas. Along the banks of the Rio São Francisco, small mills of the same type developed, and encouraged the dissemination of cane fields on the banks and on the islands of the river. The cane that these fields produced arrived at the mills by canoes. Crato, in the Cariri of Ceará, and Triunfo, in the Serra da Baixa Verde, were and are, producing centers of raw sugar that even today is largely consumed in the Sertão. It is used to sweeten dishes or is directly mixed with manioc meal. Illustrious travelers, the Englishmen Koster[22] and Gardner[23] tried the raw sugar and referred to it favorably.

Labor relationships in these humid areas differed from those predominant in the *caatinga*. The mill owners, though not having the credit and economic means of those from the Zona da Mata, tried to organize plantations of the same type. Thus they used slaves; they also tried to interest free men in cultivating sugarcane to be crushed for half-shares in their mills. In the eighteenth century, then, in the humid portions of the Sertão, cane growers followed the pattern that growers two centuries earlier had established under the captaincy of Duarte Coelho in Pernambuco. The sugarcane cycle in the cool mountains of the Sertão, as in the wet areas of Paraíba, took place like a miniature in time and space of the sugarcane civilization of the Zona da Mata. Improvements and innovations reached the Sertão decades late; at times the mills of the humid areas of the Sertão were assembled with crushing mills, kettles, and furnaces that, after long years of use in the Zona da Mata, had been replaced by others that were newer or larger. Raw sugar, a product destined for local consumption, did not bring high prices; the capacity of the mills was small; consequently, the cane fields did not expand. The number of slaves (even in the eighteenth and nineteenth centuries) rarely exceeded twenty in the mills of even the richest property owners. Normally the owner had only twelve to fifteen slaves per mill,[24] which compelled him, especially in the periods of planting and harvesting, to resort to agricultural and wage laborers.

Irineu Pinheiro, after close investigation of the old archives of the Cariri, emphasized that the small number of slaves was the result of their high price; a century ago they cost hundreds of *mil-réis*. The distance from the coast and wretched roads hindered the export of agricultural products (which were sold only on the regional market), impeded the expansion of crops, and prevented the landowner from accumulating the necessary capital for the acquisition of a large number of slaves. This accounts for the low number of slaves. Also, since the owners were relatively poorer in the Cariri, there was a closer relationship between owners and slaves, and fewer social distinctions. Consider the statement of Rugendas that "on the largest fazendas the meals for the slaves are served separately, but where they are fewer in number, and principally on those remote from the rest of the country, the owners eat at the same table as the slaves."

As a result, abolition, carried out in Ceará in 1884 and in the remaining states in 1888, did not cause problems in these small sugar-producing areas where sugarcane was the most important, but not a monocultural, product.

Beginning in 1840, coffee cultivation began in the humid areas of the Agreste and in the Sertão. The small mills producing raw sugar had a serious competitor in the coffee tree, since forests and cane fields were transformed into coffee fazendas. The Ibiapaba, Meruoca, Baturité, Baixa Verde and the Cariri Mountains of Ceará itself became, for several years, important producers. They not only supplied the region; Ceará and Pernambuco became exporters of the product. In Baturité, as in Bananeiras in Paraíba, a small coffee nobility grew up: many families distinguished themselves with "elegant dress and behavior and conspicuous social prominence."[25]

At the end of the eighteenth and into the nineteenth century, there was a cotton boom and the Sertão developed rapidly. A large proportion of the cotton was used within the Sertão for hand-woven textiles. Towns like Itabaiana in the Agreste of Sergipe distinguished themselves, in the beginning of the nineteenth century (1808), by the women's artistic techniques with textiles.[26] A large part of the cotton crop, however, like that from the Pajeú Valley, was sent across the *caatinga* for a hundred leagues to Recife, from whence it was shipped to be processed eventually on British looms.

Cotton growing, once the first years had passed, did not require as many slaves as sugarcane cultivation and resulted in the development of wage labor in the Sertão. Actually, in an area in which almost every decade there was a serious drought (decimating the cattle and causing the migration of the most substantial property owners), slaves were not optimal laborers. Because of the short vegetative cycle of cotton, slaves would spend a large part of the year without anything to do, without producing enough to pay for their support. During droughts, they were sold at extremely low prices to other regions of the country or they died of starvation. For that very reason, in Ceará in 1872, there were only 31,915 slaves, only 4.4 percent of the total population of 721,688.[27] During the drought of 1877, the majority of the slaves of the region began to be sold to the coffee fazendas of southern Brazil, which were eager for laborers.

The wages paid to the workers varied greatly during the year, according to the law of supply and demand, or from one year to another, according to circumstances of the winter rains and, consequently, the prospects for agricultural production.

During the period of the United States' Civil War, for example, at the height of the cotton rush, the daily wage reached 1$280 *mil-réis*. It is true that wage laborers gained little of the wages, because the cultivation of subsistence crops had been practically abandoned and foodstuffs, brought in from other states, were extraordinarily high priced.[28] To gain an idea of the value of the wages, it is enough to compare them with those paid to local laborers by IFOCS (Federal Inspectorate of Works Against the Drought) in 1924 during the construction of reservoirs in Ceará: 1$800 *mil-réis* per day.[29] This represents an increase of less than 50 percent over almost sixty years. Once the South was defeated in the United States, the demand for Brazilian cotton on the international market declined and prices fell in Brazil. The cotton fields were reduced and so were the workers' wages (to $400–500 *réis* per day). Many returned to their pre–cotton rush jobs.

After the cotton rush, the farmers of the Sertão began to regularize their life: they tilled the soil, helped one another, and tried to produce as much commercial cotton as food. During average years, the people of the Sertão customarily joined in collective labor parties to clear their plots in October, to burn the downed material in December, and to erect fences in January. With the start of the winter rains, the head of the family, aided by his wife and children, did the planting. He began with early-maturing beans, and followed with early-maturing maize,[30] squash, and watermelon. Manioc, cotton, and regular varieties of maize and beans were planted afterwards. Between the first and second plantings, the family kept the plot weeded, while the husband did wage labor on the large and medium properties. Wages were used to buy manioc meal, which, with hunted cavy meat, constituted the daily diet. By August the maize, beans, squash, and watermelon were harvested and eaten. In September they began to make manioc meal, a task in which they could count on help from family and friends. The meal was stored in sacks on a raised platform in the small wattle-and-daub house. The manioc meal was consumed frugally because the fam-

ily had to depend on it for food until April, when the subsistence plot would begin to yield squash, watermelons, and the
first bean pods. The harvest and sale of cotton allowed the poor
workers to buy clothing and other necessities for the family.[31]
This modus vivendi of the landless worker in the Sertão, in the
caatinga areas, persisted almost to the present.

Living on someone else's land, the peasant had to divide his
energies between his own subsistence plot and the fields of the
landowner. The work for the owner was, at times, paid for in
cash; in that case the squatter was required to pay rent for the
land he cultivated, either in cash or in kind. Other times he had
rent-free land to cultivate, but was obligated to give three days
of unremunerated work to the owner. The range of relationships
was large and, since these relationships still persist, they will be
examined in the next section of this chapter.

The carnauba palm, which covers extensive areas of the dry
valleys of the Açu, Apodi-Mossoró, Jaguaribe, and Acaraú rivers,
and is common in the middle São Francisco, has great importance because of the multiplicity of uses it presents. The notable
scholar Agassiz affirmed that it

> furnishes an admirable timber, strong and durable, from
> which the rafters of all the houses in this region are made;
> it yields a wax which, if the process of refining and bleach-
> ing it were understood, would make an excellent candle,
> and which, as it is, is used for light throughout the prov-
> ince; from its silky fiber very strong thread and cordage are
> manufactured; the heart of the leaves, when cooked, makes
> an excellent vegetable, resembling delicate cabbage; and,
> finally, it provides a very nourishing fodder for cattle. It is a
> saying in the province of Ceará, that where the carnauba
> palm abounds a man has all he needs for himself and his
> horse.[32]

Despite all of its uses, the carnauba palm was not given the
significance it merited and frequently during the periods of
drought the young palms were cut down and the leaves fed to
cattle. Only in the second half of the last century did the provin-
cial government begin to protect the palm, prohibiting the cutting of the tree to harvest the leaves. Entry of carnauba wax into
the international market and its increased value awakened the

interest of carnauba grove owners. Today extraction of the wax is one of the principal rural activities in extensive areas of the Sertão, including a large portion of Ceará, Rio Grande do Norte, and Piauí.

The economic evolution of the Sertaõ was similar, though not identical, to that of the Agreste. The Sertão's communication with the Zona da Mata was much more difficult: this brought about the increase of prices of the agricultural products, and made their placement on the market difficult. The Sertão remained isolated, remote from the progress being made in the more developed regions. Also in the Sertão the humid areas most favorable to agriculture constituted a small percentage of the total surface, contrary to the conditions of the Agreste. For that reason even today extensive cattle raising predominates in the Sertão, while the Agreste is dominated by farming and cattle raising. In the Agreste the economic importance of mixed farming and cattle raising is increasing, and shows a tendency to become intensive. The similarity that stands out derives from the fact that both of the regions were settled by cattle raisers. As population increased, subsistence agriculture, and later, as a complement to it, the cultivation of sugarcane and the making of raw sugar grew up. In the second half of the eighteenth century, cotton became the dominant crop in the two regions. One hundred years later, beginning in 1840, coffee arrived. It did not take land away from cotton, however, since it was only cultivated in the humid more elevated stretches. Until the 1920s, it was a product of great importance in the two regions. Today, with improved communication facilities, the Agreste has returned to mixed farming and cattle raising; and the Sertão is slowly transforming its economic and social organization.

Sharecropping and Rural Wage Labor in the Economy of the Sertão

Cattle raising is today, as in the past, the source of great wealth in the Sertão. Sometimes it is an almost exclusive activity; other times it is carried on with cotton cultivation. Fazendas, almost always located on the banks of one of the major rivers or nearby, extend for leagues into the *caatinga*. On the banks of

the São Francisco, and even more so along the Açu, Apodi-
Mossoró, and Jaguaribe rivers, inheritances have divided the
properties in such a way that they have become long and narrow, measuring a few meters in width at the river, by kilometers
in length. The area along the river, on the lowlands indicates a
property's value, the lands in the *caatinga* being almost always
worthless.

The system of cattle raising on the large fazendas of the Sertão
has changed little in recent years. In those areas in Bahia and
Pernambuco drained by the São Francisco, and in southern and
western Piauí, however, very extensive cattle raising is dominant. Open grazing there produces animals of small size and low
weight (120–35 kilograms) that only reach slaughtering weight at
six years of age.

This cattle raising does not produce large profits or incur large
expenses. The fazendeiros live, generally, in the cities of the
interior close to their fazendas, and devote themselves to other
economic activities, chiefly commerce. The fazenda is run by a
cowboy. The owner remains there only during the rainy season
(from October or November until March or April). During that
period the weather is pleasant, the *caatinga* vegetation is green,
and water is plentiful, the cows provide milk to make curd
cheese for meals, and the animals provide meat for tempting
dishes. When water begins to become scarce, it is time for the
fazendeiro to return to the city, leaving the property and the
herd in the hands of the cowboy. During the rainy season the
owner supervises the work of the cowboy, ordering the repair of
fences, corrals, and houses and buys animals from other regions
to fatten and sell to the slaughterhouse when the pasturage gets
scarce at the end of the rainy season.

In the dry season pasturage is insufficient and the cattle are
driven to the mountains. These mountains are the reason that
cattle raising exists in large areas of the Sertão. In the Bahia
Sertão, cattle from the São Francisco Valley are driven to the
mountains where the boundaries of Bahia, Goiás, and Piauí
come together. Migration takes place in accordance with the intensity of the rainy season, which is irregular in the subhumid
and semiarid climatic areas. The migration begins generally in
March or April, and the cattle commonly remain in the mountains until October. The cattle are so accustomed to this migra-

tion that many times they make the trip alone, without needing to be driven. With the start of the first rains, however, the cowboys go to the grazing area in search of the herd. If the cattle stay in the mountains during the rainy season they are attacked by a disease popularly called *toque* ("carbuncles").

From the basins of the tributaries of the São Francisco in Pernambuco the cattle also undergo seasonal migrations. Those of the lower Pajeú, for example, depending upon the rigors of the dry season, are driven to the Uma and Arapuá mountains or to the upper course of the Pajeú to Serra Talhada. There the fazendeiros rent enclosures in order not only to have water available but to take advantage of the abundant stubble of cotton, broad beans, and maize. To the upper Pajeú, chiefly the *municípios* of Tabira, São José do Egito, and Itapetim, the herds from the Cariri region of Paraíba are driven. If land is available, cattle are driven to the banks of the São Francisco where, generally, feed grasses are cultivated.

The fazendas are very large in the Sertão where 10 hectares of land are necessary to support one head of cattle. (In the middle São Francisco, upstream from the confluence with the Rio Grande, 3–6 hectares are sufficient for each animal.) Creole cattle are dominant, as in the Bahia Sertão; however, owners are trying to improve the herds by introducing Zebu bulls of the Cyr and Nelore races.

In the Paraíba Valley the cattle spend the rainy season along the river and the dry season in the Teixeira, Jacararé, and Poção mountains. Open grazing is practiced along the river, whereas in the mountains the cattle are pastured in harvested fields, grazing on the stubble of crops.[33]

The Chapada do Araripe is a point of convergence of cattle from Pernambuco as well as from Ceará. Cattle are driven there in May,[34] in the dry season and are driven out with the first rains to avoid the *toque* disease. Thus throughout the Sertão seasonal migration is a practice that is repeated nearly every year.

The central figure in the operation of a fazenda is the cowboy, who looks after the herd, administers the property, and, in the absence of the owner, gives orders to the workers. The cowboy is sometimes paid through receipt of one-fourth of the calves, foals, and kids born on the fazenda, the dividing-up being done randomly on a day when the owner is on the fazenda. In its most liberal form, the livestock of the cowboy are raised along with the other animals as if they belonged to the fazenda. Others, however, believe that animals grow faster "when within sight of their owners." Since the owner is absent the majority of the time, he fears that during periods of drought his livestock may not get the attention given to the livestock of the cowboy. Thus, the owner requires that the cowboy sell him his animals, just after they are divided up. Thus there is eliminated the possibility of the cowboy one day also becoming a fazendeiro, with his own herd. With the introduction of Zebu bulls from India, which improved the herds and increased the value of the meat, the fazendeiros abandoned the traditional system and began to pay the cowboy a weekly wage (it rarely reaches the level of the minimum wage). In 1960, in the Chapada do Apodi in Rio Grande do Norte, the old "one-fourth" system was still in full operation; even the milk and cheese produced during the rainy season were given to the cowboy, who could use them for his table and sell the excess in the local market. It should be made clear that fresh milk in the Sertão only has commercial value around the large cities; at the more distant fazendas it is made into curds and rennet cheese. Cheese, raw sugar, and goat meat constitute the typical food of the Sertão; it is far superior in nutritive value to the manioc and dry fish consumed in the Zona da Mata.

At first glance it appears that the cowboy has an easy life since the cattle are raised by open grazing; however, the work is hard and continuous. The cowboy spends most of his time on horseback riding all over the fazenda inspecting the pastures, fences, and watering places. On the seasonal migrations, he drives the cattle to and from distant locations, and at times during the dry season, visits the mountains to check on the condition of the herd. During the rainy season, with the cattle gathered on the best areas of the fazenda, he rounds up the calves in the afternoon so they can spend the night in an enclosure, and milks the cows in the morning. The cowboy's family takes charge of making cheese and curds. The cowboys also tend to the repairs of fences and corrals, but do little work on the wattle-and-daub house where they live. This came about especially when the landowners eliminated the "one-fourth" division because the cowboy considered it a reduction of his wages.

It is also the task of the cowboy, assisted by friends from surrounding fazendas, to round up the cattle into corrals and brand
them with the mark of the landowner. The cowboy has the job
of breaking in the young horses, a dangerous activity.

The dry season, however, is the worst period in the life of the
cowboy. The seasonal migration is not always made, there being
fazendas on which it is necessary only during the driest years.
When the migration is not made, the livestock must be fed. In
those regions, like the Moxotó Valley in Pernambuco, cacti generally are abundant (for that reason the areas are called "spiny
areas"). When there is stubble of cotton, beans, broad beans,
and maize, it is used in cattle feeding. At times cotton seed or
branches of certain trees such as the *caatingueira, umbuzeiro,
jurema, ingazeira,* and *angico* are used. The trees must be cut
by the cowboy. The cacti, such as the *mandacaru* and, in the
driest years, the *facheiro* and the *xiquexique,* have to be burned
to destroy the spines before being given to cattle. The *macambira* bromeliad, besides being burned, must be cut up before it
is fed to animals. At times the starving animals eat live cacti.
This can be fatal to the animals if the cactus chosen is the small
and spiny *quipá.*

Tending cattle in the *caatinga* of thorny brush and spiny cacti
requires that the cowboy have appropriate apparel. To herd the
cattle the cowboy always dresses in a hat, jacket, trousers,
chaps, and gloves, all leather. He always wears spurs and carries
in his hand a slender leather whip.

The greatest problem the cowboy faces is finding water. At
times the cattle must be driven tens of kilometers to the watering places. As a result, the practice of leaving the cattle without
water for forty-eight hours and then digging water holes in the
riverbeds grew up. Water holes are deepened in proportion to
the drop in the water table; they are almost always fenced on
one side to prevent the animals from breaking down the banks.
Cattle drink the water, and urinate and defecate near the water
hole, thus transmitting the diseases they carry. Athanassof, in a
report to the state of Pernambuco in the last years of the decade
1921-30, called attention to the practice of using water holes that
could infect the entire herd and spread the most harmful epizootic diseases.[35]

In some areas wells are being dug that considerably improve

conditions of cattle raising. Since 1950 this has occurred on the Chapada do Apodi, where the water table is at a depth of only 70 meters. The importance of water is such that on the fazendas the well and pump house, alongside the watering troughs, are the only masonry buildings.

Besides the cowboys, the fazendas have some workers drawing cash wages; among them the oxcart drivers stand out. Their importance comes from the traditional use of the oxcart, though that importance is diminishing year by year with the opening of new roads and the increase in the number of trucks. The oxcart driver, wearing a leather apron and hat, and carrying a stick on his shoulder, slowly drives the carts pulled by two or three oxen over the roads of the *caatinga* and is aided in his work by his sons ten years or older, who learn from their father the ways of an occupation that has been handed down from generation to generation. It has been the truck, in recent decades, that has been the great conqueror of the Sertão. It has been breaking down age-old social structures and transforming the way of life in which those structures developed.

The cattle drovers also constitute another profession on its way out. Their area of activity is limited to the most remote locations, because of the competition of the highways for transporting the cattle to the distant cities.

The locations today with the greatest amount of work for drovers are the following: the Piauí Sertão, drawing drovers from the city of Araripina in Pernambuco; the north of Bahia in the Sertão of Rodelas and Raso da Catarina, creating demand in the cities of Parnamirim, Salgueiro, and Arcoverde in Pernambuco and across the São Francisco River in Glória and Barra de Tarrachil; trails from northern Minas Gerais and southern Bahia that converge on Propriá and extend in Sergipe through Simão Dias; and those that Propría itself draws from Caruaru, Maceió, and Recife.

The cattle drovers live in the cities and towns where it is easy to obtain work and spend their lives moving over the Sertão, earning wages. Generally they drive the cattle on foot, having, however, along with the cattle, some horses on which they can ride for a few hours during the trip.

At times the drovers reside on a fazenda and plant food crops; they live in a thatched lean-to. The beds they have are very poor, made of a frame suspended on forked sticks; at the noon meal the entire family gathers around the earthen clay pot and eats with their fingers. The only meal of the day is almost always made up of beans, manioc meal, salt and pepper, at times served with meat.

It is customary for the property owners of fazendas with better soil to permit the squatters and those of the nearby towns and cities to plant crops. In such areas tree cotton is cultivated; it is planted every three or four years in association with beans and maize. Many times the landowners themselves make large plantings with the help of wage laborers.

The majority, however, prefer to turn the land over to the peasants, as in the Agreste, for the planting of cotton and cereals, using the fields in the two driest months of the year to pasture cattle. Despite tree cotton being a permanent crop, the cattle limit themselves to eating the leaves, and the plants vigorously grow new leaves with the first rains. The land generally is not rented, the owner preferring to turn it over to peasants on a sharecropping basis. Among those arrangements the "half" system stands out. It is in general use in the Rio Grande do Norte Sertão; the owners furnish land and seed, financing the peasant during the growth of the crops. After the harvest, they receive as payment one-half the cotton crop and the stubble. The sharecropper retains the other half of the cotton, and all of the maize, beans, and broad beans, as well as the squash, watermelons, and melons.[36] When the fields are planted on riverbanks, the owner requires the equal division of all the crops.

In some areas of the Sertão, under similar conditions to those just mentioned, there is used a system whereby two-thirds of the production goes to the landowner. It is interesting that in Paraíba this is called "halving."[37] In Piauí the system of "one-fourth" is not only used for livestock, but is extended to agriculture. Thus, at the beginning of the rainy season the sharecroppers receive from the fazendeiros the areas to be cultivated along with the seed of maize, beans, broad beans, cotton, etc. It is the responsibility of the sharecroppers to clear the plot, plant, and weed; in case it is necessary to exterminate ants or use herbicides, the chemicals are furnished by the owner. At the time of harvest, the sharecropper pays 240 to 480 kilograms of the crop from each *tarefa* of land. In the case where the sharecropper owes money to the landowner, his share may cover the debt, but it must be paid in cash.

The bondage typical of the Zona da Mata is also found in the Agreste and the Sertão. Under it the peasants are obligated to give to the landowner one day per week of free labor. This is the infamous bondage against which the Peasant Leagues fought so hard. It is a personal obligation. In some regions, the peasant may not pay another to carry out the task; he has to do it personally, as homage to the landowner. If one takes into account the value of a day of labor, and the fact that the peasant gives fifty-two days of labor to the owner, one concludes that he pays an exorbitant rental for a small plot of land and for the thatched hut in which he lives and at times built.

In the labor relationships discussed above, one sees that the peasant, not owning land, subjects himself to truly stringent contract conditions. One must also remember that, in a semiarid region, the peasants are subject to the loss of their labor if the rainy season is irregular. The will of the landowner is like a sword of Damocles over the head of the peasant. The peasant does not have a written contract, does not possess guarantees of remaining on the land, can be evicted at any moment, and can only find work elsewhere under the same situation.

Some areas of the Sertão, as they develop, are changing the characteristic structure of three centuries of land exploitation. Jacaré dos Homens, Major Isidoro, Batalha, Palmeira dos Índios, and Pão de Açúcar, *municípios* in the Alagoas Sertão, are largely developing beef and dairy cattle, which are fed on cultivated *palma* cactus. In the city of Batalha there is even a modern dairy that buys, from its município alone, almost all of the approximately 11,500 liters of milk that it uses daily. Nearby the fazendas, besides raising cattle with a high percentage of Holstein blood, fatten cattle brought from northern Minas Gerais and from southern Bahia, destined for consumers in Recife and Maceió. On these fazendas, which fatten from four to five thousand cattle per year, they use wage labor. The workers who tend the cattle on a permanent basis are squatters from nearby cities and towns. They are paid to plant and care for the *palma* fields. Generally the men dig the holes and the women plant the "ears" of *palma*. The wages for women are two-thirds the wages paid men. The squatters do not have the right to cultivate the

land for themselves and are obligated to provide five days of
work per week. And the large and medium property owners will
not sell land to the squatters.

The day's work begins at sunrise and continues until 10 A.M.,
when there is a one-hour rest for the first meal, consisting of
cowpeas, manioc meal, and coffee, prepared in the field. The
second meal is in the evening, at home, made up of the same
items, augmented by small pieces of meat or dried fish following
market days. Working conditions are so difficult that most of the
peasants of the Sertão try to migrate to southern Brazil; a large
number of trucks leave each week for that destination. This migration terrifies the fazendeiros. The development of cattle raising, increasing the milk and meat production, is bringing about a
greater monetary circulation and gradually eliminating the traditional forms of sharecropping.

Efforts to improve the productivity of cattle raising based on
palma cultivation and to create more dairying are being made in
the Cariri of Paraíba and the Acaraú Valley in Ceará,[38] relatively
close to the large northeastern cities of Recife and Fortaleza.
Certainly if these plans are successful, similar transformations
will be felt in the labor relationship.

On the banks of the São Francisco River and on the islands in the
river, agricultural activities have developed considerably in recent
years, thanks to irrigation. The chief irrigated crops are onions, sugarcane, and fruit. Riverbank cultivation, carried on since the colonial
period, has considerably expanded since irrigation began, thanks to
the lifting of water from the river by water wheels.[39] In 1951
motor-driven pumps were put in and in more recent years electric
pumps have been used. The abundance of water and the agricultural
development is creating jobs for landless workers, under more stable
conditions and with possibilities of higher income, compared to the
work in cattle raising. The largest profits, however, remain with the
property owners, who do little farming.

The sharecroppers receive from the owner the land, water,
onion seed (being charged 50 percent of the price of it), a cash
advance until the crop is harvested, fertilizer, and insecticide.
The crop must be sold to the landowner at the current market
price. The sharecropper is responsible for clearing the land and
applying water for some ten days, using infiltration and flooding.
Water is raised from the river by mechanical as well as manual

means, in the latter case in cans or gourds. Seed is imported from the Canary Islands since local seed does not produce quality onions acceptable on the urban markets. After the initial irrigation comes the application of goat manure and seeding. Twenty to forty days thereafter, the onions are transplanted to the final beds; three to four months later they are harvested. The two weedings that the onion fields require are done by hand, by women and children. After harvest the onions are placed on a raised platform where they are kept moist for five to seven days. Then the onion tops are braided into strings some 80 centimeters long and the onions thus are shipped by truck to southern Brazil and sold. When a property owner himself grows onions, which is not common, he uses wage labor in accordance with his greater or lesser need for help. Onion growing has given excellent returns to individuals, chiefly landowners not in the habit of investing their capital. Cabrobó has distinguished itself as a major onion center of the Northeast. This has been accompanied by the large sale of trucks and pistols, since the onion growers measure social status in relationship to the quantity of trucks and pistols they possess.

Sugarcane is widely cultivated on the riverbanks and in irrigated areas. After onions, it is the most important crop found along the banks of the river and on the islands. Small mills, powered by oxen or horses, by diesel engines or by electricity, transform the cane into raw sugar, which is sold throughout the Sertão. It is interesting that former animal-powered mills are converted directly into electrically powered ones. The planting of cane is generally done by sharecroppers who receive land from the owner and whose cane is transported free to the mill. They cultivate, weed, and cut the cane, and after the crushing, the sugar is divided equally between the mill owner and sharecropper. The sharecropper sometimes receives his share in sugar, sometimes in cash. When property owners cultivate sugarcane, they pay laborers the same wages as they pay for growing onions.

The relationship between landowner and sharecropper is the same as previously mentioned with regard to the growing of manioc, rice, beans, maize, cotton, and other products cultivated along the banks of the São Francisco. The permanent crops of oranges, mangoes, bananas, etc., are planted only by the landowners.

Beside the irrigation projects in the São Francisco Valley, a large sugar factory, with a production capacity of about one million sacks per year, has been built. It is one of the largest in the Northeast. Also being developed, thanks to the actions of SUDENE and CODEVASF, the Bebedouro project; this includes the cultivation of pasture aimed at beef production. Already established is the growing of table and wine grapes.

Along the São Francisco River there are important cottage industries: the making of lace, weaving of hammocks, and the extraction of salt, widely used not only in the home but also to salt fish. Fishing has expanded considerably and the processing of fish by traditional methods is being greatly improved, since the product is entering the rural consumer market of the entire Northeast (in proportion to the decreasing consumption of dried cod and sun-dried meat because of the high price levels these products have reached).

The traditional process of extracting salt is interesting. Pieces of clay and salty earth are removed from the low-lying areas along the banks of the São Francisco during the period of low water. The material is placed in a clay pot with a hole in the bottom; this is supported by a tripod made of sticks. Sand is placed in the pot along with the salty clay and water. The water dissolves the salt, which filters through the sand and drops into a vessel which sits below on a trivet. Once obtained, the salty water is heated over a fire until it evaporates, leaving the salt in the bottom of the pan. The salt is then put into sacks, washed to remove impurities, and dried in the sun for twenty-four hours. The clay, after the salt has been extracted, is piled around the tripod to serve as a windbreak. Generally, it is possible to obtain an average of 1 kilogram of salt from 18 kilograms of salty clay.

In the dry valleys of Rio Grande do Norte and Ceará the major interest of the large property owners is to return to the exploitation of carnauba wax. That extractive industry occupies a majority of the labor force for a few months each year. Its influence on the landscape is very significant, since the palm occupies, from the Açu to the Paraíba valleys, all of the river lowlands that drain toward the north coast. In the Açu Valley (downstream from the city of Açu), in the Apodi Valley (near the city of Mossoró), and in the Jaguaribe Valley (near Russas and Limoeiro do Norte), they form authentic gallery forests, which, where the floodplains are very wide, may be kilometers in width. There is complete dominance of native carnauba palms. It has been calculated that in the Açu lowlands alone there are six million carnauba palms; they occupy an area of about 25,000 hectares, or about 62.5 percent of the total area. On more favorable soils the trees are so dense that it is difficult to walk through the groves, and it is both difficult and dangerous to cut and harvest the leaves. On the floodplains, however, there exist wide areas not covered with carnauba palms. These are used by the local people to grow subsistence crops, build houses, and dry the carnauba leaves. Many of these clearings resulted from the destruction of the trees in the past, when carnauba wax did not have great economic value. Innumerable palms were cut down to clear the land for agriculture, chiefly cotton, during those periods when that fiber brought a high price. Also in the drought periods, when shortages of cattle feed existed, it was customary to cut the young carnauba palms and feed the leaves to the herds. Today, the exploitation of the carnauba palm gives the landowners profits almost equal to those provided by the coffee fazendas of São Paulo and Paraná. The natural carnauba groves are protected, and the palms are planted in the clearings that exist on the floodplains and tablelands.

Carnauba wax passed through a critical phase in the period 1966–69; its harvest was uneconomic because the cost of production was higher than the value of the product. The landowners began to harvest leaves only once every two years in order to obtain greater production and compensate for the low price. There were even landowners who were ready to cut down the trees and plant crops that would bring greater income. In recent years the Bank of Brazil has interceded, increased the price of the product, and caused a rise in production.

The carnauba groves do more than characterize the landscape and the agricultural calendar: the land tenure system is directly linked to them and to the lowlands. Wax is the only product of the infertile tablelands. Old land grants, divided by a sequence of heirs into narrow strips that run from the riverbank towards the interior, caused the pattern dominant today of narrow holdings with a frontage of a few meters and a depth of 3–4 kilometers. The owners' houses are placed at the side of the road, which is almost parallel to the river. The houses are so close together that it gives the impression of a real village. I know of one extreme case in which a property is 19 meters wide by 6 kilometers in length. The number of small property owners is great, but they do not occupy more area than the larger property owners. Fazenda Itu alone has 12,000 hectares, including lowlands, tablelands, small lakes, etc. The Piató Lake area is very subdivided, but consists primarily of one holding of 500 hectares. The entire Açu lowland contains about 40,000 hectares. The land tenure system of the Açu is repeated in the Apodi and Jaguaribe valleys.

The area occupied by the carnauba groves and the multiple uses of the palm products give rise to the idea that there is a carnauba civilization that demands a detailed survey: a true inventory that looks at it from the point of view of economic importance, the cultural, anthropological, and sociological influences, and the historical aspects.

The wattle-and-daub houses are often made with trunks and leafstalks of the carnauba, then covered with mud; the roof is frequently made with palm leaves placed over pieces of carnauba trunk; the windmills that raise water are made with boards or strips from the trunk; the panniers in which goods are transported on horseback and mule are made of hides and leafstalks of the palm; the straw, after extracting the wax, supports an important cottage industry of bags and hats. If the wax extraction is done mechanically, leaving the straw unusable for that industry, it is used as a soil cover, preventing the loss of moisture by evaporation and the growth of weeds in the cultivated fields. Wax, the chief product, is a source of income for the property owners and of employment for three to four months each year for the workers. The carnauba is a plant of multiple uses in a region of scanty resources. For these reasons one talks in Brazil of a carnauba civilization, along with the leather, sugarcane, gold, and coffee civilizations.

The carnauba palms only occupy workers during the harvest, from September to December, rarely until January or February, since the trees are almost always native and there is no weeding. A few plantings were made beginning in 1935 and they were intensified after World War II, when the price of the wax was high. I do not believe that the plantings have increased significantly; the tradition of exploiting native trees and the long period of waiting for the first production (about six years on the lowlands and twenty years on the tablelands) keep conservative property owners from expanding. Only when the forest is very large is it customary to cut the underbrush of the carnauba grove; this is infrequent since there are few plants that can grow in the shade of the palms. When the grove is new, it is customary in the summer to drive cattle in so that they can browse on the natural vegetation; when the grove is mature, however, the lower vegetation dies out and the association between cattle and carnauba ceases.

During the short period of about five months, however, there is much work in the harvesting of the wax. Property owners often find themselves with a lack of labor, because the carnauba harvest coincides with the period of salt extraction on the coast. Salt is another important regional product. The poor people divide up, some preferring to work in the carnauba groves, others going to the saltworks.[40] Even those who prefer to work in the carnauba groves, however, move to the saltworks in December when the cutting of leaves is well advanced and jobs are growing scarce. Thus the poor participate and provide labor for the two principal extractive industries of the Northeast.

The harvest of carnauba wax is very complex. Pimentel Gomes made clear[41] it is done in six steps: cutting, drying, beating, melting, cooling, and classifying.

Cutting is done by workers specialized in the handling of a brush hook attached to a long pole that is about 15 meters long and very light. The cutter must be sufficiently adroit to cut the leaves without damaging the tree and without having them fall on his head. The wage of a cutter, determined by the number of leaves cut, varies according to whether the winter was good or bad. In the first instance, the cutter, who is also a sharecropper, gets a good harvest and demands higher wages; in the second instance, having gotten little or nothing from his agricultural activities, he is at the mercy of the owner of the carnauba grove.[42]

The cutters take the lower leaves of the palm but always leave the youngest leaves so as not to kill the tree. Another worker gathers up the leaves, ties them in bundles, and generally using donkeys, transports them to the *estaleiro*, the place where they are spread out to dry. There the wax gets mixed with a large amount of impurities. Exposed to wind, the leaves lose 20–30 percent of the wax they contain. Those who work at this job, generally women and children, receive wages considerably lower than those of the cutters.

After a few days, when the leaves are dry, they are carried to a wooden shed where the processing machinery is kept. When machines are not available, the traditional process of beating is used. This has almost disappeared in the Açu Valley, but is still in general use in the Jaguaribe Valley. The traditional process has the great advantage of leaving the straw in good enough condition to be used in the making of bags, hats, mats, and for thatching roofs. The process, however, is disadvantageous because it causes a drop in wax production per leaf. The majority of property owners, however, remove the wax with machines powered by diesel engines of 5–12 horsepower. There are also in the region entrepreneurs who own a machine and move from one holding to another to extract the wax of the small property owners' crop. These entrepreneurs contract with landowners to extract the wax, charging a rate per *arroba*. Sometimes, however, the contract is made on a share basis, two-thirds of the wax going to the property owner and one-third to the machine owner.

The machines are operated under the direction of a competent operator who is capable of making small repairs if necessary. He has under his supervision a worker who carries the leaves from the *estaleiro* to a bench, where they are ready to be fed into the machine; another worker removes the leaves from the bench, putting them three at a time into the machine; yet another worker removes the straw residue from the machine and carries it to a field. The operator is the best paid of the crew, while those who carry leaves to and straw from the machine receive wages that correspond to about 50–60 percent of those paid the operator.

The melting process is done by a waxmaster, an assistant, and a presser. After being melted, the wax is cooled in receptacles of various sizes. It is moved next to the warehouses of the exporting companies, which sometimes find it necessary to purify the wax. Soon after it is classified into different types. Wax from new leaves is of highest quality and considered as first or second class; that from mature leaves is classified as fat, fatty, or sandy. Wax prices in favorable periods guarantee the producers a considerable profit. Depending on the extent of their carnauba groves, they may reside elsewhere, either in the principal cities of the region, such as Açu, Mossoró, Aracati, Russas, Limoeiro do Norte, etc.; in state capitals such as Fortaleza or Natal; or even, for the very rich, in Recife or Rio de Janeiro. The owners need only go to the carnauba groves during the harvest.

Once the harvest season of carnauba wax is over, and the period of salt extraction as well, the squatters attend to their subsistence crops on land along the riverbanks and lakes. Among the significant lakes are those of Piató and Ponta Grande; the latter is located entirely within the area of Fazenda Itu, a large holding of more than 12,000 hectares. The agricultural calendar depends more on the fluctuation of water levels in the rivers and lakes than on the rainy season. In general, however, planting is begun in January and February with the associated cultivation of beans and cotton. These crops are planted first because the soils first exposed are sandy and these crops grow well on sandy soils. With the lowering of the water level are exposed, chiefly on lake shores, clay soils that become parched by the sun, where the melons, watermelons, squash, and maize are planted in good years. Sorghum is planted in the poor years. Sorghum, because of the shade it casts, impedes association with other crops. Along the shores, rice has been cultivated since 1956. On the lowlands irrigated cultivation of other crops, including papayas and bananas, has become the practice. The landowner prohibits the sharecroppers from growing permanent crops to avoid complications if he wants to evict them, and requires from them one-half of the cotton and one-third of all other products. The sharecroppers still are required to sell their cotton to the landowner and pay interest on money advanced to them during the growing period. When a dry year occurs, production is small. The income generated is insufficient to pay the debts to the fazenda. Thus the sharecroppers must remain on that fazenda and try to make the payment the following year.

The sharecroppers follow traditional practices in their work; a hoe or a pointed stick of strong wood is used to dig the soil and form planting mounds that are long and fairly high, where sorghum seed is planted along with a little sand. The planting depth must be relatively deep so that birds cannot eat the seed. Despite the use of traditional practices, the shoreline soils and the bottoms of the dry lakes are so fertile that one can obtain, on an average, 5,000 kilograms of sorghum or 3,500 kilograms of rice per hectare. The sharecroppers have in cotton their cash crop, selling it shortly after the dividing-up. The other crops are used to feed the family; some are stored for the summer; only in years of good production is there a surplus to sell. The process by which they store certain crops (such as beans) is interesting; they are placed in old kerosene cans in which only a small hole has been made. After the can is filled, the hole is stopped up with soap; in this way the beans are preserved for an extended period. The crops from the fields, along with fish caught in the rivers and lakes, constitute the typical diet, and only once a week is meat eaten.

The lack of credit is a serious problem for the sharecropper, since the loans he receives from the landowner or merchant are very expensive. In research done in the Açu Valley in 1960, I gathered information from a sorghum planter, at Lagoa do Canto da Velha Joana, whose production was sold in advance. The merchant who financed the planting did it with the condition that the sorghum be sold in advance for a price 40–50 percent below the market price. It is interesting to observe how this African crop, one of the principal foods used by the population of the Sudan and south of the Sahara, has dispersed widely in Açu Valley of the Northeast. It is called the "plant for bad years" because it has a vegetative cycle shorter than maize. Once planted, it grows rapidly, being harvested in eighty to ninety days. If the soil remains damp, it produces a resprouted crop after twenty-five days and a second after an additional twenty-five days. Sorghum flour is the base for a series of regional dishes similar to those made with maize. Sorghum is a crop to which the state governments of the Northeast should turn their attention and try to diffuse in the semiarid areas of the various states. It is resistant to drought and grows with minimal amounts of rainfall. Sorghum could be an indispensable food not only for humans but for livestock, for it is also an excellent fodder. It is widely cultivated in the Sudan (where there is a veritable sorghum civilization), in India, China, and central parts of the United States. It could provide cattle, as already emphasized by the American scientist Klare S. Markley, in a report of the Bank of the Northeast, with an excellent fodder, rich in protein. He considered it, as a fodder crop, superior to *palma* cactus, so widely diffused.[43] I also believe that the diffusion of sorghum cultivation is one of the steps toward the development of livestock raising in the Northeast and, consequently, to the recovery of the regional economy.

The great adversary of sorghum and rice is birds, which eat the seed. When the grain is ripening, it is necessary to station children in the fields with slingshots to chase away the ravenous birds.

The property owners also cultivate these products and they as well as the sharecroppers customarily hire workers who were paid, in 1959, Cr$40.00 old cruzeiros per day plus meals. Among the sharecroppers, these wage laborers eat their meals in company with their bosses; this does not happen when they work for the large or medium property owner.

Irrigation of the lowland with water from the alluvial water table, which is about 7 meters deep, has been carried on for years. This permits the cultivation of bananas and other fruits, vegetables, rice, and even sorghum. During the Kubitschek presidency, the government began to finance landowners who wished to acquire pumps. Many small property owners bought the pumps. In the Açu and Apodi valleys, various areas were irrigated and cultivated, giving to the visitor a magnificent impression of abundance. Afterwards, the maintenance of the pumps, the replacement of worn and broken parts, which could only be purchased in Recife or in São Paulo, and the lack of technical assistance curbed the agricultural boom. The Bishop of Mossoró, Eliseu Mendes, who was a great stimulus to agricultural improvement in the Apodi and Açu valleys, also was transferred out of the region. Thus the farmers lost a true and enthusiastic defender of their interests. As a result, the situation of those who cultivate land in the area of the carnauba groves is very precarious.

Another interesting agricultural activity occurs on the riverbeds, and takes advantage of springs which exist near the town of Governador Dix-Sept, on the bank of the Rio Apodi. The riverside dwellers cultivate garlic and onions in the bed of the river.

When the water level of the river drops, leaving the riverbed almost entirely exposed, the riverside dwellers make seedbeds in which they mix sand with goat manure, abundant in the region.

The seedbed is always 9 hand-spans wide by 20 in length. The grouping of twenty, thirty, forty, or even fifty seedbeds is called a *lastro*. Generally, wage laborers are contracted to make the *lastro*. Each worker prepares from five to six seedbeds daily. Afterwards they work the soil; the water level in the alluvium reaches the surface by capillary action. In June and July they personally plant the white and red varieties of garlic that will be harvested in October and November. Four weedings take place during those four months. The wife and small children of the riverside dweller are charged with watering the plants, using a watering can, twice a day, in the morning and afternoon.

In October and November, when they harvest the garlic, they plant red, white and milky varieties of onions. These are harvested three months after planting and they need two weedings during that period. After the harvest, in January and February, the river begins to rise and occupies the entire bed, scattering the sand and destroying the seedbeds, which will only be remade after the next rainy season. The garlic and onions are shipped by truck to be sold in Fortaleza, Natal, Recife, and Salvador. Thus there has developed, in the small area of the bed of the river, an agricultural gardening in which the squatters work alongside their families. It constitutes a small agricultural island in the immensity of the *caatinga* where less demanding but more extensive livestock raising is dominant. The town of Governador Dix-Sept in this region is exaggeratedly dubbed the "garlic capital," since it is actually located in an area dominated by goat raising.

In the Cariri and other cool mountains there is a great contrast with the neighboring Sertão. The inhabitants of these green oases in the midst of the gray desert of *caatinga* generally do not even like to be referred to as sertanejos. They feel that there is a greater similarity between their secluded places with the distant Zona da Mata than with the surrounding Sertão. The contrast is determined by the presence of mountains. The Cariri area is located at the foot of the Chapada do Araripe, on the Ceará watershed, and the cool mountains are found over the portions that are highest and most exposed to the moist winds, as in Triunfo. The area also has generally heavy and dark soils underlying rock being exposed at the surface only in the most irregular areas; luxuriant vegetation where the native forest has not yet been destroyed and where there is very dense second growth on recently cultivated land; and agricultural activity that substitutes for the typical livestock raising of the Sertão. Among these oases within the semiarid peneplain, the Cariri and the Triunfo region stand out. They have large areas (7,649 and 500 square kilometers).

Successive inheritance has led to the repeated subdivision of old land grants and the formation of a large population of small landowners. In order to gain an idea of this fact, it is sufficient to point out that the mills producing raw sugar in the Cariri are called *sítios*. The small landowner generally devotes himself to mixed farming, growing maize, beans, rice, manioc, and peanuts; in the more humid areas they even cultivate sugarcane, which is crushed at a nearby mill for shares as payment. Hence the high-elevation floodplains of the perennial streams, or those that do not completely dry out in summer, are almost always occupied by cane fields. In the Cariri regulations control the use of water for irrigation.

The mills that produce raw sugar are powered by animals, or steam or diesel engines. In those areas where rural electricity has been installed, electrical energy is used. The wooden mills powered by oxen are becoming scarce, being confined to the base of the poorest mountains or to the most remote humid areas of the Piauí Sertão. These small mills are quite numerous; in 1956 there were 113 in Triunfo, with a production capacity of each that ranged from three hundred to four hundred loads of raw sugar per year.[44] In the Cariri, in the *município* of Crato alone, there were in 1958 a total of seventy-three functioning mills, of which sixty-seven were driven by diesel engines, three by water, and three by oxen.[45] Today most of those mills have been shut down, and construction of a sugar factory in the Ceará portion of the Cariri is planned. In general terms, the labor relationships of these areas are similar to those that existed in the Zona da Mata before the sugar factory boom. The squatters live over the properties in wattle-and-daub houses, having around the house small areas where they cultivate for themselves some cotton and subsistence crops. The property owner does not take a share of these crops, but requires a certain number of days of labor per week at a rate less than that paid to outside laborers. It is only sugarcane, also being planted by the squatters, that requires payment of shares for crushing. The squatters are paid less than the workers who do not reside on the property because rent for the house and plot of land is considered payment. During the harvest season, the squatters are required to give five to six days of labor per week. As in the Zona da Mata, migrant laborers who come from the neighboring *caatinga* in search of work are also used.

During the harvest the workers who spend most of the year with a hoe tending the cane fields, begin to take on diverse jobs. Some serve as animal drivers, driving the horses and donkeys that transport the cane from the fields to the mills. Some work as cane cutters, and earn wages based on production. Some are cane feeders, who with a slip can lose an arm in the crushing machinery; carriers, who pick up bundles of cane from the *picadeiro* and place them on a bench near the crusher, within reach of the cane feeder; machinists, who care for the engine and verify and control the pressure of the kettle; sugarmasters, who test the juice while it is cooking, determining the moment at which it should be transferred from one boiler to another, and from the last one into the raw sugar forms. Others serve as sugarmaster's assistants, tending the kettles, and as bagasse removers, carrying the cane residue from the crusher to the dumping area, where it is left in the sun to dry. The description of the duties of the various workers who toil in a mill making raw sugar is very reminiscent of the detailed description of the colonial mills made at the beginning of the eighteenth century by the astute Jesuit Antonil.

These workers, performing jobs for the entire day, at times work more than ten hours at a stretch, and draw daily wages according to their specialties and their individual production. These wages do not even provide them conditions of modest existence. The contribution of subsistence crops to the support of the squatters, so stressed by the apologists of the current social structure in the rural Northeast, is almost insignificant. The cultivated plots of the squatters are small, about a third to a half hectare, and are planted every year, without land rotation or fertilizer. Beside this, the squatters generally have only a few days to tend their small plots. It is fitting to emphasize that the experiment stations are still not the least concerned with subsistence agriculture; instead they are trying to select seed from varieties that are the most productive and best adapted to the environment. There is no systematic study of the pests that attack the crops, or a technical orientation aimed at educating the peasant so he is more identified with the crops he plants and with the environment in which he lives. The concern of these experiment stations is exclusively with large-scale farming for export, and, to a minor degree, with fruit trees, also of interest only to the property owners.

As necessary as a reform of the structure, is the pressing need to reform the thinking of the people. It is imperative to educate the people so that they learn to manage the land in the best possible way, permitting them to produce the maximum amount with a minimum of erosion.

6

The Middle North: Maranhão and Piauí

The French and Portuguese Conquest

In the settlement of the Middle North two areas stand out. The coast, initially disputed between the French and Portuguese, was occupied by settlers coming from Olinda, and was the starting point for the conquest of all the northern coast and the Amazon region. At the same time, groups of cowboys and cattle raisers from Bahia ascended the rivers of the eastern watershed, the Itapecuru, Vaza Barris, Paraguaçu, and so forth. They crossed the interfluves between the headwaters of those rivers, the Chapada Diamantina, and the headwaters of the right-hand tributaries of the São Francisco. After conquering the valley of that great river, they ascended the tributaries of the left bank, crossed the plateaus that separate Piauí from Bahia, and spread over the lands drained by the Rio Parnaíba. They dominated Piauí, and even today southern Piauí and the southern part of Maranhão have great Bahian influence. These two streams of settlement (from Pernambuco and from Bahia) dominated the colonial period.

The coastal portion of the Middle North was not integrated into Portuguese America until the seventeenth century. The attempt to settle the hereditary captaincies completely failed north of Itamaracá; for nearly a century the French, allied with the Tupinambás, controlled that portion of the Brazilian territory, developing a trade of local products for European goods of low value.

178

At the end of the sixteenth century they established a colony, Equatorial France, in what is today Maranhão, and constructed on an island their capital, São Luís. There they remained for more than twenty years, until the Portuguese, led by Jerônimo de Albuquerque from Pernambuco, expelled them, and occupied the capital.

Occupation of the Territory

For a long time this new captaincy remained very poor. Its economy was based on subsistence agriculture and on the capture of Indians (who were used for agricultural work or were sold as slaves to more prosperous areas such as the captaincy of Pernambuco).[1] The prevailing winds and ocean currents hindered both communication by sea with Portugal and the integration of Maranhão into the Portuguese colonial system of an economy entirely directed toward supplying an external market with tropical products. It remained in a secondary position within the Brazilian colonial structure: a supplier of manpower to the sugarcane region in the Sertão and of hides and meat to the dynamic Zona da Mata. Settlement initially was limited to the coastal areas and the more easily defended Maranhão lowland. There were trails that extended long distances from the coast, by which the Indian slave hunters gained access to the interior to search for their commercial products and also by which Indians many times descended to make war on their enemies. Those battles between colonists and Indians were the cause of tremendous disagreement between the colonists and the Jesuits. The latter wanted to catechize the Indians and gather them into villages, and they tenaciously opposed their enslavement.

Thus, according to the writings of Maurício de Heriarte,[2] at the end of the eighteenth century settlement was restricted to the area near the Gulf of Maranhão and São Luís Island; there were cattle fazendas among the lower courses of the Grajaú, Pindaré, Mearim, Itapecuru, and Munim rivers, just as elsewhere in the Northeast, and near the prosperous town of Alcântara. Sugarcane was cultivated to produce sugar and brandy in twenty mills and twenty-six small crushers. These were primarily located on São Luís Island, near Alcântara, or in the

Itapecuru Valley. Also of some importance on São Luís Island was tobacco raising. Other agricultural activities included cattle raising (chiefly in the lowland, which was flooded during the rainy season) and large plantings of fruit trees for the local population. The forests permitted lumbering.

Commerce was chiefly done by barter, the circulation of money having little importance. The creation in 1756 of the General Commerce Company of Grão-Pará and Maranhão, an effort to improve the economy of the colony prompted by the dynamic government of the Marquis of Pombal, would transform Maranhão into a producer of commodities for export. It stimulated the development of rice and cotton cultivation, products that had great demand on European markets. Because of the decimation of the native peoples, hunting Indians was in decline. In order to transform Maranhão into an exporting zone, the Company tried to regularize the commercial traffic with Europe, the potential consumer of tropical products, and with Africa, supplier of the necessary manpower for the development of the agricultural activities. The Company even began to extend credit to the colonists so they could purchase Negro slaves, selected cotton and rice seed, and be able to extend the settlement and occupied area along the banks of the navigable rivers. The Company guaranteed a reasonable price, seldom complied with, for the agricultural products, and furnished the imported products that came to be consumed by the class of people enriched by the new political economy, chiefly landowners and high officials. The expanded consumption of rice and cotton in Europe, which was going through the Industrial Revolution, greatly stimulated the economic growth of the captaincy. By the end of the colonial period, it was one of the richest in Brazil. Even today the large mansions of São Luís attest the grandeur of those days.

Increased settlement would create serious problems for an economy oriented toward external markets, since transportation facilities between the interior and the coast were lacking. The rivers, despite their heavy flow, had very irregular regimes, with great drops in water level and rapidly silting riverbeds, especially after the clearing of the forests. The soil originated in decomposing Tertiary rock, was very siliceous, and subject to a very prolonged rainy season; it soon became leached, forcing the tenant farmers to seek new land. As far back as the beginning of the nineteenth century,[3] Governor Bernardo José da Gama expressed concern about this.

Settlement expanded so much that settlers from the Northern Littoral who ascended the rivers found Bahian settlers and cattle raisers already established along the upper Itapecuru and the middle Parnaíba. Moving ahead of the cowboys of the important families of Bahia (especially the Garcia D'Ávila), or employed by them, the Bahians established corrals in the *caatinga* where they raised beef cattle, sheep, and goats, and cultivated small, fenced subsistence plots (since the livestock grazed in the open), and drove the livestock from the driest to the most humid areas during the dry periods. From the animals they got everything they needed, according to Capistrano de Abreu, who wrote of the leather civilization. And they received cash wages if they were free men. Generally the cowboys could use cows' milk and received one calf of every four born, a practice used today in the more distant areas where the creole cattle breeds, of low value, predominate. The cattle raisers supplied meat and work animals to the coastal region, which exported sugar, tobacco, and hides. They drove the cattle hundreds of leagues (drives lasted months) from the production to the consuming areas. The contrast between the cattle-raising area, which occupied practically all of the southern and central portion of Piauí and southern Maranhão to Pastos Bons, and the production area of rice, cotton, and sugarcane, chiefly dominant in the Itapecuru Valley, was extreme.

Extensive livestock raising on open range required few laborers.[4] The work was neither continuous nor sedentary, as in agriculture, so little slave labor was used. The cowboy was an independent man with the power to make decisions not only because he was free, but also because he was a great distance from his boss. Further incentive was the possibility of becoming a fazendeiro in view of the remuneration system and the practice of large property owners renting *sítios*, plots of about a square league, under a system of emphyteusis.

In the Itapecuru Valley of Maranhão, however, agriculture was carried on by large property owners, who used slave labor, with the aim of meeting the demand for tropical products on the international market. Out of that came the great interchanges of the golden period between São Luís and the African coast; that city carried on an intensive slave traffic equal to that of Recife, Salvador, and Rio de Janeiro, the principal production centers of the eighteenth century. The importation of Negroes ethnically modified Maranhão, which today is largely made up of Negroes and Mulattoes, and which led Caio Prado Júnior to state that cotton, despite being white, made Maranhão black.[5]

The importance of the northern part of Maranhão as a region of speculation,[6] that is, a region in which the Europeans established an economy based on the export of tropical products, grew: by the end of the eighteenth century the captaincy of Maranhão was, after Pernambuco, the greatest exporter of cotton, and an important exporter of rice and hides. Thus, part of southern Maranhão, having closer access to the sea via the north, avoided the influence of Salvador. In order to have an idea of the economic growth of Maranhão and, consequently, of the Middle North in the second half of the eighteenth century, it is sufficient to point out that the export of cotton by the General Commerce Company began in 1769 with 130 sacks, and would reach, in 1800, 29,799 sacks. Rice, after the introduction of new seed and the establishment of rice mills, would have significant growth; its exports increased from 2,847 *arrobas* in 1766 to 102,944 in 1774, and reached 360,000 in 1777. Exported through São Luís were 21,810 skins in 1760, and 31,625 in 1767; this dropped in 1771 to 11,460 skins.[7]

At the beginning of the nineteenth century Maranhão was one of the most prosperous captaincies of Brazil, benefiting from the policy of King João VI that opened Brazilian ports to friendly nations. São Luís became a city with a rich bourgeoisie; linked to Portuguese interests, they tried to remain loyal to Lisbon. Property owners, farmers, and popular groups from the interior fought for independence. The events of the regency period, when a large part of the poor population of the interior (cowboys, artisans, and slaves) spontaneously started the so-called Balaiada revolt, created serious problems and disrupted the rural and export economies. Even so, during the second reign, despite the constant struggle between the merchants and farmers, the region stood out because of its ever-increasing agricultural production. In the second half of the nineteenth century, Maranhão distinguished itself by its production of cotton, sugar, and rice as export products, and of manioc and maize as subsistence crops. Sugarcane was cultivated chiefly in the more humid areas, the Pindaré Valley, where slave labor was used on a large scale. In 1860 there were in Maranhão 410 sugar mills, 284 of which were steam powered.[8] The cotton cultivated in the Itapecuru Valley boosted the production in Maranhão to 460,000 *arrobas* in 1875. The cotton growers utilized a lesser amount of labor and the product was of inferior quality if compared to other regions of the Northeast. Processing methods were outdated. Sawmills were used for the removal of the seeds, and these cut and shredded the fiber. Rice, requiring better soil, was cultivated on recently cleared land. Distance and freight costs destroyed its competitive position on international markets. It changed from an export crop to one for internal consumption, and was thus removed from competition with sugarcane and cotton in the struggle for land and labor.

Unlike Maranhão, Piauí continued to be dedicated entirely to livestock raising. Live cattle were shipped to Bahia or processed into sun-dried meat. Sun-dried meat was exported to Pernambuco and Bahia by ship. The shops for preparing the meat were of great importance in the eighteenth century, chiefly in the Parnaíba and Jaguaribe valleys. The great droughts at the end of that century decimated the herds, and the business competition from southern Brazil in the nineteenth century brought about the decline and disappearance of the shops.

The Problem of Labor

During the colonial period all agricultural activity was dependent upon slave labor, initially Indian and later Negro. During the earliest times, when the Middle North was not integrated into the export economy, agriculture was of relatively minor importance and required little labor. The Indians were sufficient to take care of necessities. Subsequently, the expansion of cultivated area, and the possibility of exporting slaves to Pernambuco and Bahia, led the slave hunters to intensify their preying upon the Indians, aggravating the differences between the colonists and the Jesuits. Slave-hunting expeditions went farther inland, seeking out Indians in the remote places to which they had retreated.

With the creation of the General Commercial Company of Grão Pará and Maranhão, trade with Africa began on a large scale and Maranhão began to receive large numbers of Negro slaves. It stands to reason that the number of Negroes imported each year varied with the demand for products from Maranhão on the European market and with the expansion of agriculture. It is known, however, that in the eight-year period from 1812 to 1820, some 36,456 slaves entered through the port of São Luís, an average of 4,500 per year. Those slaves were most common in the Pindaré Valley, where sugarcane cultivation developed, but also were very common in the Itapecuru-Mirim Valley, a zone of cotton production. Slaves were considered valuable possessions with which the fazendeiros needed to make good, in a few years, the investment made by purchasing them. Thus, they were made to work twelve to fourteen hours per day, depending on the requirements of the crops. The slaves revolted, many times resisting their captivity or escaping to the forest where hunting and fishing, and cultivated manioc constituted their diet.

They called their communities *quilombos*. They were so numerous that during the Balaiada revolt, one of the most influential leaders was a black named Cosme, chief of a *quilombo*.

The poor free population seldom worked on the large landholdings, since in the humid tropical region there was an abundance of food provided by nature and few advantages offered by working for the fazendeiros. Living in the midst of a babassu palm grove, the rural poor obtained food through hunting, fishing, and the collecting of babassu nuts, and by cultivating small fields of manioc, maize, or rice. They remained isolated from the small cities, living in a closed subsistence economy.

The abolition of slavery in 1888 seriously affected the economic situation of the agricultural areas, although it only indirectly affected livestock raising. With emancipation, the Negroes left the fazendas and sugar mills. They hid away in the babassu groves and forests, easily drawing from them their sustenance. There was abundant unoccupied government land, from which the Indians had already been removed but which the colonists had not yet occupied for agriculture, and they were able to live in a closed, nonmonetary subsistence economy. The sugar mills and fazendas felt the effects of the lack of manpower and declined; some were abandoned. In the livestock-raising

area, however, the number of slaves was very small and the labor requirements were low; consequently, the abolition of slavery only had indirect effects. The economic disorganization of the agricultural area, which had consumed meat and required work animals, reduced the demand for these products.

Current Agricultural Systems

In analyzing the agricultural systems and labor problems of the Middle North, one can clearly distinguish two regions: one in which livestock raising dominates, the region of older settlement; and that of recent settlement, in which agriculture dominates.

In the region of older settlement, the large property owner maintains a large fazenda, practices the open grazing of cattle, and employs cowboys to watch over the cattle on their movements in search of pasture, or migration to distant locations such as Piauí, southern Maranhão, or the Maranhão coastal lowland, when drought occurs. Needing supplementary feed for the cattle during the period when pasture is poor, and food for the people of the fazenda, the owner allows peasants to cultivate portions of his land with cotton and subsistence crops such as maize, beans, and manioc, or he rents land under a sharecropper arrangement. The cost of rent or the sharecropping arrangement on the part of the fazendeiro has varied considerably over time and geographic space, according to the bargaining power that each possessed. Thus, when there is abundant land and a lack of manpower, the contracts are more favorable to the peasants. The owner's relationship with the cowboys and workers devoted to caring for the herd is the same as in the Sertão.

In the lowlands of the Parnaíba River and its principal tributaries, the Gurgueia, Piauí-Canindé, and Poti, there are extensive carnauba groves, true gallery forests, which in the same manner as in Ceará and Rio Grande do Norte, are exploited for the foreign wax market and have great importance in the Piauí economy. In 1970, Piauí produced 4,085 tons of carnauba wax, valued at Cr$8,363,000, and representing about 20 percent of Brazil's production. Carnauba wax was almost totally exported through the port of Luís Correia, reaching the city of Parnaíba, the important commercial and processing center, via the Parnaíba River. Construction of a road between Teresina and Fortaleza, however, made it possible for the capital of Ceará to capture within its economic sphere of influence a large part of the land south of the road, taking from Piauí's only port a large part of its traffic. This provoked a deceleration in the population and economic growth of the city of Parnaíba.

In the northeastern part of Maranhão, babassu palm groves are dominant, and the poor people who live there depend in large part on the gathering of babassu nuts. Lands formerly cultivated with cotton and rice are almost exhausted and the babassu groves dominate the landscape. The large property owners, almost always merchants, government employees, or industrialists from the cities of the region, exploit the land they own, developing extensive livestock raising and some complementary commercial activities. By and large, they do not build comfortable houses on the fazendas, but establish a small supply station where they sell products from the urban areas, such as salt, gunpowder, common fabrics, medicines, etc., and buy local products, such as hides, babassu nuts, and so forth. The owners allow local peasants, or those from elsewhere in the Northeast who migrate from the densely populated eastern portion, to establish themselves on the land, since they gather the babassu nuts, extract the kernels, and deliver them to the supply station, where they are purchased at an established price (generally lower than the market price). Payment is not made in cash, the peasant having to take in trade for the kernels the articles he needs. The owner establishes the prices of the products that he sells and buys, raising the former and lowering the latter; often his profit is increased even more by the use of inaccurate scales.

The peasant, illiterate, without support, often suffering from intestinal parasites and diseases, leads a primitive life, in a straw hut that he builds in the babassu grove. Besides gathering babassu nuts, he devotes himself to hunting and fishing, and to cultivating a small plot. In the morning, after a meager breakfast, the peasant and his family collect a basket of babassu nuts, walking over trails that lead away from his house, picking up the nuts they find. They are numerous, since each palm bears an average of twelve bunches per year, and each bunch contains an average of two hundred to three hundred nuts. Each nut yields two to six kernels. The work is arduous because the palms, not being cultivated, grow irregularly, often very close to each other. Moreover, there is an undergrowth of various low- to medium-sized plants. The ground is covered with leaves and rotting nuts. Snakes are numerous, as are game animals like the armadillo, cavy, and agoute. Many workers die as a result of snake bite.

There is no selection in the gathering of nuts; some are green, some ripe, and sizes vary. In the afternoon, the gatherers return to the house, and dump the nuts on the ground where women split them to extract the kernels. The process used is manual, because nobody has developed a machine that can break the nuts without damaging them. The women sit on the ground and hold between their legs a large, sharp knife, with the blade up, place a nut over the blade, and hit it with a mallet to split it into two parts. From the split nut the kernels are extracted and placed in a container. Working all day a woman can obtain 8 or 10 kilograms of kernels. The kernels are spread out to dry and after a few days sold to the property owner, generally a merchant, who resells them to the vegetable oil factories in the principal cities. The price paid to the peasant almost always corresponds to 40 percent of the price that the property owner receives. The primitive processes of gathering and breaking the nuts, and the problems arising out of the labor relationships that exist between the peasant and the property owner, are largely responsible for the low quality of much of the babassu production in Brazil.

The lack of knowledge about babassu is startling, since it is an abundant product in the Northeast and Central-West of the country, and organization of its production could make a significant contribution to the economy. Unfortunately, agricultural geography studies of the palm have not been done, and it continues to be ignored in terms of the areas it occupies, the climatic and soil conditions that would give greater productivity, the spacing necessary between palms to stimulate greater production, and a more rational process of gathering the nuts. Still, it is difficult to find a better process of gathering the nuts in a spontaneous tropical forest, and the development of a machine to break the nuts would provoke considerable unemployment among the rural people.

Very diverse problems exist in the area of recent settlement in northeastern Maranhão, partly in the Middle North and partly in the Guiana Maranhense. The Amazon forest there is being destroyed by migrants, who follow the route of new telegraph lines and roads as they open up new areas, clear the forest by the slash-and-burn method, and plant rice. These lands, originally belonging to the government and now largely controlled by SUDENE and companies that obtained subsidies from SUDAM (Superintendency for the Development of the Amazon), are being appropriated and the forest cleared. In the period of spontaneous settlement, very intense in the 1960s, the peasants from elsewhere in the Northeast migrated to Maranhão in search of virgin forest land. Upon finding it, they built a small hut, cleared a field in the forest, burned the brush and trees, and prepared the field for planting. In the soil covered with ashes and among the tree trunks, they planted rice, being financed by the owners of the rice mills, to whom they paid high interest and promised to sell their harvest. The following year, because the soil was less fertile, the peasants planted manioc in the same field and cleared a new plot in the forest on which to plant rice. They moved forward each year, making new clearings, and carrying out what might be called "migratory agriculture." The lands left behind are being occupied by merchants, rice millers, or government officials, who fence the land for cattle raising. Thus, there is taking place the devastation of the forest and an expansion of rice cultivation and livestock raising. The timber is not used; most of it is burned, and in that way a valuable resource is destroyed. The poor peasant, thus, clears areas for the rich livestock raiser to occupy. Land titles are difficult to obtain, and the land remains in the hands of the livestock raiser.

SUDENE, since its first Directorate Plan, has been trying to establish a program of settlement and colonization in an area of more than 30,000 square kilometers given to it by the state of Maranhão. SUDENE hopes permanently to settle peasants, financing the effort through a cooperative policy to organize production. It has conducted experiments with an eye to introducing in the area new tropical commerical crops, such as bananas, that could easily be sold on the international market. Problems related to getting the necessary financial support, the low fertility of leached soils, the transportation difficulties from the production area to the ports, and administrative problems have impeded the project, which is now being reformulated. After the opening of the Belém to Brasília highway and, more recently, the Belém to São Luís highway, and with the facility of obtaining credit as a result of the provisions of Articles 34/18, through the approval of agriculture and livestock projects by SUDENE and SUDAM, companies from the Southeast Region of Brazil, chiefly São Paulo, are establishing fazendas in the area, furthering the deforestation, planting pasture grasses, and introducing Zebu beef cattle. The project involves the creation of extensive fence systems, within which the technical practices followed are far superior to those in use in the region. In this way the fazendeiros try to obtain a product for the large urban consumer centers within Brazil and also have acceptance on international markets. High meat prices on the international market have stimulated Brazil to become an exporter, although the expansion of livestock raising is creating serious unemployment problems, since it is prompting the migration of people from rural to urban centers where there is no work.

Maranhão is the fifth largest producer of rice in Brazil. In 1970 production reached 675,553 tons, valued at Cr$144,565,000 and represented 9 percent of Brazil's production. Maranhão rice, however, cultivated traditionally and without selection of varieties, milled in primitive facilities, is of lower quality than rice from Rio Grande do Sul and the lower São Francisco Valley; it is sold, thus, for lower prices. Maranhão rice, however, has a large market in the Northeast and Southeast, thanks to this lower price and to the expansion of the urban population of the lower-middle and middle classes. What is needed now is a policy of assistance to the small producer that would effectively guarantee him low-interest agricultural credit, a minimum price, technical assistance, and the guarantee of title to land he clears while following a conservationist orientation. Otherwise, within a few years the large livestock raisers will have occupied the production areas of the Middle North, substituting grazing land for rice fields. A cooperative system with ample official support would be able to improve the crops and the living conditions of the small farmer, thus contributing to an increase in their standard of living and economic role as consumers, as well as improving the food supply for the urban centers.

Tentative Solutions to the Agrarian Problem

Colonization Plans

Since the nineteenth century, following the example of southern Brazil, the states of the Northeast have been concerned—though sporadically—with the problem of colonization. The Northeast is traditionally a region that imports foodstuffs and, consequently, has a population that is undernourished. The formation of a class of small landowners in the rural areas, isolated among large sugarcane holdings, could help solve the problem of supplying foodstuffs to the urban centers and to the sugarcane area itself. Rural property owners, however, have had difficulty in complying with governmental orders that besides sugarcane they also cultivate foodstuffs, chiefly manioc. This concern distressed Maurício de Nassau in the seventeenth century, during the height of Dutch domination, which he administered, and more recently worried Luís Cavalcânti, governor of Alagoas. In early 1962 he met in the governor's palace with sugar factory owners of the state in order to urge them to cultivate manioc.

In the first half of the last century, a colony of German farmers was established in Pernambuco on the Cova da Onça sugar mill in an attempt to increase the production of foodstuffs. Those Germans, however, after a few years were entirely integrated into traditional practices, subsisting on manioc meal and devoting themselves to making charcoal to earn a cash income.

More recently, colonies have sprung up and rapidly declined in almost all of the states of the Northeast. Generally they were

190

established without following an overall colonization plan, many times without receiving agronomic assistance from the state governments, and without having organized the marketing of their products. That happened in the colonies founded in Pernambuco after 1948 (the year of the creation of the Directorate of Lands and Colonization, part of the Secretary of Agriculture).[1] In Rio Grande do Norte, the Japanese and Brazilian Pium colony, which in 1959 began to furnish fruits and vegetables to Recife, is today in decline. In Penedo, Alagoas, the Pindorama colony has for two decades faced nothing but problems. Only the passion fruit juice industry and the production of coconuts have permitted the colony to survive a long, difficult period. But the emphasis on those products (aimed at increasing the income of the colony, which is supported by the Directorate) has resulted in inattention to subsistence crops and the creation of an atmosphere of distrust between the colonists and the directors of Pindorama.

Because of the aggravated living conditions of rural people and the precarious conditions under which food is supplied to the large cities of the Northeast, in 1960 colonization began to be looked at as a front to be attacked as much by SUDENE, in relationship to the entire Northeast, as by CRC (Resale and Colonization Company), as far as the state of Pernambuco was concerned.

Indeed, SUDENE was created at an opportune time, with the aim of coordinating the application of public funds in the Northeast and trying to save the region from the scourge of underdevelopment (which victimizes it more than the droughts). SUDENE mobilized its technical personnel with the aim of carrying out a survey of the possibilities and needs of the region in an extensive and discerning study. They neglected to consult, however, the technicians who for some years had worked in the region and knew it reasonably well. This resulted in the delay that occurred at the beginning of its activities, and the shock, sometimes, over the plans that were formulated. I also believe that SUDENE neglected somewhat the human problem, which, as emphasized by Caio Prado Júnior in 1943,[2] should have been a primary concern of the technicians and the governors, and have held priority even over certain basic problems (such as industrialization). Indeed, we cannot be a strong and developed country, with a population that is diseased, undernourished, and illiterate. If one reads the Directorate Plan of SUDENE, one sees that in analyzing the regional problems, the agency is concerned with expansion of the agricultural frontier, marketing of foodstuffs through the reorganization of the network of warehouses and silos, industrialization, rational exploitation of mineral resources, and the improvement of transportation and communication systems, public health, and basic education. All these aspects will contribute to improving the living conditions of poor people, but they do not offer direct measures for improving, in the short run, living conditions of the rural population. These measures, more often than not, seek long-term transformation of subhuman living conditions; but it is not known whether SUDENE will be able to achieve the end it strives for. It is fitting to stress that the improvement of production techniques, the increase of profits from the land, without complementary measure to protect the rural workers, has, until now in Brazil, only channeled more money into the pockets of the rich property owners, thus perpetuating the conditions of those who slave on the land under the most precarious living conditions.

Conceding the existence of a high population density and of an archaic and obstructive land-tenure system, SUDENE believes that the solution to the agrarian problems must be found in the increased supply of land: in the opening up, thanks to modern technology, of new agricultural area. For that reason it advocates the opening of new agricultural area in Maranhão and southern Bahia, in the humid valleys, the irrigable strips along the large rivers and the reservoir basins, as well as the partial conversion of the sugarcane zone into a food-producing zone,[3] taking advantage of unoccupied government lands in humid areas of various Northeastern states. On these lands, which consist of 13,000 hectares in Alagoas, 9,430 hectares in Paraíba, and 3,068 hectares in Pernambuco,[4] some 1,774 families, a total of 8,870 inhabitants, could be located. SUDENE is also trying to increase the irrigable areas in the semiarid interior, by taking advantage either of the waters of the São Francisco or those contained in the reservoirs constructed by DNOCS (National Department of Works Against the Drought); this amounts to more than 250,000 hectares. The lands to be improved are distributed over diverse areas: from the Bahia Sertão, in the Rio Grande basin, and along the middle and lower São Francisco, not only in Bahia, but also in Pernambuco, Alagoas, and Sergipe. SUDENE could also take advantage of the areas located downstream from the reservoirs constructed by DNOCS, in the river valleys of the Acaraú, Curu, and Jaguaribe in Ceará; Apodi and Piranhas in Rio Grande do Norte; Paraíba in Paraíba; Pajeú and Moxotó in Pernambuco; and Vaza-Barris and Itapicuru in Bahia. The areas to be developed would have to be expropriated. With such works, SUDENE hopes to increase by 1,000 percent the area irrigated by large reservoirs DNOCS has constructed. I believe that the distribution of land in the semiarid region must ensure that sharecroppers, who cultivate another person's land through the payment of high percentages of the crop, be the first to benefit. From the planning agency they need credit at modest interest rates, broader technical assistance, a plan for marketing products under a cooperative arrangement, and an adequate storage system.

A more serious problem, however, involves the old land-tenure system in the sugarcane areas of the Zona da Mata. Considering the low income generated by the cultivation of sugarcane and the laying-off of workers during the off-season, SUDENE devised an ingenious plan. SUDENE would finance the construction of necessary irrigation works to increase the productivity of those lands. Once that agricultural improvement was accomplished, the property owners could cede part of their land, equal in value to the improvements made. Subsequently, the land would be divided into lots and handed over to the squatters, who would become small property owners dedicated to producing foodstuffs. The ceded area would be at least equal to that irrigated, and its value equal, at least, to 45 percent of the financing given for the irrigation installation.[5] The project forecasted the establishment of fifty thousand families, the irrigation of 100,000 hectares, and a total investment of Cr$5,810,000 over five years.[6] The location of small landowners in the Zona da Mata, where they could receive technical assistance and credit through SUDENE, was one of the most sensible measures of the agency. The location of these centers in the most densely populated area and close to such important urban centers as Recife, Salvador, Maceió, João Pessoa, and Natal, would promote, if the marketing of the agricultural production were organized, an appreciable improvement in the supply of foodstuffs to the urban centers and would create a small middle class of farmers whose standard of living would soon contrast with the rural wage earners, demonstrating to them the need to fight for better living and working conditions. Mindful of those possibilities, the large agricultural companies tried to mechanize their operations, decreased the number of hired laborers, and, in order to diminish the strong social tensions in the countryside, paid higher wages. The increase in wages, even today well below the minimum, and the increase in foodstuff production in the region, provoking a lowering of their prices, would bring better living conditions, not only to the small landowners, but also to the wage laborers. It would have improved the most miserable living conditions in the Northeast, those dominant in the Zona da Mata where the greatest riches are produced, but where that wealth benefits only a small number of inhabitants.

Economist Celso Furtado, first head of SUDENE, did not take into account the customary inclinations of the sugar factory owners of the Northeast: always distrustful of large-scale technical plans and ever hungry for land. They were not concerned with vertical growth, or with small landowners in their vicinity and peasant sugarcane workers being transformed into prosperous truck farmers by SUDENE. Such a plan was introduced at the beginning of 1962. It still has not been executed.

It was difficult for the sugar factory owners to understand that a decrease in the area of land they owned, could, through irrigation, bring about an increase in production. Certainly the existence of small farms, with owners in good economic conditions, alongside their lands, stealing away the cheap labor they utilized, seemed dangerous to them. The success of small farmers near latifundia could contribute a great deal to the lessening of social tension, as Celso Furtado points out. But it could also awaken in the landless workers a desire to own land. This two-edged sword is what the large property owner always looks at with dread. Accordingly, the sugar factory owner remains ready to hamper whatever experiment he judges dangerous to the current agrarian structure.

In my view, the large landowners' desire to maintain their extensive latifundia aginst expropriation results as much from the status attributed to land as to a defense against inflation. While currency is devalued, often at high rates (according to official statistics, it was 44 percent in 1976), land increases in value, guaranteeing the landowner an authentic monetary correction. To date the large landowners have succeeded in neutralizing the actions of various governmental agencies aimed at correcting the distortions of the land-tenure system. In 1968, GERAN (Executive Group for the Rationalization of Agroindustry in the Northeast) was created in order to rationalize the sugarcane industry and free lands for distribution to small farmers. The first surveys were made, but when it began to acquire excess lands, the program was stopped. Afterward, the PROTERRA program was instituted; it was aimed at expropriation of excess lands on holdings considered latifundia, in order to establish medium properties. The program has been implemented with great caution. Thus far only the expropriation of the small Crauatá factory in the Pernambuco Agreste has been carried out. Most of its lands were divided into parcels and sold as small- and medium-sized properties.

Furtado considered Maranhão a favored area because it experienced spontaneous migration from the semiarid zone of the Northeast, and had an abundance of unoccupied government land. Rainfall permitted a peasant agriculture that was reasonably profitable. SUDENE planned to obtain donations of extensive areas in Maranhão: in the west, on the Rio Pindaré; in the upper Mearim; and, later, in the Gurupi Valley, in the forest zone. These lands were to be divided into parcels and given to families brought from the semiarid zone. To guarantee the success of this undertaking, Ambassador Merwin Bohan, special representative of President John F. Kennedy, went to the region in order to channel funds from the Alliance for Progress and foodstuffs from the Food for Peace program.

According to SUDENE's Five Year Plan for 1961–65,[7] about 5,000 families a year would be transferred to the region drained by the Turi and Gurupi rivers, where unoccupied land was donated by the state of Maranhão to SUDENE. The families would be recruited from among volunteers, each family having to have at least four members, and no school-age children. That measure was aimed at involving, chiefly, young couples so the SUDENE would not have to build schools immediately. The problem of education could be put off for two or three years. These families would be transported to Maranhão beginning in August, after the rainy season, and would be used initially in the construction work of SUDENE itself: road building, well digging, construction of houses and warehouses, and so on. Wages thus earned could support the families for the first few months. Afterward, they would occupy parcels of land and begin to cultivate annually 5 hectares, practicing a land rotation of eight years, typical in Maranhão.[8] Ten hectares would be conserved as native babassu palm groves, thus avoiding the task of clearing, and the gathering of babassu nuts would supplement the income of the colonists.

The procedure for distributing land included a concession for a minimum of ten years; the parcel could not be rented to a third party. In case the land could not be used by the recipient himself, it was to be returned to the public agency that gave the concession.

The total investment in the project was to be about Cr$183,-000,000 at 1960 prices. This perfectly drafted plan, however, had to undergo serious modifications to be realistic. The Northeasterners, harassed by want, did not wait for the call for volunteers by SUDENE. They began to move on their own, under precarious conditions, to the publicized "Canaan" of Maranhão. SUDENE found itself with serious problems. Without any assistance, many families were locating along the roads, practicing their traditional forms of agriculture. SUDENE had hoped to establish only a pioneer nucleus of fifty families in the area, with the basic objective of studying the behavior of a heterogeneous group confronted by a large colonization plan. It is appropriate to emphasize Gilberto Freyre's point—made to the SUDENE council—that the elaboration of plans of the agency must also include the participation of social scientists: sociologists, anthropologists, geographers, etc., and not only agronomists, physicians, and statisticians. The complexity of social problems must be understood in its totality.

I believe it was reasonable that SUDENE try to rationalize a natural migration to areas where there was unoccupied land, giving to the migrant more humane living conditions, and also preventing the depletion of the soils in Maranhão through a traditional itinerant agriculture of low productivity. However, I believe that those colonists are going to be located in areas distant from the principal consuming centers and that their products will arrive at those centers, if they arrive at all, at very high prices. I do not understand how one can put into effect in the Northeast, where there is annually a crisis in the supply of foodstuffs and where SUDENE itself intends to extend a great network of warehouses and silos, a program of colonization without linking it to the problem of food supply for the urban centers, urban centers that will grow considerably, most certainly due to the policy of industrialization defended by SUDENE itself.

The removal of 5,000 families of four members each, or 20,000 people annually from the semiarid zone to Maranhão, is not going to alleviate the poverty of the rural population. Those 20,000 people represent only 0.2 percent of the total population of the Sertão and Agreste.

The SUDENE project in western Maranhão did not achieve the planned results. Plots of land were demarcated and given to peasants, a system of rural credit and technical assistance for them was established, an agricultural cooperative was created in the area, in a place called Zé Doca, but only a few of the peasants benefited from the overall program. Today, the majority of the unoccupied government land in western Maranhão has been the object of various programs that have permitted the establishment of very large holdings, thousands of hectares in area, aimed chiefly at the development of cattle raising and the exploitation of tropical woods. Thus the migrants from elsewhere in the Northeast, ever more numerous, have to seek lands farther and farther west, in the neighboring states of Goiás and Pará.

SUDENE deserves credit, in turn, for its attitude when it tried to increase the network of warehouses and silos that would have an essential function of storing the agricultural products of the rural property owners, from the harvest season, when they are abundant, until the off-season, when they become scarce and increase in price and benefit only the middlemen. SUDENE did not overlook the existence of two companies already devoted to that purpose, one in Pernambuco, another in Bahia. It planned to expand the network then in existence, from fifteen warehouses with a capacity of 75,360 tons to sixty warehouses with a capacity of 265,000 tons. Table 6 shows how the warehouses were to be distributed in the various states.

TABLE 6
Storage Warehouse Projects of the Northeast

State	Number	Capacity (metric tons)
Maranhão	6	46,000
Piauí	8	29,000
Ceará	10	49,000
Rio Grande do Norte	6	40,000
Paraíba	10	52,000
Pernambuco	11	66,000
Alagoas	10	26,000
Sergipe	4	10,000
Bahia	21	83,000
TOTAL	86	401,000

Source: *Plano Qüinqüenal de Desenvolvimento para o Nordeste (1961-1965)*, SUDENE, Recife, 1961.

The warehouses in Pernambuco and some in Bahia were already constructed while those in other states were to be built. A good network of general warehouses would improve the condition of the producer, owner or renter, since it would free him from the greediness of the middlemen and would guarantee a rational food supply for the urban centers. In order for the system to function well, however, it was necessary that partisan politics be eliminated. Administration had to be in the hands of dedicated technical personnel, competent and chiefly concerned with social aspects of the problems and with the solution of the human problems.

Furtado was again correct when he declared that it would be necessary to create the conditions for rapid and effective change in the anachronistic agrarian structure of the country. Bold actions were needed, among them constitutional modifications that would permit the realization of agrarian reform and modify, at its roots, the state administrative mechanism, financial system, and banking structure.[9] Indeed, reforms were made, such as the promulgation by President Castelo Branco of the Land Statute Law, whereby the development of a land redistribution policy and a cooperative organization was allowed. It happens, however, that the process, today directed by INCRA, has been moving very slowly, and the problem of the land-tenure system continues to be one of the most serious of the country.

CRC was a state agency organized by Governor Cid Sampaio

in Pernambuco, much poorer and with much more modest plans than SUDENE. Urged by the Peasant Leagues of Francisco Julião, the governor formed CRC when he had to expropriate the Galiléia sugar mill, and shortly thereafter the Barra and Terra Preta mills, all located in the *município* of Vitória de Santo Antão, a zone of influence of the peasants and squatters subject to bondage labor. The CRC tried to orient the disorganized colonization that had been attempted since 1948, directing the landless workers to expropriated or unoccupied lands. When José Rufino sugar factory of Cabo was expropriated in order to establish an industrial district, the slope areas and those most remote from the Rio Pirapama were sold to the CRC so that some colonists could be settled on those lands. In that industrial district there was, among other industries, a synthetic rubber factory that constituted one of the major concerns of the state of Pernambuco.

The district was organized as a result of a law approved on December 26, 1959, with the following purposes:

1. Execute directly or indirectly the colonization plans and re-sale of material goods elaborated by the state.
2. Acquire adequate areas for sale to tenant farmers and for the establishment of colonies.
3. Construct dams and reservoirs, principally in the Sertão and Agreste, and make other necessary improvements for the development of agriculture, directly or under agreements with the state public agencies, following the plans and directives of the Secretary of Agriculture.
4. Resell materials for agriculture and livestock raising, exclusively to farmers and livestock raisers.[10]

The plans of CRC were very modest; they intended to establish only 5,000 families, over a period of five years. Recognizing in the Pilot Plan the miserable conditions dominant in the rural sector of Pernambuco and the need to form a solid nucleus of small property owners, they tried to improve not only the living conditions in the rural areas, but also the food supply of the urban centers. The establishment in colonies of 1,000 families per year represents a drop in the bucket for a state that has, according to CRC more than two million rural workers.[11]

One of the great concerns of the CRC Pilot Plan was to use the unoccupied state lands available in the three natural regions.

This overlooked the fact that those of the Sertão, due to climatic conditions and distance from the large consumer centers, would not provide much hope for families located on them. Moreover a large portion of the available land in the Sertão is thought to be occupied by 4,000 peasants who could regularize their situation and become property owners. CRC forecast the establishment of five colonies in 1962, colonies to be located at different locations in Pernambuco. Table 7 lists the planned colonies.[12]

TABLE 7
Distribution of Colonies of the Resale and Colonization Company (CRC)

Colonies	Number of Families to be Included
Chapada do Araripe Group	3,000
Tabuleiros do Litoral Group	700
Old Colonies Group	150
Galiléia	150
Zona da Mata and Agreste Group	1,000
TOTAL	5,000

The groupings in the Table were to contain various individual colonies, that is, seven in the Tabuleiros do Litoral group, five in the Old Colonies group, and ten in the Zona da Mata and Agreste group. In the Chapada do Araripe group, the 3,000 families were to be distributed into twenty-five settlements. Afterwards, 3,400 hectares of land were acquired near the city of Cabo, some 30 kilometers from Recife. It was part of expropriated land from José Rufino sugar factory, and it was intended to establish 340 families there.

Source: Projecto de Colonizacão, no. 2, State of Pernambuco, Recife, 1961.

Several of the colonies were established in poor locations. More than 50 percent of the families were to be located in the portion of the state where there is a lack of water, where the soils are poor, and where the consumer market is very distant, just to take advantage of the unoccupied lands. The placement of the colonists on the Chapada do Araripe was not justified in view of the low productivity of the land and the long distance from consuming centers (which led to high transportation costs), even though colonization was carried on to stimulate the cultivation of cotton, sisal, and other xerophytic plants, as well as extensive livestock raising, as stated in the Pilot Plan of CRC.

The Tabuleiros do Litoral, where CRC intended to locate 700 families, are known for their low soil productivity; they are located near the larger cities and within densely populated areas, but have remained untilled, surrounded by cultivated fields like the cane fields of the lowlands and the coconut groves of the with fertilizer the infertile soils can be improved and that in Alagoas, the tablelands are being taken over by sugarcane. But why select negatively, choosing the poorest areas for colonization? Would it not be more attractive to acquire areas on the lowlands or more fertile slopes, where the plots could be smaller? It would be promising for the colonists to have less land giving greater production, than a greater area of land with lesser production.

Galiléia sugar mill was known to have poor and eroded soils. The members of the Peasant Leagues who fought against the family that owned it were so numerous that CRC itself wanted to remove some of them to other mills. This provoked serious clashes between CRC and the Peasant Leagues, since the Peasant Leagues looked on that idea as a policy to try to break up their headquarters, and to separate their leaders in order to weaken their activities in the rural area. The Peasant Leagues also believed that the problem at Galiléia need not be resolved only in terms of its agrarian aspects. They felt it was possible to direct a portion of the workers toward small industries and tertiary service activities. The problems reached such a serious state that CRC resorted to the courts to clear out the supporters of the Leagues. The peasants still refused to withdraw from the land because CRC did not have available other areas for them. Some were left in the cities, without a means of subsistence, as in Terra Preta. Many of them as well, because of age, physical defects, and the fact that they had not served in the military could not be allocated any of the CRC plots. The requirements of CRC would have, in fact, been reasonable if the agency had been distributing land in unpopulated areas. But they could not be justified when the agency was expropriating densely populated sugar mills and refraining from giving land to renters or squatters who were already using it. If the renters and squatters who pressed for the expropriation, the very men who had cultivated the land for decades, organized and struggled against the landowner to win the expropriation, and then were ousted from their plots because they were more than fifty years old, suffered from some disease, had not served in the military, or lacked a certificate stating that they were not individuals of "difficult adaptation," then the positive social aspects of the agency's expropriation were negated.

The colonies at Cabo, Vitória, Guabiraba, and Bonito were the most promising, in my view, since they were located in a humid area, with moderately good soils and a high population density. Unfortunately, however, they included fewer than 300 families, only about 6 percent of the families to be settled in colonies by the CRC.

The size of the plots was to vary in keeping with their locations and the natural conditions: from 5 to 10 hectares, if located entirely on irrigated land; from 10 to 20 if located on upland areas that were partially irrigable; from 20 to 30 if located on lands in the Zona da Mata and Agreste, and from 30 to 50 hectares when located in the Sertão, away from any reservoir basin. I believe the size the plots of land should be larger. A family can survive cultivating 5 hectares a year, but only with difficulty, only when they plant with crops of high value such as onions, flowers, or grapes, can it give to the family a standard of living above miserable. That is especially true when, in the event of the death of the head of the family, two sons, neither having other jobs, begin to farm the land jointly, since the land cannot be subdivided. The size of land parcels is one of the most serious problems facing the organizers of colonization and the directors of agrarian reform. In such matters the participation of a geographer in the planning is indispensable; no one can designate better the regions and subregions into which an area should be divided. A parcel of a certain size may be small in one region but very large in another. With 5 hectares, however, the parcel will always be small, always a minifundium in Pernambuco, since only in exceptional cases and with difficulty can it support a family. Never, no matter how good the land, should one consider plots of fewer than 15 or 20 hectares.

CRC imposed sensible conditions on awarded parcels of land when they required that perspective colonists have at least five years experience as farm workers. Moreover, they could not already be a rural property owner, merchant, industrialist, member of the armed forces, public servant, and so forth. I cannot understand, on the other hand, how CRC could require the colonists to prove that their past life did not prompt them to be considered individuals of "difficult adaptation." It fell to CRC to determine, in the initial years, if the colonists were or were not adaptable to the conditions. How can one require of a simple peasant, who often does not have proper identification, and is not legally married, the presentation of such a document? That item would permit the directorate of CRC in the future, in the event of political influence in the administration, examples of which unfortunately we are not free of, to begin to use that requirement to veto the entry into the colonies of individuals of diverse political parties. It would not be desirable to facilitate the entry of politics into such programs because that would be likely to destroy the best ventures.

The colonists selected would receive their parcels of land under lease for a period of three years, and on the plots they had not only to plant crops, but also construct a house, fence in the plot, heed the regulations, fulfill their financial commitments, and so forth. After three years they could buy the land, paying annual installments not only for the land but also for the improvements. The colony would only be independent when all of the parcels of land had been paid for in full and the colonists were in a condition to direct it.

Supervised rural credit and technical orientation would be given to the colonists; CRC had contracts for that purpose with ANCAR (Rural Credit Agency for the Northeast). One should not forget, however, that those institutions have reduced staffs, generally operating with a small number of people, as already observed in relation to ANCAR when I studied the tobacco-growing area of Ubá in the forest region of Minas Gerais. It was intended that the colonists utilize the existing warehouses and silos of eleven distribution centers for various cities located in the three natural regions of Pernambuco; they were Ingàzeira, Arcoverde, Caruaru, Garanhuns, Limoeiro, Ouricuri, Salgueiro, São José do Egito, Serra Talhada, Timbaúba, and Vitória de Santo Antão.

I believe that CRC needed to open new colonization fronts in land areas that were more productive and better located, a point of view with which the directors agreed. In 1961 CRC acquired 1,106 hectares in Vitória de Santo Antão, 1,129 hectares in Guabiraba, and 3,400 hectares in Cabo, and intended to acquire 1,500 hectares more on Assunção Island, at Cabrobó, where the cultivation of onions was giving good returns.

Sociologist José Artur Rios did not agree with various aspects of that colonization plan. After visiting the colony of Terra Preta, at Vitória de Santo Antão, he declared that "any agrarian reform, no matter how advanced it is, is reduced, in practice, to a colonization project."[13] I do not share that point of view after having traveled over various parts of Brazil, since the process of dividing up land and of colonization with technical and social assistance to the colonists is very slow and generally reaches only a small percentage of the rural population. That must have concerned the abovementioned sociologist, who, after making an apology about the Terra Preta colony, emphasized the necessity of more projects like Terra Preta. Isolated in a zone of latifundia, they are insignificant, but, duly structured in large areas, with technical and financial support, they could lead to profound modification in the agrarian situation of the entire Northeast. Could it be that the illustrious sociologist believed that the large property owners would consent to the multiplication, within their midst, of experiments like Terra Preta? It is known that colonies are subject to alternating phases of progress and decline, in accordance with those who administer them, or to the greater or lesser demand for their products on the market. A colony, made up of small land parcels, can hardly survive and maintain an economic organization for itself alongside large properties. For José Artur Rios, a colonization plan would need to group its activities on two large fronts: a colony could be established, aimed at the economic uplift and social equilibrium of the rural peasant, or concern itself with the food supply of the cities. Of course, the two purposes are complementary.

In my opinion, CRC should concern itself less with colonization on the Chapada do Araripe and focus its attention on Cabo where there is an available area of 3,400 hectares located only 30 kilometers from Recife; on Cova da Onça in Jaboatão, where there are 253 hectares; on Pau-Brasil, Água Preta, and Palmares, where 122 hectares are available; followed by the colonies of Olho d'Água in Angelim, Sertãozinho in Maraial, and Bolandeira in Canhotinho, which contain a total of 7,309 hectares relatively close to Garanhuns; and with the colonies of Vitória de Santo Antão and Guabiraba, which have 200 hectares and are located between Recife and Caruaru, less than 100 kilometers from one of the two principal cities of Pernambuco.

I also feel that we can only achieve better results through the modification of our old land-tenure system. Colonization as Celso Furtado wished[14] requires a constitutional reform that would permit easy expropriation of land, when it is in the social interest. Although expropriation is regulated by Article 141, Paragraph 16, of the Constitution of 1946, the colonization projects have to be timid, seeking out unoccupied government lands, and putting the small property owner in unfavorable conditions in face of the large property owners. Having the colonies located in remote areas, or those that are least fertile, takes away from them whatever chance of victory in the struggle between the small and large farmers that, can be said, reflects all of the agricultural history of Brazil. This struggle up to now has been favorable to the large farmer, to the growing of commercial export crops, linked to latifundium, and, initially, to slavery (afterwards substituted by wage labor).

It is fitting to emphasize that CRC, after the governorship of Cid Sampaio, began to concern itself more with the problems of resale of land, leaving colonization in a secondary position. Thus, during the administration of Governor Miguel Arraes, a policy of acquisition of the agricultural production of the small property owners, at compensatory prices, was launched. This forced the middlemen, merchants who acquired the agricultural products in the countryside and sold them on the urban markets, to pay higher prices, in order to benefit the small farmer. After 1964 CRC began to give more attention to the sale of insecticides, fertilizer, agricultural implements, etc., to the farmers. It was eventually incorporated, along with other related state companies, into a new state agency.

Attempts to Organize the Rural Masses: the Peasant Leagues and the Unionization of Rural Workers

The difficult, and worsening, situation in which the landless workers of the Northeast found themselves after 1950 made them seek for themselves a solution to replace colonization. Colonization, as it was conceived by SUDENE and CRC, and in the face of the means that either had available, would be, if successful, a long-term solution that would benefit only a small number. The absolute majority of the peasants would continue to drift along, as has occurred to the present, under subhuman living conditions. That fact has been perceived not only by the students of our social problems, such as the politicians and clergy, but by the people themselves. The spirit of revolt has been expressed from time to time in the most diverse locations of the Northeast, and embryonic forms of organizations have arisen daily. The landowners were alarmed, fearing the peasant reaction, fearing an agarian reform prepared by politicans and technicians, and dreading the plans for economic recovery with nothing aimed at improving the productivity of their land, so that they could release for subsistence crops areas formerly occupied by the large-scale crops, chiefly sugarcane.

In 1962, the governor of Rio Grande do Norte himself stated: "Either one finds a solution through massive financial measures to ameliorate the situation in the Northeast, or we will not reach January 1, 1963, without a violent disturbance that may be bloody. Anyone who does not believe it should put a calendar in their pocket and wait and see." He continued, "Either the elites decipher the Northeast of 1962, opening a door of hope, or they will be responsible, because they were warned, for the unpreventable revolution."[15] The superintendent of SUDENE, author of and responsible for the Development Plan of the Northeast, speaking to the same reporter declared, "If one takes into account that three-fourths of the Northeasterners go hungry every day of the year, that such misery results from the Northeasterner not having an opportunity to utilize his work capacity, and that, at the same time, the best lands in the Northeast are underutilized and that capital generated in the region tends to emigrate, it results in an economic system that is socially doomed, and needs to be modified at its foundations. But, it is not possible to change the foundation of an economic and social organization except through revolutionary means. Historically, those transformations occurred spontaneously and cataclysmically. Today, we are in a position to diagnose a historical situation, to identify its predominant tendencies, and to regulate its development. Therefore, we are in a position to direct a revolution." In a later article,[16] Celso Furtado, illustrious economist, declared there to be a basic duality in the Brazilian revolution, since, although the urban workers had the right to organize and to participate in an open society, "the rural workers did not possess any rights and were not able to make legal claims. If they organized themselves, it was concluded that it was done with subversive aims. The conclusion, which we need to remove, is that Brazilian society is rigid in its largest segment: that formed by the rural sector." It is interesting that, knowing the reality of the rural Northeast, Celso Furtado did not remember to try to get to the bottom of the urgent needs of the rural workers and to advise attention to the most urgent demands as a necessity so that the protection of the labor laws would be extended to cover them, and not just try to regulate the rental and sharecropping contracts in the countryside. Those were problems that concerned the Ministry of Agriculture in 1963. In the agrarian reform project the Ministry sent to the Congress, it tried to regulate the relationships in Articles 29 through 38.[17]

Federal Deputy Aberbal Jurema, after carrying out legislative inquiries in the interior of Pernambuco, understood the difficult situation being experienced, and the oppression of the renters and others, because of the high rent charged and the low wages being paid. He proposed to the Federal Chamber of Deputies "a change in, and not a reform of, the agrarian structure of the country," and that the sugar factories be transformed "into cooperative centers, chiefly so that we are able to resolve the social catastrophe of the Northeast."[18] Jurema affirmed in the Federal Chamber of Deputies that "we must state loud and clear that Francisco Julião with his Peasant Leagues, was ahead of time, through the social facts, the laws, or better the reality of the Northeastern worker, with which he organized the Leagues before the legislation reached the countryside, because the Leagues already existed."

The continuous aggravation of the crisis, of the growing difficulties of day-to-day living, put the rural workers in a mood of revolt, of despair. Galiléia mill, like others located in marginal areas, distant from the factories, was being shut down in the 1930s, when the sugar prices were low; the property owners began to rent out the land to individuals, who began to plant fruit trees and cereals destined for the food supply of Recife and other urban centers in the Northeast. The landowners began to live in the city on the income, sporadically visiting the property. A trusted overseer charged the annual rents, supervised the fulfillment of the work obligation or bondage, and served as an intermediary between the absentee owner and those who worked the land.

In the post–World War II period, high sugar prices and the

building of roads stimulated an expansion of the capacity of the factories, which, reequipped, began to gain more land for the planting of sugarcane. That expansion was made at the cost of the disappearance of the small mills. The mills became suppliers of sugarcane to the factories, at the expense of the peasants, who were expelled from their land in order that the cane fields could expand imperialistically over lands the peasants had tilled for decades. I personally witnessed the destruction of old orchards and coffee plantings because of the ruthless thirst for land in the *municípios* of Vicência and Amaraji.

The peasants, badgered by the landowners, resorted to the courts; the legal process, however, was slow, and only with difficulty were they able to pay a lawyer for any length of time. Although they remained on their plots of land, they were constantly threatened by the guards and wage laborers of the property. Few resisted to the end. It was that difficult situation that led the renters of Galiléia mill to organize, under the direction of their own overseer, a beneficent society called The Agricultural and Livestock Society of the Planters of Pernambuco.[19]

The organization of that society irritated the son of the mill owner. Seeing in the nascent cooperative spirit of the peasants a danger to his inheritance, he tried to evict them. They refused to obey him, leading the property owner to start eviction proceedings. Seeking a lawyer to defend themselves, the peasants ended up in the office of Francisco Julião, a recently elected state deputy. He was the only member of the Socialist party in the Chamber of Deputies; he resolved to defend the peasants for free, since they could not pay, offering as an explanation that, as a state deputy he received a good salary. Taken by surprise, Julião certainly did not have a plan to resolve the agrarian problems of the Northeast;[20] he knew, however, the rural environment, for he was the son of a sugar mill owner, and, while defending those from Galiléia, he observed that identical cases were springing up all over the state and that the problem that before was only legal, had become social. He believed that the matter had left the jurisdiction of judges and lawyers and was then a matter for the legislature. For that reason, utilizing his mandate, he began to fight in the Chamber of Deputies and in the press against the bondage practice. He believed that his chief mission was to awaken the great mass of peasants to the struggle, to make them aware of their power and their needs, and to forestall the attempts to solve the agrarian problems in ivory towers by intellectuals and politicians who almost always ignore the peasant reality. To better structure the struggle of the peasants, the society founded by the peasants of Galiléia was legalized on January 1, 1955, it having previously existed without legal standing. Despite continuing to be called The Agricultural and Livestock Society of the Planters of Pernambuco, the same organization was known throughout Brazil as the Peasant Leagues. That name was so well accepted that in Paraíba the word "peasant" identified the members of the Leagues. In order to forestall the eviction of the peasants of Galiléia, Julião presented to the Chamber of Deputies a draft bill expropriating the mill. This was approved and signed by the governor of Pernambuco.

The example of Galiléia was a lighted fuse, and in 1960 the Leagues already had members in twenty-six *municípios* in the Zona da Mata, Sertão, and Agreste of Pernambuco.[21] In Paraíba large chapters sprang up in *municípios* such as Santa Rita, Sapé, Mamanguape, Guarabira, Pirpirituba, Espírito Santo, and other smaller places. The chapter at Sapé was one of the most important, with nearly 7,000 members. In 1964, the Peasant Leagues had influence in all of the Northeast, since their chapters were numerous in Piauí and Ceará, where the various *município*-level associations met together, forming a federation, and in the state of Bahia in the São Francisco Valley. In Alagoas, the first chapters were founded in Viçosa and Atalaia. In some states (such as Piauí and Paraíba) the Leagues had depended upon the understanding of the governors, but had encountered a serious reaction on the part of the large property owners.

Julião accepted everyone's support, reaching the point of once stating: "We do not see enemies in the soldier, priest, student, industrialist, or Communist; the enemy is the large landowner." Accused by some of being a mystic and of using mysticism to mislead the peasants, he affirmed: "Pope John XXIII was the first pope to come from a peasant background. The encyclical that he has just issued is proof that the Pope has approved of the Peasant Leagues. We use in our exhortation the words of the Bible. Yes, because the Bible is a revolutionary book." He did not hesitate to advise his followers to take part in the rural unions that the priests were founding in the various parishes. Undeniably, Julião had leadership ability and emerged as an authentic leader. His influence was continually increasing, and his prestige was on the rise among the peasants, squatters, and small landowners. Obviously, the Leagues had greater support in the areas where the peasants and squatters were dominant, the organization being almost nonexistent in the region where the cane fields of the factories predominated and where the proletarization of the people was more complete. For that reason, in the recommendations on agrarian reform of the Brazilian Institute of Democratic Action, the Leagues were accused of "carefully avoiding a threat to the interests of the large property owners or provoking the rural masses against the area of low production and decadent exploitation."[22] As I see it, that fact derived from the peasants being men who had something of their own, a few belongings to protect, and having a higher cultural level and better conditions for resistance, as long as they held their plot of land. Also, having their own crops, they remained attached to their *sítios*, where they may have been born. These were men easily recruited into the Peasant Leagues. As for the wage laborers, they were veritable nomads. They worked on the mills and lived in what were many times old slave quarters, staying there only a few days, before departing for another location. They owned almost nothing except for a few rags. It was difficult for the wage laborers to relate to a chapter of the Leagues, for they never stayed in one place. Some withdrew from the Leagues, fearing the reaction of the property owner and his employees, which almost always manifested itself in the form of violence. In 1961 in southern Pernambuco a squatter was branded with a branding iron as if he were an animal, and in April 1962, João Pedro Teixeira, the leader of the peasants in Sapé, Paraíba, was assassinated, and it was said to have been ordered by a rural property owner. In March 1962, the Leagues launched a "Denunciation to the People" about the persecution of peasants by the authorities of Rio Formoso.

One should not conclude, however, that there was no influence of the Leagues in the cities where they did not have chapters, since Julião himself stated, referring to his organization: "The movement grew in a disorderly way. It is now that we are attempting a survey of the people. There is not in the entire Zona da Mata or in most of the semiarid interior of the Northeast a peasant who is not now potentially a member of the Leagues. In whatever state of the Northeast, even where the Leagues were not established, it is common for the wronged peasant to say to the foreman or boss, 'Thank Jesus Christ that the Leagues are coming. It will be our freedom.' " Military leaders, who were very concerned about the operation of the Leagues, believed that there were thirty to thirty-five thousand followers in Pernambuco and about eighty thousand in all of the Northeast.[23]

One of the most frequent accusations made about Julião by the intellectuals and technicians of the right and center was that he did not want to resolve the agrarian problems, that he was a simple demogogue creating turmoil and trying to guarantee his seat as a deputy. They also said that he had no program. Julião, the deputy and writer, however, in his public proclamation on agrarian reform, declared that he wished to awaken the masses so that they could participate in the solutions to their problems, solutions that would change the Brazilian agrarian structure. He believed that the experiences and demands for rights of those who tilled the soil had to be taken into account when one made an agrarian law. His general ideas, however, were revealed in a document read on September 15, 1961, when the campaign for agrarian reform was being initiated.[24] After criticizing the plans of SUDENE, the Agrarian Review of São Paulo, and CRC, Julião presented what he called the "Ten Commandments" of the Peasant Leagues. They are as follows:

1. The States, using the constitutional prerogatives consigned to them for levying local taxes (which, after a conference would pass to the jurisdiction of the *municípios*), need to increase the taxation of land, up to now ludicrous, "changing from the current practical inexistence of land taxes to its highly progressive regulation by a realistic valuation of property and dividing the taxes on the basis of the area of each establishment."

2. At the federal level there must be executed a systematic organization of all those who wish to resolve the agrarian problem, aiming, at once, "to fight for an amendment of the constitution to define a fair price, so as to restrain speculation and to permit the payment of indemnity in bonds or notes of public debt."

3. The necessity that there be legislated, at once, based on

Article 147 of the Constitution of 1946, an attempt to reach a "regulation of rental and of sharecropping in the long and medium term, also considering the possibility of exceptions, in the case of adequate utilization of lands to be defined." He pointed to Resolution 6, of August 7, 1957, of the Urbanization Company of the New Capital, on the utilization of land in the Federal District, as an acceptable model for that legislation.

4. Utilization, to the maximum, of mixed production cooperatives, whose economy could be strengthened based on processing and industrialization.

5. Establishment of effective sanctions, by taxation and other means, against monopolistic concentration of land.

6. Approval of colonization programs if there is "donation of lands in usufruct or surrounded by property titled to cooperative peasant associations; self-administered and with wide participation of the colonists in all phases of the agricultural activities; repudiation of land speculation."

7. Complete application to the rural population of the rights assured in the constitution, of labor legislation, and other laws that benefit urban workers with "guarantees of civil and political rights, suppression of evictions, private police forces, and all offenses of a physical nature to the security of the rural workers."

8. Elimination of abuses through intermediaries by the cooperative organizations that guarantee the supply of food and raw materials and organize the marketing of the products.

9. "Restructuring of sugarcane cultivation: (a) utilization of 10 percent of the area forecast for that crop by the Cane Statute for the cultivation of food crops, on continuous areas of lands, of adequate conditions of fertility, by means of government planning, in the form of cooperative peasant associations; (b) agricultural zonation aimed at diminishing the area of sugarcane cultivation but increasing productivity through improved technology; (c) conjoined unionization of peasants and wage earners in the National Council and in the Regional Institute of Sugar and Alcohol."

10. Stimulate as "a finishing touch for all these measures" the creation of Peasant Leagues throughout the country be-

cause they "are law and order against the latifundium, which is anarchy and disorder."

Some of these ideas were accepted by the Ministry of Agriculture in the draft of the law that was sent to Congress. Thus the necessity of an increase in land taxes with progressive taxation that would increase in proportion to the increased size of property was recognized, as were legal regulation of contracts of rental and sharecropping; extension of labor legislation to rural workers; and, in addition, adoption of a concise process "for the resolution of lawsuits involving property owners, renters, sharecroppers, and workers in the rural zone."[25]

I believe, however, that of all the items, numbers 5 and 6 were those that Julião stuck to most as principles, since he always emphasized the necessity of giving land to the peasants, exclaiming that "the parcel of land that is given to the rural worker is like a branch extended to someone who is drowning in a river." Land, he believed, would make it easier to organize credit at modest rates of interest, to give technical agricultural orientation, and to establish the cooperatives that would market the products.

One can see that Julião's program differed from those of SUDENE and CRC: he intended to benefit not only a small portion of the mass of rural workers, but, in one form or another, all those who tilled the soil. His program was not a rigid scheme to be applied to the most diverse geographic regions, which would be a catastrophe in a region as diverse as the Northeast or, even worse, in a continental-sized country like Brazil. Certain measures, such as the increase of land taxes, unionization of rural workers, explicit regulation of rental and sharecropping contracts, respect for the rights of cooperatives, elimination of private police forces, etc., were recognized as pressing and necessary, theoretically, by almost everyone. Rare were those who publically affirmed support for the maintenance of the status quo. It stands to reason that the application of these general principles must be made, considering the local conditions, so that the agrarian reform not fail, so that within a few years one need not reform the agrarian reform. It is very true that there should be a supervisory organization to administer the application of the modification to the land-tenure structure, and that such an organization and its legislation be sufficiently dynamic to keep up with the evolution of the problem and to provide solutions that are compatible in space and time, to the problems that arise.

The conservatives frequently accused the Peasant Leagues of inciting the workers against the landowners and alleged that they were responsible for fires in the cane fields. Julião defended himself against that accusation, asserting that terrorist actions were not part of his aims. In fact, every year fires were breaking out, as they do today, burning hundreds, sometimes thousands of tons of cane, causing financial losses to the property owners; the burned cane must be crushed within two or three days and the factories deduct about 10 percent from its value. One should emphasize, however, that these fires very often were caused by sparks from the locomotives of the railroads, or even by the cane cutters themselves who, without any political orientation, start a fire in a cane field in order to achieve higher production, since it makes the cane much easier to cut. Frequently, the landowner or factory owner will direct the setting of fire to the cane field in a certain area, in order to speed up the cane supply, since that speed-up would compensate for the 10-percent decrease in the value of the product. I believe that in some cases a wronged worker, or one who judged himself to be wronged by his bosses, would seek revenge by becoming an arsonist, but these were sporadic cases that did not justify the atmosphere of fear that led many people to declare that the fires were organized in advance and set from airplanes (as was reported in the press during the 1962 harvest).[26] Imagination, and many rumors, were aimed at creating irreconcilable differences between the Peasant Leagues and the government to provoke their repression. Peasants said to be arsonists, when imprisoned by the police, did not reveal any participation by the Peasant Leagues in the setting of fires.[27]

The most serious clash occurred in Paraíba at the Miriri mill—between members of the Peasant Leagues and the owner of the latifundium of 15,000 hectares. The majority of the squatters gave one day of labor per week as payment of rent on a *sítio* of a half hectare. Alerted that one day of bondage labor per week was equivalent to fifty-two days per year and that the current wages for those fifty-two days represented Cr$6,240 per year, a sum of money that in two years would correspond to the value of the land they were cultivating, the tenant farmers were stirred up. They began to seek the right to pay the rent in cash, eliminating the bondage labor. The landowner rejected the proposal and threatened to evict squatters who were affiliated with the Leagues. From that a disagreement between the squatters and the guards of the owner arose, resulting in fights in which two of the owner's henchmen were killed with knives and axes, and an administrator, a guard, and two peasants wounded from pistol shots. Concerning the clash, the chief of police of Paraíba said: "The appeal to the police for a solution to the problems with the Peasant Leagues is annoying and short-sighted. That practice is defended only by the Fascist organizations that attribute to armed forces the solution of all problems. Instead of calling for the assistance of the police, the appeal should be addressed to the National Congress and to the agencies of economic development." The leader of the State Assembly declared in the name of the government that the crimes of Miriri were attributed to "a structure that is deemed to be outmoded and whose reform must be urgently undertaken."[28]

From those statements one can conclude that the state of Paraíba was convinced of and understood that the question was not a police matter, but that the social problems had to be solved. Only the large property owners who were least enlightened fought desperately, evicting from their lands the influential members of the Peasant Leagues, in an attempt to stem the rising tide that they represented.

With the overthrow of the João Goulart government in April 1964, the Peasant Leagues, considered subversive, were banned, and the majority of their leaders imprisoned. Francisco Julião lost his office as a state deputy and his political rights for ten years; he gained asylum in the Mexican embassy, from which he left the country for exile. His activities in the rural sector of the Northeast were finished.

The regimentation of the rural masses, however, was not only done by politicians like Julião. The church entered into the dispute over the control of the masses and priests and bishops began to organize rural unions. In some *municípios* the church began to act, orienting the peasants and defending them in the struggle against the large property owners when clashes broke out. Some young priests, behind the shield of the encyclical "Mater et Magistra," of Pope John XXIII, which affirmed that "the tillers of the soil should feel solidarity between one another and cooperate in the creation of cooperative enterprises and professional associations or unions,"[29] tried to bring together the rural people who followed their advice.

Among the clerics pledged to the organization of the peasants, the most famous was the young priest Antônio Melo, from the city of Cabo, in Pernambuco. His fame, like that of Julião, spread over the entire country. According to the Recife newspapers of April 7, 1962, Governor Magalhães Pinto of Minas Gerais, on visiting Pernambuco, showed interest in meeting him. They had a long conversation at the Recife airport about the agrarian problems of the Northeast. Melo was young, eager, and courageous, and was the leader of the peasants of his parish, who had strong disagreements with the land administrators of José Rufino factory, after its expropriation by the state and the attempt to evict the squatters from the land. His fame began when the COPERBO (Pernambucan Synthetic Rubber Company) began to try to evict from the lands that they sold to CRC, the workers who, logically, would become colonists. In 1962, the government offered each one Cr$30,000, in exchange for their fields, their houses, and their departure. The squatters refused and unjust force was used; Melo, who had just helped the workers of the Tibiri sugar mill, linked to the Peasant Leagues, came to their assistance. Once the struggle began, he tried to reach an understanding with the mayor, with the deputy elected by the *município*, and with the newspapers, but without results. He turned against the governor, alleging that since he was elected by the people it was his obligation to resolve the social problems. Supporting the peasants was the Young University Catholics organization, which filled the streets, held meetings, and promised to unite with the workers if the police were used against them. It called everyone's attention to the injustices that the government wished to perpetuate. After all that agitation, the government yielded, and announced that the peasants could remain in their houses until they could be conveniently established in their final locations.[30]

Journalist Mauritônio Meira, with rare intelligence, focused on the fact that Melo had definite ideas that he made plain without evasion: "It is as much a mistake to organize peasants according to Bolshevist theory, as according to Catholic theory," and he added, "the peasant has nothing to do with ideological struggles. He has to demand his rights and fulfill his obligations." Despite disagreeing ideologically with Julião, the journalist declared that he was contributing positively "by the awakening of conscience that was aroused in the peasants." He concluded with statements such as: "An agrarian revolution is necessary, but we should not start from the preconceived idea that it must be done peacefully, as the capitalists say, or by force, as the Communists wish. The nature of a revolution is dictated by the historical circumstances. If it cannot be made peacefully, then we will have to confront the reality of a fight."[31]

In the well-known Seridó Valley, in Rio Grande do Norte, Monsignor Emerson Negreiros unionized the rural workers, and braved the wrath of the property owners (who constantly threatened him). He, however, was eager and courageous, was supported by the Bishop of Natal, and confronted the attacks of his enemies and continued to unionize the peasants, at the same time giving them medical and dental assistance. He declared: "The church must become more courageous and more Christian, and combat the latifundium." It was not only those clerics of the Northeast who turned toward the problems of the people and tried to give them the help they needed. A few bishops became famous because of the struggle that they confronted in favor of the rural workers, including Avelar Brandão, of Teresina; Severino Mariano of Pesqueira; José Terceiro of Penedo; and José Tavoura of Aracaju. Influential people were displeased with the Bishop of Penedo's greater concern with helping the colonists of Pindorama than with the prayers of the cathedral, and with the idea that he devoted more time to problems of the earth than of the heavens. But he, unconcerned, moved heaven and earth to obtain credit, fertilizer, plows, and technical help for the peasants of his diocese. In 1964 there were in the Northeast tens of rural unions awaiting recognition by the Ministry of Labor, it being the responsibility of the minister to carry out, with dispatch, recognition of them. I believe that the priests moved with such enthusiasm toward unionization of rural workers because they understood that if the church continued to spurn the earthly problems they would lose the support of the men of the countryside, precisely those with whom they had the greatest influence.

This rural unionization movement was greatly strengthened in 1963 with the promulgation of the Rural Labor Statute, which granted to rural workers rights similar to those enjoyed by urban workers. In that year, numerous rural worker unions were founded, chiefly in Pernambuco, when the then Governor Miguel Arraes, elected by a coalition of leftists, permitted the rural workers to organize themselves into unions and associations that could exercise the right to strike (up to that time a right only exercised by the urban workers). In other states, the Statute was being applied with greater or lesser intensity and the landowners were compelled to respect the rights granted to the workers by the new law. Above all, the application of the minimum wage to the rural areas considerably improved the buying power of the agricultural workers; this was reflected in the commerce between the urban centers and the rural areas. In 1964, with the overthrow of the João Goulart government and the removal of the governors of Pernambuco and Sergipe, the Ministry of Labor intervened in many unions, and the leftist leaders, considered subversive, were removed. The unions were given new leaders, who were more concerned with demands for rights (chiefly the minimum wage, vacations, and so forth) than with political matters. The unions continued to supervise the application, in the rural sector, of the labor legislation and to furnish medical and social assistance to its members. Its power, however, was not sufficient to avoid the acceleration of the process of proletarization and the eviction of workers from the sugar mills and fazendas, as well as their concentration in areas peripheral to the cities. They live in cities today, many working outside the jurisdiction of the labor legislation that was to protect their rights, waiting for eventual work, while some intermediary arranges for them to supply the labor demand of the nearby landowners. Thus, the use of itinerant workers has intensified, accentuating a social problem of grave consequences. This problem is linked to the acceleration of the proletarization of the rural workers and will be resolved only when there is an agrarian reform that gives to the worker a fair share of the results of his labor.

Glossary

(The definitions are those that have a direct relationship to subjects included in the text. Many of the words have other connotations, but no attempt has been made to include them.)

ABCAR: (Associação Brasileira de Crédito e Assistência Rural), Brazilian Association of Credit and Rural Assistance.

Agreste: the region of the Northeast between the well-watered Zona da Mata and the semiarid Sertão.

almanjarra: the large, wooden mechanism for turning the cane crusher of an animal-powered sugar mill (*engenho*).

alqueire: a measure of weight equal to 240 kilograms.

ANCAR: (Associação Nordestino de Crédito e Assistência Rural), Rural Credit Agency for the Northeast.

angico: a tree of the family Mimosaceae, *Piptadenia* spp.

arroba: a measure of weight equal to 15 kilograms.

avelós: a tree of the family Euphorbiaceae, *Euphorbia gymnoclada.* It is planted as a living fence in the Northeast.

babassu: a tree of the family Palmae, *Orbignya speciosa.* The seed contains an edible oil.

bandeirante: explorer, frontiersman, and hunter of Indians.

braça: a measure of distance equal to 2.2 meters.

brejo: a moist area with a permanent water supply.

caatinga: drought-resistant thorn scrub vegetation of the interior parts of the Northeast; the areas characterized by such vegetation.

caatingueira: a small tree of the family Caesalpiniaceae, *Caesalpinia pyramidalis.*

CHESF: (Companhia Hidrelétrica do São Francisco), São Francisco Hydroelectric Company.

219

CIBRAZEM: (Companhia Brasileira de Armazenamento), Brazil Warehousing Company.

CIDA: (Comitê Interamericano de Desenvolvimento Agrícola), Inter-American Committee for Agricultural Development.

CNG: (Conselho Nacional de Geografia), National Council of Geography.

CODEVASF: (Companhia de Desenvolvimento do Vale do São Francisco), Development Company of the São Francisco Valley.

COPERBO: (Companhia Pernambucana de Borracha Sintética), Pernambucan Synthetic Rubber Company.

corumba: a migrant worker from the *caatinga* area.

CRC: (Companhia de Revenda e Colonização), Resale and Colonization Company.

cruzeiro: the Brazilian money unit that replaced the *mil-réis* in 1942. In 1967, 1,000 old cruzeiros became 1 new cruzeiro. One cruzeiro is written Cr$1.00.

CVSF: (Commissão do Vale do São Francisco), São Francisco Valley Commission. Became CODEVASF.

DNOCS: (Departamento Nacional de Obras Contra as Sêcas), National Department of Works Against the Drought.

engenho: an old-fashioned sugar mill; also used to designate the entire landholding.

engenhoca: a very small sugar mill, used mostly for the manufacture of brown sugar.

estaleiro: a cleared, level area where carnauba palm leaves are spread in the sun to dry.

facheiro: a tall plant of the family Cactaceae, *Cereus squamosus.*

fazenda: a large rural landholding devoted to ranching or crop production.

fazendeiro: owner-operator of a fazenda.

foreiro: a peasant who resides on a large holding and is obligated to provide the owner with a few days of free labor each week in return for the use of a small plot of land.

furão: a type of digging stick of Indian origin used in place of a hoe on soft lowland soils.

GEPA: (Grupo Executivo de Produção de Alimentos), Executive Group for Food Production.

GERAN: (Grupo Executivo de Racionalização da Agroindustria do Nordeste), Executive Group for the Rationalization of Agroindustry in the Northeast.

IAA: (Instituto do Açúcar e Alcool), Alcohol and Sugar Institute.

IBC: (Instituto Brasileiro de Café), Brazilian Coffee Institute.

IBGE: (Instituto Brasileiro de Geografia e Estatística), Brazilian Institute of Geography and Statistics.

IBRA: (Instituto Brasileiro de Reforma Agrária), Brazilian Institute of Agrarian Reform.

IFOCS: (Inspectoria Federal de Obras Contra as Sêcas), Federal Inspectorate of Works Against the Drought. Became DNOCS.

INCRA: (Instituto Nacional de Colonização e Reforma Agrária), National Institute of Colonization and Agrarian Reform.

INDA: (Instituto Nacional de Desenvolvimento Agrícola), National Institute of Agricultural Development.

ingazeira: a small tree of the family Mimosaceae, *Inga* spp.

jurema: a small tree of the family Mimosaceae, *Mimosa verrucosa.*

lastro: a term to designate a group of seedbeds planted in the bed of a river.

macambira: a plant of the family Bromeliaceae, *Bromelia laciniosa.*

mandacaru: a tall plant of the family Cactaceae, *Cereus Jamacaru.*

mangabeira: a tree of the family Apocynaceae, *Hancornia speciosa.* It bears an edible fruit.

mil-réis: lit. 1,000 *reais;* the Brazilian money unit until 1942.

miradouro: in the Cariri region of Ceará, a spring with a small volume of water.

mocó: a variety of tree cotton grown in the Northeast for its long, silky fiber.

município: an administrative subdivision of a state, equivalent to a county in the United States. The name of the *município* and its seat are the same.

nascente: in the Cariri region of Ceará, a spring with an abundant volume of water.

olho d'água: in the Cariri region of Ceará, a spring with a moderate volume of water.

paçoca: dried meat pounded in a mortar with manioc meal.

palma: a plant of the family Cactaceae, *Opuntia* spp. It is cultivated as cattle feed in the Northeast.

picadeiro: a term used to designate the portion of the sugar mill where the cut cane is stored before being crushed.

PROTERRA: (Programa de Redistribuição de Terras e de Estímulo à Agro-Indústria do Norte e Nordeste), Program of Land Redistribution and Stimulus to Agroindustry in the North and Northeast.

quadra: a measure of area equal to 1.21 hectares.

quilombo: a settlement of fugitive Negro slaves.

quipá: a plant of the family Cactaceae, *Opuntia inamoena.*

réis: lit. plural of *real;* former Brazilian money unit. One hundred *réis* is written $100.

sertanejo: resident of the Sertão.

Sertão: the semiarid region of the Northeast to the west of the Agreste.

sítio: a small farm plot.

SUDAM: (Superintendência do Desenvolvimento da Amazônia), Superintendency for the Development of the Amazon.

SUDENE: (Superintendência do Desenvolvimento do Nordeste), Superintendency for Development of the Northeast.

SUPRA: (Superintendência da Reforma Agrária), Superintendency of Agrarian Reform.

tabuleiro: a low coastal plateau.

tarefa: lit. task; a measure of area that varies greatly in size.

terra firme: land of a river basin not subject to seasonal flooding.

terra roxa: reddish-purple soil of high fertility derived from basalt.

toque: popular term referring to inflammation of subcutaneous tissue of cattle; carbuncles.

travessão: a divide made of barbed wire, stones, closely spaced plants, or a trench, separating grazing areas from cultivated areas.

umbuzeiro: a small tree of the family Anacardiaceae, *Spondias tuberosa.* It bears an edible fruit.

usina: a modern sugar factory; also used to designate the entire land-holding.

vazante: a term to designate agriculture practiced on a riverbed during the dry season of low water.

verdão: a variety of tree cotton grown in the Northeast.

xiquexique: a low plant of the family Cactaceae, *Cereus Gounellei.*

Zona da Mata: the region of the Northeast along the humid east coast. Its name derives from the former forest cover.

Notes

2 The Northeast: Region of Contrast

1. "Divisão Regional do Brasil." *Revista Brasileira de Geografia* 3, no. 2, pp. 343 ff.

2. *La Géographie: Guide de l'Etudiant*, pp. 17 ff.

3. *O Rio Comanda a Vida: Uma Interpretação da Amazônia.*

4. With respect to this see Gilberto Freyre, *Nordeste: Aspectos da Influência da Cana na Vida e na Paisagem do Nordeste do Brasil;* Djacir Meneses, *O Outro Nordeste. Formação Social do Nordeste.*

5. Annual precipitation averages 1,066 millimeters in Ceará-Mirim, 1,854 in Mamanguape, and 1,692 in João Pessoa. *Atlas Pluviométrico do Brasil (1914–1938)*, Rio de Janeiro, 1948.

6. The sugarcane rivers of the Northeast have been studied geographically by teams from the Joaquim Nabuco Institute of Social Research. The work of those teams resulted in the publication of four monographs in the series *Os Rios do Açúcar do Nordeste Oriental: Vol. 1, O Rio Ceará-Mirim*, 1957; *Vol. 3, O Rio Paraíba do Norte*, 1959, both by Gilberto Osório de Andrade; and *Vol. 2, O Rio Mamanguape*, 1957; *Vol. 4, Os Rios Coruripe, Jiquiá e São Miguel*, 1959, both by Manuel Correia de Andrade.

7. Orlando Valverde, "O Uso da Terra no Leste da Paraíba," *Revista Brasileira de Geografia* 13, no. 3, p. 51.

8. Manuel Correia de Andrade, *O Vale do Siriji (Um estudo de Geografia Regional)*, pp. 22–23.

9. Lysia Bernardes, "Tipos de Clima do Brasil," *Boletim Geográfico* 9, no. 105, p. 991.

10. Inês Amélia Leal Teixeira Guerra, "Tipos de Clima do Nordeste," *Revista Brasileira de Geografia* 18, no. 4, p. 450.

11. Vasconcelos Sobrinho, *As Regiões Naturais de Pernambuco, o Meio e a Civilização*, p. 37.

12. Manuel Correia de Andrade, *O Vale do Siriji (Um estudo de Geografia Regional)*, and "Caracterização da sub-região da mata seca em Pernambuco," *Anais da Associação dos Geógrafos Brasileiros* II, part 1.

13. Alfredo José Porto Domingues, "Aspectos físicos do Litoral e Mata da Grande Região Nordeste," *Enciclopédia dos Municípios Brasileiros* 4, p. 124.

14. *Municípios* in Alagoas such as Palmeira dos Índios, Arapiraca, Junqueiro, Limoeiro de Anadia and Anadia, placed by the IBGE in the Alagoas Sertão, do not have characteristics of the Sertão, being more typically like the Agreste, but an Agreste that is more humid and devoted to agricultural activities than the traditional Pernambuco Agreste.

223

15. "Resolução no. 461 de 7 de julho de 1955," *Boletim Geográfico* no. 134, Conselho Nacional de Geografia.

16. It should be made clear that in the Northeast a *"brejo"* is a humid area almost surrounded by or adjacent to the semiarid *caatinga.* Thus a *"brejo"* is that region where there is no dry season, where water is available all year. The term does not have the same meaning in southern Brazil where it refers to a swampy area.

17. There are numerous bibliographic items on the Paraíba *brejos,* among them the following works stand out: José Américo de Almeida, *A Paraíba e os seus problemas,* 2d ed., Manuel Correia de Andrade, *O Rio Mamanguape,* and the works of Nilo Bernardes, "Observações sobre a paisagem agrária no município de Areia," Mário Lacerda de Melo, "Aspectos da Geografia Agrária do Brejo Paraibano"; and Heloísa Carvalho, "Areia, Aspectos da sua Geografia Urbana"; all published in the *Anais da Associação dos Geógrafos Brasileiros* 6, part 2, besides Orlando Valverde, "O Uso da Terra no Leste da Paraíba," *Revista Brasileira de Geografia* 17, no. 1.

18. Louis Lombard, who traveled over the region at the end of the last century (1896), gave witness to this fact in the article "Explorações Geográficas e Geológicas," *Revista do Instituto Archeológico, Geográphico e Histórico Pernambucano* 12, no. 66, pp. 89–111.

19. Manuel Correia de Andrade, *Aspectos Geográficos do Abastecimento do Recife.* unpublished manuscript.

20. Mário Lacerda de Melo, "Um Brejo de Pernambuco (A Região de Camocim de São Félix)," *Boletim Carioca de Geografia* 18, nos. 3–4.

21. With respect to the Serra de Ororobá, see Manuel Correia de Andrade, *A Serra de Ororobá: Contribuição ao estudo dos níveis de erosão do Planalto da Borborema* and Hilton Sette, *Pesqueira: Aspectos de sua Geografia Urbana e de suas relações inter-regionais.*

22. Mariano Feio, "Notas acerca do relevo da Paraíba e do Rio Grande do Norte," *Boletim Geográfico* 13, no. 128, acknowledges that there are two plateau surfaces on the Borborema, one at an elevation of 450–550 meters and another at 650–750 meters; Gilberto Osório de Andrade, in *A Superfície de aplainamento pliocênica do Nordeste do Brasil,* acknowledges the existence of the Borborema Plateau at an average elevation of 150 meters.

23. Walter Albert Egler, "Contribuição ao Estudo da Caatinga Pernambucana," *Revista Brasileira de Geografia* 13, no. 4.

24. Nicolau Athanassof, "Indústria Pastoril," p. 225.

25. *Anuário Estatístico do Brasil 1957,* p. 10.

26. Rodolpho Theophilo, *História da Seca do Ceará (1877–1880),* p. 7.

27. "Resolução no. 461, de 7 de julho de 1955," *Boletim Geográfico* no. 134, Conselho Nacional de Geografia.

28. Mauro Mota, *O Cajueiro Nordestino: Contribuição ao seu estudo biogeográfico.*

29. José Antônio Gonsalves de Mello, neto, *Tempo dos Flamengos,* p. 45.

30. Pascoale Petrone, *A várzea do Açu,* p. 26.

31. See Wilhelm Kegel, *Contribução ao estudo da bacia costeira do Rio Grande do Norte.*

32. Lysia Bernardes, "Tipos de Clima do Brasil," *Boletim Geográfico* 9, no. 105.

33. Inês Amélia Leal Teixeira Guerra, "Tipos de Clima do Nordeste," *Revista Brasileira de Geografia* 18, no. 4.

34. Caio Prado Júnior, *Formação do Brasil Contemporâneo. A Colônia,* p. 40.

35. Irineu Pinheiro, *O Cariri,* p. 8.

36. Ibid., pp. 16–17.

37. Ibid., p. 21.

38. Manuel Correia de Andrade, *Paisagens e Problemas do Brasil,* 3d ed., pp. 86–95.

39. Otávio Guilherme Velho, *Frentes de Expansão e Estrutura Agrária,* pp. 93 ff.

40. Concerning the characteristics of the shantytowns, there is an interesting book by Gilberto Freyre, *Mocambos do Nordeste. Algumas notas sobre o tipo de casa popular mais primitivo do Nordeste do Brasil.*

41. *La Campagne: Le fait rural a travers de monde.* p. 64.

42. In this respect see Caio Prado Júnior, "Contribuição para análise da Questão Agrário no Brasil," *Revista Brasiliense* 28, p. 203.

43. Mário Lacerda de Melo, *Paisagens do Nordeste em Pernambuco e Paraíba*, pp. 114 ff, makes clear the position of secondary crops in relation to sugarcane.

44. Manuel Figueiroa, *Cuestones de Política Agrícola Regional no Nordeste*, p. 107.

45. *Land Tenure Conditions and Socio-economic Development of the Agricultural Sector - Brazil*, p. 126.

46. Concerning the formation of this group see Gilberto Osório de Andrade, *O Rio Paraíba do Norte*, p. 115.

3 Land Tenure and Labor in the Zona da Mata and Eastern Littoral

1. Oliveira Lima, "A Nova Lusitânia," in *História da Colonização Portuguesa*, vol. 3.

2. Francisco Adolpho Varnhagen, *História Geral do Brasil*, vol. 1, p. 124.

3. Manuel Diégues Júnior, *População e Açúcar no Nordeste do Brasil*, p. 43.

4. Letter published in *Revista do Instituto Histórico e Geográfico Brasileiro* 15, p. 14.

5. Maurício Goulart, *A Escravidão Africana no Brasil*, pp. 17 ff.

6. Pita Rocha, *História da América Portuguesa*, p. 81.

7. Letter of 15 April 1549, published in *História da Colonização Portuguesa*, vol. 3, pp. 318–19.

8. Frei Vicente do Salvador, *História do Brasil*, p. 201.

9. Ibid., p. 203.

10. Ibid., p. 204; Alfredo Carvalho, *Aventuras e Aventureiros no Brasil*, pp. 49–97.

11. Caio Prado Júnior, *Evolução Política do Brasil: Ensaio de Interpretação Materialista da História Brasileira*, p. 32.

12. Frei Vicente do Salvador, *História do Brasil*, p. 220; Barbosa Lima Sobrinho, *Pernambuco e o São Francisco*, pp. 36–39.

13. Costa Porto, "Sobre velhos engenhos," *Jornal do Comércio* 14 January 1962.

14. Pero de Magalhães Gandavo, "História da Província de Santa Cruz," in Assis Cintra, *A Nossa Primeira História.*

15. Fernão Cardim, *Tratados da Terra e da Gente do Brasil*, p. 290.

16. Adrien van der Dussen, *Relatório sobre as capitanias conquistadas no Brasil pelos holandeses (1639).*

17. Letter of 24 November 1555, transcribed in *História da Colonização Portuguesa*, vol. 3, p. 320.

18. José Antônio Gonsalves de Mello, neto, "Notas acerca da introdução de vegetais exóticos em Pernambuco," *Boletim do Instituto Joaquim Nabuco de Pesquisas Sociais* 3, pp. 33–138.

19. Agostinho Marques de Perdigão Malheiro, *A Escravidão no Brasil: Ensaio Histórico-Jurídico-Social*, vol. 1, p. 138.

20. Pero de Magalhães Gandavo, "História da Província de Santa Cruz," in Assis Cintra, *A Nossa Primeira História*, p. 78.

21. Ibid., p. 294.

22. Letters of 23 August 1608, published in *Anais da Biblioteca Nacional* 57, p. 37.

23. Ambrósio Fernandes Brandão, *Diálogos das Grandezas do Brasil*, p. 99.

24. Manuel Diégues Júnior, *População e Açúcar no Nordeste do Brasil*, pp. 43 ff.

25. Opinion of José Antônio Gonsalves de Mello, neto, *Tempo dos Flamengos*, p. 150;

José Honório Rodrigues and Joaquim Ribeiro, *Civilização Holandesa no Brasil*, p. 92. The Pernambuco historian Alfredo Carvalho acknowledges in *Estudos Pernambucanos*, that the desire to find gold mines also had an influence on the decision for that invasion.

26. Gilberto Freyre, *Casa-Grande & Senzala*, 4th ed., *Sobrados e Mocambos, Ordem e Progresso*, and *Nordeste* are the books principally devoted by the sociologist from Apipucos to the social formation of the sugar civilization of the Northeast.

27. José Antônio Gonsalves de Mello, neto, *Tempo dos Flamengos*, pp. 152–53; José Honório Rodrigues and Joaquim Ribeiro, *Civilização Holandesa no Brasil*, pp. 254 ff.

28. Adrien Verdonck, "Memória oferecida ao Senhor Presidente e mais Senhores do Conselho desta Cidade de Pernambuco sobre a situação, lugares, bem como de Itamaracá, Paraíba e Rio Grande, *Revista do Arquivo Público* 4, no. 6, pp. 613–28.

29. Flávio Guerra wrote an essay, *Arrecife de San Miguel*, about the population of Recife in the pre-Dutch period.

30. Manuel Diégues Júnior, *O Banqüê nas Alagoas*, pp. 25 ff.

31. See C. R. Boxer, *Os Holandeses no Brasil (1624–1654)*, p. 200.

32. Adrien van der Dussen, *Relatório sobre as capitanias conquistadas no Brasil pelos holandeses (1639)*.

33. José Antônio Gonsalves de Mello, neto, *Tempo dos Flamengos*, pp. 163–65.

34. Adrien van der Dussen, *Relatório sobre as capitanias conquistadas no Brasil pelos holandeses (1639)*, p. 91.

35. José Antônio Gonsalves de Mello, neto, *Tempo dos Flamengos*, p. 210.

36. Hermann Watgen, *O Domínio Colonial Holandês no Brasil*, pp. 486-87.

37. Adrien van der Dussen, *Relatório sobre as capitanias conquistadas no Brasil pelos holandeses (1639)*, pp. 93–96.

38. José Antônio Gonsalves de Mello, neto, *Tempo dos Flamengos*, p. 221.

39. Ibid., p. 208.

40. C. R. Boxer, *Os Holandeses no Brasil (1624–1654)*, pp. 192–93.

41. José Antônio Gonsalves de Mello, neto, "Um Regimento de feitor-mor de engenho em 1663," *Boletim do Instituto Joaquim Nabuco de Pesquisas Sociais* 2, p. 83.

42. C. R. Boxer, *Os Holandeses no Brasil (1624–1654)*, pp. 188–89.

43. Ibid., p. 160; José Antônio Gonsalves de Mello, neto, *Tempo dos Flamengos*, p. 175.

44. Ibid., p. 189.

45. Caio Prado Júnior, *História Econômica do Brasil*, pp. 81 ff.

46. "Idéia Geral da Capitania de Pernambuco e das suas Anexas . . .," *Anais da Biblioteca Nacional* 40, pp. 1–113.

47. Felisberto Firmo de Oliveira Freire, *História de Sergipe (1575–1855)*, p. 205.

48. "Idéia Geral da Capitania de Pernambuco e das suas Anexas . . .," *Anais da Biblioteca Nacional* 40, p. 36.

49. Gilberto Freyre, *Nordeste*, 2d ed., p. 124.

50. André João Antonil, *Cultura e Opulência do Brasil por suas Drogas e Minas*, pp. 74 ff; Luís dos Santos Vilhena, *Notícias Seteropolitanas e Brasílicas*, vol. 1, pp. 182–83; Barbosa Lima Sobrinho, *Problemas Econômicos e Sociais da Lavoura Canavieira*, 2d ed., pp. 9 ff, all analyze these problems.

51. L. F. Tollenare, *Notas Dominicais*, pp. 93–95.

52. Ibid., p. 94.

53. Ibid., p. 96.

54. Ibid., p. 77.

55. Manuel Diégues Júnior, *População e Açúcar no Nordeste do Brasil*, pp. 69 ff.

56. José Antônio Gonsalves de Mello, neto, "Um Regimento de feitor-mor de engenho em 1663," *Boletim do Instituto Joaquim Nabuco de Pesquisas Sociais* 2, pp. 80–87.

57. André João Antonil, *Cultura e Opulência do Brasil por suas Drogas e Minas*, p. 84.

58. Ibid., p. 91.

59. Ibid., pp. 105–81; L. F. Tollenare, *Notas Dominicais*, pp. 54–55.

60. L. F. Tollenare, *Notas Dominicais*, p. 94.

61. Irineu Ferreira Pinto, *Datas e Notas para a História da Paraíba*, vol. 1, p. 190; Henry Koster, *Viagens ao Nordeste do Brasil*, pp. 426–28.

62. Gileno de Carli, *Geografia Econômica e Social da Cana-de-Açúcar no Brasil*, pp. 29, 72.

63. "Idéia Geral da Capitania de Pernambuco e das suas Anexas . . .," *Anais da Biblioteca Nacional* 40, p. 30.

64. Henry Koster, *Viagens ao Nordeste do Brasil*, p. 440.

65. Manuel Diégues Júnior, "O Banguê em Pernambuco no século XIX," *Revista do Arquivo Público* 7–10, nos. 9–12, p. 23.

66. Apolônio Peres, *A Indústria Açucareira em Pernambuco*, p. 33.

67. Manuel Correia de Andrade, *O Vale do Siriji (Um estudo de Geografia Regional)*, p. 57.

68. Gilberto Osório de Andrade, *O Rio Ceará-Mirim*, p. 33.

69. Celso Mariz, *Evolução Econômica da Paraíba*, p. 78.

70. Manuel Diégues Júnior, *O Banguê nas Alagoas*, p. 92.

71. Apolônio Peres, *A Indústria Açucareira em Pernambuco*, p. 57.

72. Gilberto Osório de Andrade, *O Rio Paraíba do Norte*, p. 115.

73. Manuel Diégues Júnior, *O Banguê nas Alagoas*, pp. 112–13.

74. Gilberto Freyre, *Um Engenheiro Francês no Brasil*, pp. 178 ff.

75. Estêvão Pinto, *História de uma Estrada de Ferro do Nordeste*, p. 62.

76. Henry Koster, *Viagens ao Nordeste do Brasil*, p. 346.

77. Daniel P. Kidder, *Reminiscências de viagens e permanência no Brasil (Províncias do Norte)*, p. 109.

78. Jean Nieuhof, *Memorável Viagem Marítima e Terrestre ao Brasil*, p. 284.

79. Irineu Joffily, *Notas sobre a Paraíba*, p. 144.

80. Gileno de Carli, *Geografia Econômica e Social da Cana-de-Açúcar no Brasil*, p. 15.

81. Celso Mariz, *Evolução Econômica da Paraíba*, p. 41.

82. F. A. Pereira da Costa, *Anais Pernambucanos* 6, p. 83; and *O Algodão em Pernambuco. Vista histórico-retrospectiva*, p. 11.

83. Henry Koster, *Viagens ao Nordeste do Brasil*, p. 103.

84. With respect to this see Gilberto Osório de Andrade, *O Rio Paraíba do Norte*, pp. 105–6; Manuel Correia de Andrade, *O Vale do Siriji (Um estudo de Geografia Regional)*, p. 62; Celso Mariz, *Evolução Econômica da Paraíba*, p. 22; Irineu Pinto, *Datas e Notas para a História da Paraíba*, vol. 2, p. 210; Lyra Tavares, *A Parahyba*, pp. 539, 543, 603–4.

85. Manuel Diégues Júnior, *O Banguê nas Alagoas*, pp. 87–88.

86. José Saturnino Costa Pereira, *Apontamentos para a formação de um roteiro das Costas do Brasil*, p. 118.

87. Ibid., pp. 22–23.

88. Ibid., p. 290.

89. Manuel Diégues Júnior, *População e Propriedade da Terra no Brasil*, pp. 19–20.

90. Gileno de Carli, *Geografia Econômica e Social da Cana-de-Açúcar no Brasil*, pp. 32–33.

91. Ibid., pp. 221–23.

92. Henrique Augusto Millet, *O Quebra-Kilos e a Crise da lavoura*, p. 35.

93. Robert Avé-Lallemant, *Viagem pelo Norte do Brasil, no ano de 1859*, vol. 1, p. 337; José Pereira Rêgo, *Memória Histórica das Epidemias que têm Reinado no Brasil*, p. 1235.

94. Luís da Câmara Cascudo, *História do Rio Grande do Norte*, pp. 45–48.

95. Ibid., pp. 188–89; Gilberto Osório de Andrade, *O Rio Ceará-Mirim*, pp. 28–29.

96. Celso Mariz, *Evolução Econômica da Paraíba*, pp. 37–38.

97. José Américo de Almeida, *A Paraíba e seus problemas*, pp. 208–9.

98. Henrique Augusto Millet, *Auxílio à Lavoura e Crédito Real*, published by *Journal do Recife*, p. 33.

99. Henrique Augusto Millet, *O Quebra-Kilos e a Crise da Lavoura*, pp. vii, 3 ff.

100. Thomaz do Bom Fim Espíndola, *Geografia Alagoana ou Descripção Physica, Política e Histórica da Província das Alagoas*, p. 97.

101. Gileno de Carli, *Geografia Econômica e Social da Cana-de-Açúcar no Brasil*, p. 49.

102. Manuel Diégues Júnior, *População e Açúcar no Nordeste do Brasil*, p. 183.

103. Gileno de Carli, *Aspectos da Economia Açucareira*, p. 18.

104. Gileno de Carli, *O Açúcar na Formação Econômica do Brasil*, pp. 28–29.

105. Gileno de Carli, *Aspectos da Economia Açucareira*, p. 9.

106. Gileno de Carli, *O Açúcar na Formacão Econômica do Brasil*, pp. 32–33.

107. Gileno de Carli, *O Processo Histórico da Usina em Pernambuco*, p. 18.

108. Craveiro Costa, *Alagoas em 1931*, pp. 78–79.

109. Manuel Correia de Andrade, *O Vale do Siriji (Um estudo de Geografia Regional)*, pp. 86 ff.

110. Orlando Valverde, "O Nordeste da Mata Pernambucana (A região de Timbaúba)," *Boletim Carioca de Geografia* 13, nos. 1–2, p. 42.

111. *O Estado de Sao Paulo* 27 January 1973.

112. Gilberto Osório de Andrade, *O Rio Paraíba do Norte*, p. 126.

113. Mário Lacerda de Melo, *Pernambuco: Traços de sua Geografia Humana*, p. 92; and *Paisagens do Nordeste em Pernambuco e Paraíba*, p. 112.

114. Mário Lacerda de Melo, "Aspectos do 'habitat' rural no Nordeste do Brasil," *Anais da Associação dos Geógrafos Brasileiros* 10, part 1, p. 251.

115. Humberto Bastos, *Açúcar & Algodão*, p. 96.

116. In that period dried codfish sold for Cr$3.50 per kilogram, coffee for Cr$2.80, sugar for Cr$1.00, butter for Cr$9.50, and sun-dried meat for Cr$3.80. Manioc meal was sold for Cr$0.80 per liter and beans for Cr$1.40.

117. Gileno de Carli, *Aspectos Açucareiros de Pernambuco*, p. 19.

118. Mário Lacerda de Melo, "Fisionomia do 'habitat' rural no Baixo Ceará-Mirim," *Anais da Associação dos Geógrafos Brasileiros* 10, part 1, pp. 272 ff.

119. Caio Prado Júnior, "Contribuição para análise da Questão Agrário no Brasil," *Revista Brasiliense* 28, pp. 179–80.

120. Gilberto Osório de Andrade, *O Rio Ceará-Mirim*, p. 53.

121. Daniel P. Kidder, *Reminiscências de Viagens e Permanência no Brasil (Províncias do Norte)*, p. 106.

122. Mário Lacerda de Melo, *Paisagens do Nordeste em Pernambuco e Paraíba*, pp. 78–85; Hilton Sette, "Aspectos da Atividade Pesqueira em Pernambuco," *Anais da Associação dos Geógrafos Brasileiros* 11, part 1, pp. 235 ff.

4 Property, Polyculture, and Labor in the Agreste

1. Elias Herckmann, "Descrição Geral da Capitania da Paraíba (1639)," *Revista do Instituto Archueológico, Histórico e Geográphico Pernambucano* 31, pp. 239–65.

2. Manuel Correia de Andrade, *O Rio Mamanguape*, p. 25.

3. Hilton Sette, *Pesqueira: Aspectos de sua Geografia Urbana e de suas relações inter-regionais*, p. 40.

4. *Documentação Histórica Pernambucana*, vol. 1, pp. 4, 91, 93, 171, 173; Irineu Joffily, *Notas sobre a Paraíba*, pp. 31–32.

5. Irineu Joffily, *Notas sobre a Paraíba*, pp. 126 ff.

6. Luís da Câmara Cascudo, *Tradições Populares da Pecuária Nordestina*, pp. 13–25.

7. Manuel Diégues Júnior, *Regiões Culturais do Brasil*, p. 154; Caio Prado Júnior, *Formação do Brasil Contemporâneo*, p. 187.

8. Luís da Câmara Cascudo, *História do Rio Grande do Norte*, p. 116.

9. Irineu Joffily, *Notas sobre a Paraíba*, p. 117.

10. Mário Lacerda de Melo, *A Serra Negra, uma 'ilha' na caatinga*, p. 150.

11. "Idéia Geral da Capitania de Pernambuco e das suas Anexas . . .," *Anais da Biblioteca Nacional* 40, pp. 100 ff.

12. *Anais Pernambucanos* 6, p. 83.

13. Celso Furtado, *A Operação Nordeste*, p. 22; and *Formação Econômica do Brasil*, p. 81.

14. Henry Koster, *Viagens ao Nordeste do Brasil*, pp. 451, 455.

15. F. A. Pereira da Costa, *O Algodão em Pernambuco. Vista histórico-retrospectiva*, p. 17.

16. L. F. Tollenare, *Notas Dominicais*, pp. 112 ff; Henry Koster, *Viagens ao Nordeste do Brasil*, p. 462.

17. Henry Koster, *Viagens ao Nordeste do Brasil*, pp. 103–17.

18. Ibid., pp. 268–72.

19. Horácio de Almeida, *Brejo de Areia*, pp. 147–48.

20. Irineu Joffily, *Notas sobre a Paraíba*, pp. 115–16.

21. Rodolpho Theophilo, *História da Seca do Ceará (1877–1880)*, p. 27.

22. Henrique Augusto Millet, *Os Quebra-Kilos e a Crise da Lavoura*, p. vii.

23. Henrique Augusto Millet, *Auxílio à Lavoura e Crédito Real*, p. 33.

24. Celso Mariz, *Cidades e Homens*, pp. 93–94.

25. Henry Koster, *Viagens ao Nordeste do Brasil*, p. 463.

26. Celso Mariz, *Cidades e Homens*, pp. 95 ff.

27. Manuel Correia de Andrade, *O Rio Mamanguape*, pp. 43 ff.

28. Horácio Almeida, *Brejo de Areia*, pp. 147–65.

29. José Américo de Almeida, *A Paraíba e os seus problemas*, p. 208.

30. Horácio de Almeida, *Brejo de Areia*, pp. 154–55.

31. Manuel Correia de Andrade, *O Vale do Siriji (Um estudo de Geografia Regional)*, p. 64.

32. Augusto Ramos, *O Café no Brasil e no Estrangeiro*, pp. 259–65.

33. Nilo Bernardes, "Observações sobre a paisagem agrária no Município de Areia," *Anais da Associação de Geógrafos Brasileiros* 6, part 2, pp. 60–62.

34. Mário Lacerda de Melo, "Um Brejo de Pernambuco (Região de Camocim de São Félix), *Boletim Carioca de Geografia* 18, nos. 3–4, pp. 19–20.

35. There are three types of *palma: palma graúda (Opuntia Ficus indica* Mill), *palma redonda (Opuntia* sp.) and *palma miúda (Napolea Cachenilifera* Salm-Dick).

36. The problem of migration of Northeasterners was studied in 1953 by Sousa Barros, *Éxodo e Fixação* and by Lopes de Andrade, *Forma e Efeitos das Migrações no Nordeste;* and more recently by the Joaquim Nabuco Institute of Social Research, in the series *As Migrações para o Recife*, composed of four essays: Mário Lacerda de Melo, *Estudo Geográfico;* Antônio Carolino Gonçalves, *Aspectos do crescimento urbano;* and Paulo Maciel, *Aspectos econômicos*, all published in 1961; and José Lavareda, "Migrações internas no Nordeste - Caruaru um dos seus centros detentores," *Boletim do Instituto Joaquim Nabuco de Pesquisas Sociais* 9, pp. 7 ff.

37. Nilo Bernardes, "Observações sobre a paisagem agrária no Município de Areia," *Anais da Associação dos Geógrafos Brasileiros* 6, part 2, p. 57; Orlando Valverde, "O Uso da Terra no Leste da Paraíba," *Revista Brasileira de Geografia* 17, no. 1, p. 75.

38. Manuel Correia de Andrade, *O Rio Mamanguape*, p. 53.

39. Mário Lacerda de Melo, "Um Brejo de Pernambuco (Região de Camocim de São Félix)," *Boletim Carioca de Geografia* 18, nos. 3–4, p. 31.

40. Manuel Correia de Andrade, *Anadia, um município do Agreste Alagoana.*

41. Manuel Correia de Andrade, *Aspectos Geográficos da Região de Ubá,* p. 41.

5 Latifundium, Division of Land and Labor Systems in the Sertão and Northern Littoral

1. Pedro Calmon, *História da Casa da Torre;* Luís da Câmara Cascudo, *Tradições Populares da Pecuária Nordestina,* pp. 1–7.

2. J. Brígido, *Ceará (Homens e Fatos),* pp. 65 ff.

3. André João Antonil, *Cultura e Opulência do Brasil em suas Drogas e Minas,* pp. 264–65.

4. Barbosa Lima Sobrinho, *O Devassamento do Piauí,* pp. 134–35.

5. Ibid., p. 141.

6. André João Antonil, *Cultura e Opulência do Brasil em suas Drogas e Minas,* p. 265.

7. Manuel Correia de Andrade, *A Economia Pernambucana no século XVI,* p. 63.

8. Raimundo Girão, *História Econômica do Ceará,* p. 65.

9. Irineu Joffily, *Notas sobre a Paraíba,* pp. 31 ff.

10. Capistrano de Abreu, *Caminhos Antigos e Povoamento do Brasil,* p. 57.

11. Quotation from Capistrano de Abreu, in Manuel Correia de Andrade, *Evolução e Características da Pecuária Nordestina,* p. 17.

12. J. von Spix and C. F. P. von Martius, *Viagem ao Brasil,* vol. 2, p. 418.

13. André João Antonil, *Cultura e Opulência do Brasil em suas Drogas e Minas,* pp. 268–69.

14. Luís da Câmara Cascudo, *Tradições Populares da Pecuária Nordestina,* p. 6.

15. Tadeu Rocha, "O Homem e a Técnica em Paulo Afonso," *Diário de Pernambuco* 29 April 1953; Manuel Correia de Andrade, *Evolução e Características da Pecuária Nordestina,* p. 5.

16. Raimundo Girão, *Pequena História do Ceará,* pp. 91–97.

17. Ibid., p. 59.

18. Irineu Pinheiro, *O Cariri,* p. 26.

19. Gilberto Freyre, "Estácio Coimbra, Governador de Pernambuco," p. 193.

20. José de Figueiredo Filho, *Engenhos de Rapadura do Cariri,* p. 13.

21. J. Brígido, *Ceará (Homens e Fatos),* p. 416.

22. Henry Koster, *Viagens ao Nordeste do Brasil,* p. 152.

23. George Gardner, *Viagens no Brasil,* p. 135.

24. José de Figueiredo Filho, *Engenhos de Rapadura do Cariri,* p. 24.

25. Raimundo Girão, *História Econômica do Ceará,* pp. 371–72.

26. Marcos Antônio de Sousa, *Memória sobre a Capitania de Sergipe (anno de 1808),* pp. 32 ff.

27. Irineu Pinheiro, *O Cariri,* pp. 36; 43–44.

28. Rodolpho Theophilo, *História da Seca do Ceará (1877–1880),* p. 27.

29. Paulo de Moraes Barros, *Impressões do Nordeste Brasileiro,* p. 76.

30. Rodolpho Theophilo, *História da Seca do Ceará,* p. 53.

31. Information collected in the field leads me to believe that the early-maturing beans referred to by Rodolpho Theophilo are cowpeas, that are widely grown in the Sertão. As to the early-maturing ("seven-week") maize, I did not succeed in identifying it, but I do not believe it is grain sorghum, which is much cultivated in the valleys of the Jaguaribe, Apodi, and Açu rivers, since its vegetative cycle is more than seventy-five days.

32. Luís Agassiz, *Viagem do Brasil (1865–1866)*, p. 539. (Quotation taken directly from *A Journey in Brazil*, translator's note)

33. Dirceu Lino de Matos, *Região da Baixa Mojiana (Contribuição ao estudo da Geografia Agrária do ponto de vista do uso da terra)*, p. 61.

34. Irineu Pinheiro, *O Cariri*, pp. 26 ff.

35. Nicolau Athanassof, "Indústria Pastoral," p. 255.

36. Hélio Galvão, *O Mutirão no Nordeste*, p. 47.

37. Lopes de Andrade, *Introdução à Sociologia das Secas*, p. 34.

38. Pimentel Gomes, "O Nordeste dos Geógrafos," *Observador Econômico e Financeiro* pp. 50–55.

39. José Cláudio Meira Coelho, *Irrigação na Área Pernambucana do São Francisco*, p. 13.

40. Pasquale Petrone, *A Várzea do Açu*, Associação dos Geógrafos Brasileiros, Avulso no. 2, p. 53.

41. Pimentel Gomes, *A Carnaubeira*.

42. Orlando Valverde and Miriam Gomes Coelho Mesquita, "Geografia Agrária do Baixo Açu," *Revista Brasileira de Geografia* 13, no. 3, p. 468.

43. Francisco Alves de Andrade, *Agropecuária e Desenvolvimento do Nordeste*, p. 75.

44. Mário Lacerda de Melo, *Paisagens do Nordeste em Pernambuco e Paraíba*, p. 190.

45. José de Figueiredo Filho, *Engenhos de Rapadura do Cariri*, pp. 36–37.

6   The Middle North: Maranhão and Piauí

1. Adrien van der Dussen, *Relatório sobre as capitanias conquistadas em Pernambuco pelos holandeses* (1639), p. 91.

2. *Descrição do Estado do Maranhão, Pará, Corujá e o rio das Amazonas*, p. 10.

3. Bernardo José da Gama, *Informação sobre a Capitania do Maranhão dada em 1813*, p. 10.

4. Manuel Correia de Andrade, "L'Elevaje au Nord-Est du Brésil," *Les Cahiers d'Autre Mer*.

5. Caio Prado Júnior, *História Econômica do Brasil*, p. 84.

6. Bernard Kayser, "Les divisions de l'Espace Geographique dans les Pays Sous-Developpés," *Annales de Geographie*.

7. Jerônimo Viveiros, *História do Comércio do Maranhão*, pp. 16–17.

8. Ibid., pp. 201 ff.

7   Tentative Solutions to the Agrarian Problem

1. *Plano Pilôto da Política de Colonização*, p. 20.

2. Caio Prado Júnior, "O problema 'humano' no Brasil," *Rumo* 1, no. 3.

3. *Plano Diretor para o Desenvolvimento do Nordeste*, p. 220.

4. *Plano Qüinqüenal de Desenvolvimento para o Nordeste (1961–1965)*, pp. 44–45.

5. Item published in *Diário de Pernambuco*, 4 October 1961.

6. Murilo Melo Filho, "Chuva de dólares sôbre o Nordeste," *Manchete* 1961; *Plano Qüinqüenal de Desenvolvimento para o Nordeste (1961–1965)*, pp. 34, 43.

7. *Plano Qüinqüenal de Desenvolvimento para o Nordeste (1961–1965)*, p. 21.

8. Item published in *Jornal do Comércio* (Recife), 18 February 1962.

9. Celso Furtado, "Reflexões sôbre a Pré-Revolução Brasileira," *Jornal do Comércio* 22 March 1962.

10. *Plano Pilôto da Política de Colonização*, p. 6.

11. *Companhia de Revenda e Colonização–Algumas Considerações*, p. 7.

12. *Projeto de Colonização*, no. 2. p. 3.

13. Interview published in *Diário de Pernambuco*, 24 March 1962.

14. Celso Furtado, "Reflexões sôbre a Pré-Revolução Brasileira," *Jornal do Comércio* (Recife), 22 March 1962.

15. Mauritônio Meira, "Nordeste, as vítimas da imprevisão," *O Cruzeiro*, 9 December 1961.

16. Celso Furtado, "Reflexões sôbre a Pré-Revolução Brasileira," *Jornal do Comércio* (Recife), 22 March 1962.

17. Draft of *Lei de Reforma Agrária*.

18. Aderbal Jurema, *Sindicalização rural para a mudança democrática*.

19. Antônio Callado, *Os Industrais da Sêca e os "Galileus" de Pernambuco*, p. 35.

20. Mauritônio Meira, "Nordeste, as sementes da subversão," *O Cruzeiro*, 11 November 1961.

21. The following cities in Pernambuco had offices of the Peasant Leagues: Recife, Olinda, Paulista, Igaraçu, Goiana, São Lourenço da Mata, Pau d'Alho, Limoeiro, Bom Jardim, Orobó, João Alfredo, Surubim, Jaboatão, Moreno, Vitória de Santo Antão, Gravatá, Bezerros, Caruaru, Belo Jardim, Pesqueira, Buíque, São Bento do Una, Bonito, Cortès, Escada, and Cabo.

22. Fernando Bastos de Ávila, *A Reforma Agrária; a Lei e o Plano em Recomendações sôbre a Reforma Agrária*, p. 217.

23. Mauritônio Meira, "Nordeste, as sementes da subversão," *O Cruzeiro* 11 November 1961.

24. *Dez Mandamentos das Ligas Camponesas da Opressão do Latifúndio*.

25. Armando Monteiro Filho, *Exposição remetida ao Conselho de Ministros acompanhando o anteprojeto de Lei da Reforma Agrária*.

26. Items published in *Diário de Pernambuco*, 16, 17, and 18 January 1962.

27. Items published in *Diário de Pernambuco*, 21, 28 December 1961.

28. Item published in *Diário de Pernambuco*, 18 March 1962.

29. Papa João XXIII, "Carta encíclica 'Mater et Magistra' sobre a recente Evolução da Questão Social à Luz da Doutrina Cristã," *Síntese Econômica, Política e Social* 3, no. 11 (1961).

30. Mauritônio Meira, "Nordeste, a Revolução de Cristo," *O Cruzeiro*, 2 December 1961.

31. Ibid.

Bibliography

Abreu, Capistrano de. *Caminhos Antigos e Povoamento do Brasil.* Rio de Janeiro: Edição da Sociedade Capistrano de Abreu, Livraria Briguiet, 1930.

Agassiz, Luís. *Viagens no Brasil, 1865–1866.* São Paulo: Companhia Editora Nacional, 1938.

Almeida, Horácio de. *Brejo de Areia.* Rio de Janeiro: Serviço de Documentação do Ministério da Educação e Cultura, n.d.

Almeida, José Américo de. *A Paraíba e seus problemas.* 2d ed. Porto Alegre: Livraria do Globo, 1937.

Andrade, Francisco Alves de. *Agropecuária e Desenvolvimento do Nordeste.* Fortaleza: Imprensa Universitária, Universidade Federal do Ceará, 1960.

Andrade, Gilberto Osório de. *Os Rios-do-Açúcar do Nordeste Oriental, vol. 1, O Rio Ceará-Mirim.* Recife: Instituto Joaquim Nabuco de Pesquisas Sociais, 1957.

———. *A Superfície de aplanamento pliocênica do Nordeste do Brasil.* Recife: Edição do Diretório Acadêmico da Faculdade de Filosofia de Pernambuco da Universidade do Recife, 1958.

———. *Os Rios-do-Açúcar do Nordeste Oriental, vol. 3, O Rio Paraíba do Norte.* Recife: Instituto Joaquim Nabuco de Pesquisas Sociais, 1959.

Andrade, Manuel Correia de. *A Serra de Ororobá. Contribuição ao estudo dos níveis de erosão do Planalto da Borborema.* Recife: Separata da revista *Doxa,* n.d.

———. *Os Rios-do-Açúcar do Nordeste Oriental, vol. 2, O Rio Mamanguape.* Recife: Instituto Joaquim Nabuco de Pesquisas Sociais, 1957.

———. "Caracterização da sub-região da Mata Seca, em Pernambuco." *Anais da Associação dos Geógrafos Brasileiros* 11, part 1 (1957–58).

———. *O Vale do Siriji (Um estudo de Geografia Regional).* Recife: Edição mimeografada, 1958.

———. *Os Rios-do-Açúcar do Nordeste Oriental, vol. 4 - Os Rios Coruripe, Jiquiá e São Miguel.* Recife: Instituto Joaquim Nabuco de Pesquisas Sociais, 1959.

———. "Evolução e Características da Pecuária Nordestina (Contribuição ao estudo da Geografia Pastoral no Nordeste Oriental)." *Boletim do Instituto Joaquim Nabuco de Pesquisas Sociais* 8 (1960).

———. *Aspectos Geográficos da Região de Ubá.* São Paulo: Separata no. 1, Associação dos Geógrafos Brasileiros, 1961.

———. *A Economia Pernambucana no século XVI.* Recife: Arquivo Público Estadual, 1962.

233

————. *Anadia; um município do Agreste Alagoano*. Unpublished report. Serviço Social Rural, 1962.

————. *Aspectos Geográficos do Abastecimento do Recife*. Recife: Relatório de Pesquisa realizada para o Instituto Joaquim Nabuco de Pesquisas Sociais, 1961, 1963.

————. "L'Elevaje au Nord-Est du Brésil." *Les Cahiers d'Autre Mer* 21 (1968).

————. *Paisagens e Problemas do Brasil*. 3d ed. São Paulo: Editora Brasiliense, 1970.

Antonil, André João. *Cultura e Opulência do Brasil em suas Drogas e Minas*. São Paulo: Companhia Melhoramentos de São Paulo, n.d.

Anuário Estatístico do Brasil. Rio de Janeiro: Conselho Nacional de Estatística, 1957.

Anuário Estatístico do Brasil. Rio de Janeiro: Conselho Nacional de Estatística, 1961.

Athanassof, Nicolau. "Indústria Pastoril." *Boletim da SAIVOP* (1927).

Atlas Pluviométrico do Brasil (1914–1938). Rio de Janeiro: Divisão de Águas, Secção de Hidrologia do Departamento Nacional de Produção Mineral, Ministério da Agricultura, 1948.

Avé-Lallemant, Robert. *Viagem pelo Norte do Brasil, no ano de 1859*. Rio de Janeiro: Instituto Nacional do Livro, 1961.

Barbosa Lima Sobrinho, Alexandre José. *Pernambuco e o São Francisco*. Recife: Imprensa Oficial, 1929.

————. *Problemas Econômicos e Sociais da Lavoura Canavieira*. 2d ed. Rio de Janeiro: Zé Valverde, 1943.

————. *O Devassamento do Piauí*. São Paulo: Companhia Editora Nacional, 1946.

Barros, Sousa. *Êxodo e Fixação. Sugestões para uma política de colonização e aldeamento no Nordeste*. Rio de Janeiro: Serviço de Informação Agrícola, 1953.

Bastos, Humberto. *Açúcar & Algodão*. Maceió: Casa Ramalho Editora, 1938.

Bastos de Ávila, Fernando. *A Reforma Agrária: a Lei e o Plano em Recomendações sobre a Reforma Agrária*. Rio de Janeiro: Instituto Brasileiro de Ação Democrática, 1961.

Bernardes, Lysia Maria Cavalcanti. "Tipos de Clima do Brasil." *Boletim Geográfico* 9, no. 105 (1951).

Bernardes, Nilo. "Observações sobre a paisagem agrária no Município de Areia." *Anais da Associação dos Geógrafos Brasileiros* 6, part 2 (1958).

Boxer, C. R. *Os holandeses no Brasil, 1624-1654*. São Paulo: Companhia Editora Nacional, 1961.

Brandão, Ambrósio Soares. *Diálogos das Grandezas do Brasil*. Rio de Janeiro: Dois Mundos Editora, n.d.

Brígido, J. *Ceará (Homens e Fatos)*. Rio de Janeiro: Typ. Besnard Frères, 1919.

Callado, Antônio. *Os Industriais da Seca e os "Galileus" de Pernambuco*. Rio de Janeiro: Editora Civilização Brasileira, 1960.

Calmon, Pedro. *História da Casa da Torre*. Rio de Janeiro: Livraria José Olympio Editora, n.d.

Cardim, Fernão. *Tratados da Terra e da Gente do Brasil*. 2d ed. São Paulo: Companhia Editora Nacional, 1939.

Carli, Gileno de. *O Açucar na Formação Econômica do Brasil*. Rio de Janeiro: Separata do *Anuário Açucareiro*, n.d.

————. *Geografia Econômica e Social da Cana-da-Açucar no Brasil*. Rio de Janeiro: Edição de Brasil Açucareiro, 1938.

————. *Aspectos da Economia Açucareira*. Rio de Janeiro: Irmãos Pongetti Editores, 1942.

————. *O Processo Histórico da Usina em Pernambuco*. Rio de Janeiro: Irmãos Pongetti Editores, 1942.

Carvalho, Alfredo. *Estudos Pernambucanos*. Recife: A Cultura Acadêmica Editora, 1907.

————. *Aventuras e Aventureiros no Brasil*. Rio de Janeiro: Empresa Gráfica Editora, 1929.

Carvalho, Heloísa. "Areia. Aspectos de sua Geografia Urbana." *Anais da Associação dos Geógrafos Brasileiros* 6, part 2 (1958).

Cascudo, Luís da Câmara. *História do Rio Grande do Norte.* Rio de Janeiro: Serviço de Documentação do Ministério da Educação e Cultura, n.d.

————. *Tradições Populares da Pecuária Nordestina.* Rio de Janeiro: Serviço de Informação Agrícola, 1956.

Censo Agrícola—Estado da Bahia. VI Recenseamento Geral do Brasil. Rio de Janeiro: Conselho Nacional de Estatística, 1956.

Censos Econômicos—Estado de Alagoas. VI Recenseamento Geral do Brasil. Rio de Janeiro: Conselho Nacional de Estatística, 1956.

Censos Econômicos—Estado do Ceará. VI Recenseamento Geral do Brasil. Rio de Janeiro: Conselho Nacional de Estatística, 1956.

Censos Econômicos—Estado da Paraíba. VI Recenseamento Geral do Brasil. Rio de Janeiro: Conselho Nacional de Estatística, 1956.

Censos Econômicos—Estado de Pernambuco. VI Recenseamento Geral do Brasil. Rio de Janeiro: Conselho Nacional de Estatística, 1956.

Censos Econômicos—Estado do Piauí. VI Recenseamento Geral do Brasil. Rio de Janeiro: Conselho Nacional de Estatística, 1956.

Censos Econômicos—Estado do Rio Grande do Norte. VI Recenseamento Geral do Brasil. Rio de Janeiro: Conselho Nacional de Estatística, 1956.

Censos Econômicos—Estado de Sergipe. VI Recenseamento Geral do Brasil. Rio de Janeiro: Conselho Nacional de Estatística, 1956.

Coelho, Duarte. "Cartas ao Rei de Portugal." In *História da Colonização Portuguesa,* vol. 2. Porto: Litografia Nacional, 1922.

Coelho, José Cláudio Meira. *Irrigação na Área Pernambucana do São Francisco.* Fortaleza: ETENE, 1957.

Companhia de Revenda e Colonização. *Algumas Considerações.* Recife: n.p., 1961.

Costa, Craveiro. *Alagoas em 1931.* Maceió: Imprensa Oficial, 1932.

Costa Pereira, José Saturnino. *Apontamentos para a formação de um roteiro das Costas do Brasil.* Rio de Janeiro: Typographia Nacional, 1848.

Diégues Júnior, Manuel. *O Banguê nas Alagoas. Traços da influência do sistema econômico do engenho de açúcar na vida e na cultura Regional.* Rio de Janeiro: Edição do Instituto do Açúcar e do Álcool, 1949.

————. *População e Açúcar no Nordeste do Brasil.* Rio de Janeiro: Edição da Comissão Nacional de Alimentação, 1952.

————. "O Banguê em Pernambuco no século XIX." *Revista do Arquivo Público* 7–10, nos. 9–12 (1952–56).

————. *População e Propriedade da Terra no Brasil.* Washington: Pan American Union, 1959.

————. *Regiões Culturais do Brasil.* Rio de Janeiro: Centro Brasileiro de Pesquisas Educacionais, INEP, 1960.

Documentação Histórica Pernambucana. vol. 1. *Sesmarias.* Recife: Secretaria de Educação e Cultura, Biblioteca Pública, 1954.

Dussen, Adrien van der. *Relatório sobre as capitanias conquistadas no Brasil pelos holandeses (1639).* Translation, introduction, and notes by José Antônio Gonsalves de Mello, neto. Rio de Janeiro: Edição do Instituto do Açúcar e do Álcool, 1947.

Egler, Walter Albert. "Contribuição ao Estudo da Caatinga Pernambucana." *Revista Brasileira de Geografia* 13, no. 4 (1951).

Espíndola, Thomaz do Bom Fim. *Geographia Alagoana ou Descripção Physica, Política e Histórica da Província das Alagoas.* Maceió: Typographia do Liberal, 1871.

Feio, Mariano. "Notas acerca do relevo da Paraíba e do Rio Grande do Norte." *Boletim Geográfico* 13, no. 128 (1955).

Figueiredo Filho, José de. *Engenhos de Rapadura do Cariri.* Rio de Janeiro: Serviço de Informação Agrícola, 1958.

Figueiroa, Manuel. *Cuestones de Política Agrícola Regional no Nordeste.* Recife: MINTER/SUDENE, 1972.

Freire, Felisberto Firmo de Oliveira. *História de Sergipe (1575–1855).* Rio de Janeiro: Tipographia Perseverança, 1891.

Freyre, Gilberto. *Mocambos do Nordeste. Algumas notas sobre o tipo de casa popular mais primitivo do Nordeste do Brasil.* Rio de Janeiro: Ministério da Educação e Saúde, n.d.

———. *Um Engenheiro Francês no Brasil.* Rio de Janeiro: Livraria José Olympio Editora, 1940.

———. *Casa-Grande & Senzala.* 4th ed. Rio de Janeiro: Livraria José Olympio Editora, 1943.

———. "Estácio Coimbra, Governador de Pernambuco." In *Perfil de Euclides e outros perfis.* Rio de Janeiro: Livraria José Olympio Editora, 1944.

———. *Nordeste. Aspectos da Influência da Cana na Vida e na Paisagem do Nordeste do Brasil.* 2d ed. Rio de Janeiro: Livraria José Olympio Editora, 1951.

———. *Sobrados e Mocambos.* 2d ed. Rio de Janeiro: Livraria José Olympio Editora, 1951.

———. *Ordem e Progresso.* Rio de Janeiro: Livraria José Olympio Editora, 1959.

Furtado, Celso. *Formação Econômica do Brasil.* Rio de Janeiro: Editora Fundo de Cultura, 1959.

———. *A Operação Nordeste.* Rio de Janeiro: Edição do Instituto Superior de Estudos Brasileiros, 1959.

———. "Reflexões sobre a Pré-Revolução Brasileira." *Jornal do Comércio,* (Recife) 20, 21, and 22 March 1962.

Galvão, Hélio. *O Mutirão no Nordeste.* Rio de Janeiro: Serviço de Informação Agrícola, 1959.

Gama, Bernardo José. *Informação sobre a capitania do Maranhão dada em 1813.* Vienna: Imprensa do filho de Carlos Gerald, 1874.

Gandavo, Pero de Magalhães. "História da Província de Santa Cruz." In Cintra, Assis. *A Nossa Primeira História.* São Paulo: Companhia Melhoramentos de São Paulo, 1921.

Gardner, George. *Viagens no Brasil.* São Paulo: Companhia Editora Nacional, 1942.

George, Pierre. *La Campagne. Le fait rural a travers le monde.* Paris: Presses Universitaires de France, 1956.

Girão, Raimundo. *História do Ceará.* Fortaleza: Editora Instituto do Ceará, 1947.

———. *Pequena História do Ceará.* Fortaleza: Editora A. Batista Fontenelle, 1953.

Gonçalves, Antônio Carolino. *Migrações para o Recife. Aspectos do Crescimento Urbano.* Recife: Instituto Joaquim Nabuco de Pesquisas Sociais, 1961.

Gonsalves de Mello, neto, José Antônio. *Tempo dos Flamengos. Influência da Ocupação Holandesa na Vida e na Cultura do Norte.* Rio de Janeiro: Livraria José Olympio Editora, 1947.

———. "Um Regimento do Feitor-Mor de Engenho em 1663." *Boletim do Instituto Joaquim Nabuco de Pesquisas Sociais* 2 (1953).

———. "Notas acerca da introdução de vegetais exóticos em Pernambuco." *Boletim do Instituto Joaquim Nabuco de Pesquisas Sociais* 3 (1954).

Goulart, Maurício. *A Escravidão Africana no Brasil.* São Paulo: Livraria Martins Editora, n.d.

Guerra, Flávio. *Arrecife de San Miguel.* Recife: Arquivo Público Estadual, 1954.

Guimarães, Fábio de Macedo Soares. "Divisão Regional do Brasil." *Revista Brasileira de Geografia* 3, no. 2 (1941).

Herckmann, Elias. "Descrição Geral da Capitania da Paraíba (1639)." *Revista do Instituto Archeológico, Histórico e Geográphico Pernambucano* 31 (1886).

Heriarte, Maurício de. *Descrição do Estado do Maranhão, Pará, Corujá e rio das amazonas.* Vienna: Imprensa do filho de Carlos Gerald, 1874.

"Idéia Geral da Capitania de Pernambuco e suas Anexas, extensão de suas Costas, Rios e Povoações notáveis, Agricultura, Número de suas Costas, Rios e Povoações notáveis, Agricultura, Número de Engenhos, Contractos e Rendimentos Reais, Aumentos que estas têm tido desde o anno de 1774 em que tomou posse do Governo das mesmas Capitanias o Capitam General José César de Meneses." *Anais da Biblioteca Nacional do Rio de Janeiro* 40 (1918).

João XXIII, Papa. "Carta encíclica 'Mater et Magistra' sobre a recente Evolução da Questão Social à Luz da Doutrina Cristã." *Síntese Econômica, Política e Social* 3, no. 11 (1961).

Joffily, Irineu. *Notas sobre a Paraíba.* Rio de Janeiro: Edição do *Jornal do Comércio,* 1898.

Julião, Francisco. *Dez Mandamentos das Ligas Camponeses da Opressão do Latifúndio.* n.p., n.d.

Jurema, Aderbal. *Sindicalização rural para a mudança democrática.* Speech of 26 March 1962 in the Federal Chamber of Deputies. Brasília: Departamento da Imprensa Nacional, 1962.

Kayser, Bernard. *Les divisiones de l'Espace Geographique dans les Pays Sous-Developpés.* Extrait de *l'Annales de Geographie.* Société de Géographie, Paris: 1966.

Kegel, Wilhelm. "Contribuição ao Estudo da Bacia Costeira do Rio Grande do Norte." *Boletim do Departamento Nacional da Produção Mineral* 170 (1957).

Kidder, Daniel P. *Reminiscências de Viagens e Permanência no Brasil (Províncias do Norte).* São Paulo: Livraria Martins Editora, 1943.

Koster, Henry. *Viagens ao Nordeste do Brasil.* São Paulo: Companhia Editora Nacional, 1934.

Lacerda de Melo, Mário. *Pernambuco: Traços de sua Geografia Humana.* Recife: published by the author, 1940.

————. "A Serra Negra, uma 'ilha' na caatinga." *Anais da Associação dos Geógrafos Brasileiros* 7, part 1 (1955).

————. "Aspectos do 'habitat' rural no Nordeste do Brasil." *Anais da Associação dos Geógrafos Brasileiros* 10, part 1 (1955–57).

————. "Fisionomia do 'habitat' rural no Baixo Ceará-Mirim." *Anais da Associação dos Geógrafos Brasileiros* 10, part 1 (1955–57).

————. "Aspectos da Geografia Agrária do Brejo Paraibano." *Anais da Associação dos Geógrafos Brasileiros* 6, part 2 (1958).

————. *Paisagens do Nordeste em Pernambuco e Paraíba.* Rio de Janeiro: Edição do Conselho Nacional de Geografia, 1958.

————. "Um Brejo de Pernambuco (Região de Camocim de São Félix)." *Boletim Carioca de Geografia* 18, nos. 3–4 (1961).

————. *A Colonização e os problemas agrários do Nordeste.* Recife: Edição mimeografada, Instituto Joaquim Nabuco de Pesquisas Sociais, 1961.

————. *As Migrações para o Recife. Estudo Geográfico.* Recife: Instituto Joaquim Nabuco de Pesquisas Sociais, 1961.

Land Tenure Conditions and Socio-economic Development of the Agricultural Sector - Brazil. Washington: CIDA, 1966.

Lavareda, José Hesketh. "Migrações internas do Nordeste - Caruaru um dos seus centros detentores." *Boletim do Instituto Joaquim Nabuco de Pesquisa Sociais* 9 (1960).

Lino de Matos, Dirceu. *Região da Baixa Mojiana (Contribuição ao estudo da Geografia Agrária do ponto de vista do uso da terra).* São Paulo: Edição mimeografada, 1959.

Lombard, Louis. "Explorações Geográficas e Geológicas." *Revista do Instituto Archeológico, Geográphico e Histórico Pernambucano* 12, no. 66 (n.d.).

Lopes de Andrade. *Introdução à Sociologia das Secas*. Rio de Janeiro: Editora A. Noite, n.d.

———. *Forma e Efeito das Migrações do Nordeste*. Paraíba: A União Editora, 1952.

Lyra Tavares, João de. *A Parahyba*. Parahyba: Imprensa Oficial, 1910.

Macedo, José Norberto de. *As Fazendas de Gado do Vale do São Francisco*. Rio de Janeiro: Serviço de Informação Agrícola, 1952.

Maciel, Paulo. *Migrações para o Recife. Aspectos Econômicos*. Recife: Instituto Joaquim Nabuco de Pesquisas Sociais, 1961.

Mariz, Celso. *Evolução Econômica da Paraíba*. João Pessoa: A União Editora, 1939.

———. *Cidades e Homens*. João Pessoa: A União Editora, 1945.

Meira, Mauritônio. "Nordeste, as sementes da Subversão." *O Cruzeiro* (11 November 1961).

———. "Nordeste, a revolução de Cristo." *O Cruzeiro* (2 December 1961).

———. "Nordeste, as vítimas da imprevisão." *O Cruzeiro* (9 December 1961).

Melo Filho, Murilo. "Chuva de dólares sobre o Nordeste." *Manchete* 10 (1961).

Meneses, Djacir. *O Outro Nordeste. Formação Social do Nordeste*. Rio de Janeiro: Livraria José Olympio, 1937.

Millet, Henrique Augusto. *Auxílio à Lavoura e Crédito Real*. Recife: Typographia do *Jornal do Recife*, 1878.

———. *O Quebra-Kilos e a Crise da Lavoura*. Recife: Typographia do *Jornal do Recife*, 1878.

Monteiro Filho, Armando. *Anteprojeto de Reforma Agrária (Aumento da produtividade e humanização do Homem do Campo)*. Rio de Janeiro: Serviço de Informação Agrícola, 1962.

Moraes Barros, Paulo de. *Impressões do Nordeste Brasileiro*. São Paulo: Oficinas Gráficas Monteiro Lobato, 1924.

Nieuhof, Jean. *Memorável Viagem Marítima e Terrestre ao Brasil*. São Paulo: Livraria Martins Editora, 1942.

Oliveira Lima. "A Nova Lusitânia." In *História da Colonização Portuguesa*. vol. 3. Porto: Litografia Nacional, 1922.

Perdigão Malheiro, Agostinho Marques de. *A Escravidão no Brasil. Ensaio Histórico-Jurídico-Social*. vol. 1. Rio de Janeiro: Typographia Nacional, 1866.

Pereira da Costa, F. A. *O Algodão em Pernambuco. Vista histórico-retrospectiva*. Recife: Imprensa Oficial, 1916.

———. *Anais Pernambucanos*. Recife: Arquivo Público Estadual, 1954.

Pereira Rêgo, José. *Memória Histórica das Epidemias que têm Reinado no Brasil*. Rio de Janeiro: Typographia Nacional, 1873.

Peres, Apolônio. *A Indústria Açucareira em Pernambuco*. Recife: Imprensa Industrial, 1915.

Petrone, Pascoale. *A Várzea do Açu*. São Paulo: Avulso no. 2, Associação dos Geógrafos Brasileiros, 1961.

Pimentel Gomes. *A Carnaubeira*. Rio de Janeiro: Serviço de Documentação Agrícola, 1945.

———. "O Nordeste dos geógrafos." *O Observador Econômico e Financeiro* (September 1959).

Pinto, Estêvão. *História de uma Estrada de Ferro do Nordeste*. Rio de Janeiro: Livraria José Olympio Editora, 1949.

Pinto, Irineu Ferreira. *Datas e Notas para a História da Parahyba*. Parahyba: Imprensa Official, 1908.

Plano Diretor para o Desenvolvimento do Nordeste. Recife: SUDENE, 1960.

Plano Piloto da Política de Colonização. Recife: n.p., 1961.

Plano Qüinqüenal de Desenvolvimento do Nordeste (1961–1965). Recife: SUDENE, 1961.

Porto Domingues, Alfredo José. "Características Gerais da Grande Região Nordeste." *Enciclopédia dos Municípios Brasileiros* 4 (1958).

————. "Aspectos físicos do Litoral e Mata da Grande Região Nordeste." *Enciclopédia dos Municípios Brasileiros* 4 (1958).

Prado Júnior, Caio. *Evolução Política do Brasil. Ensaio de interpretação materialista da história brasileira*. São Paulo: n.p., 1933.

————. "Distribuição da propriedade fundiária no Estado de São Paulo." *Geografia* 1 (1934).

————. "O problema 'humano' no Brasil." *Rumo* 1, no. 3 (1943).

————. *Formação do Brasil Contemporâneo. A Colônia*. São Paulo: Livraria Martins Editora, 1943.

————. *História Econômica do Brasil*. 4th ed. São Paulo: Editora Brasiliense, 1956.

————. "Contribuição para análise da Questão Agrária no Brasil." *Revista Brasiliense* 28 (1960).

Projeto de Colonização, no. 2. Recife: Governo do Estado, 1961.

Ramírez, Luís. "Carta." *Revista do Instituto Histórico e Geográfico Brasileiro* 15, (1852).

Ramos, Augusto. *O Café no Brasil e no Estrangeiro*. Rio de Janeiro: Papelaria Santa Helena, 1923.

"Resolução no. 461, de 7 de julho de 1955." In *Boletim Geográfico* no. 134 (1956).

Rocha, Pita. *História da América Portuguesa*. Salvador: Livraria Progresso Editora, 1950.

Rocha, Tadeu. "O Homem e a Técnica em Paulo Afonso." *Diário de Pernambuco* (9 April 1953).

Rodrigues, José Honório and Ribeiro, Joaquim. *Civilização Holandesa no Brasil*. São Paulo: Companhia Editora Nacional, 1940.

Salvador, Frei Vicente de. *História do Brasil*. 3d ed. São Paulo: Companhia Melhoramentos de São Paulo, 1931.

Sette, Hilton. *Pesqueira. Aspectos de sua Geografia Urbana e de suas relações inter-regionais*. Recife: Edição mimeografada, 1956.

————. "Aspectos da Atividade Pesqueira em Pernambuco." *Anais da Associação dos Geógrafos Brasileiros* 11, part 1 (1959).

Sinopse Preliminar do Censo Demográfico—Estado de Alagoas. VII Recenseamento Geral do Brasil. Rio de Janeiro: IBGE, 1961.

Sinopse Preliminar do Censo Demográfico—Estado da Bahia. VII Recenseamento Geral do Brasil. Rio de Janeiro: IBGE, 1961.

Sinopse Preliminar do Censo Demográfico—Estado do Ceará. VII Recenseamento Geral do Brasil. Rio de Janeiro: IBGE, 1961.

Sinopse Preliminar do Censo Demográfico—Estado da Paraíba. VII Recenseamento Geral do Brasil. Rio de Janeiro: IBGE, 1961.

Sinopse Preliminar do Censo Demográfico—Estado do Piauí. VII Recenseamento Geral do Brasil. Rio de Janeiro: IBGE, 1961.

Sinopse Preliminar do Censo Demográfico—Estado do Rio Grande do Norte. VII Recenseamento Geral do Brasil. Rio de Janeiro: IBGE, 1961.

Sinopse Preliminar do Censo Demográfico—Estado de Sergipe. VII Recenseamento Geral do Brasil. Rio de Janeiro: IBGE, 1961.

Siqueira, Diogo de Meneses e. "Cartas." *Anais da Biblioteca Nacional* 57 (1935).

Spix, J. von and Martius, C.F.P. von. *Viagem ao Brasil*. 4 vols. Rio de Janeiro: Imprensa Nacional, 1938.

Souza, Marcos Antônio de. *Memória sobre a Capitania de Sergipe (anno de 1808)*. n.p., n.d.

Theophilo, Rodolpho. *História da Seca do Ceará (1877–1880)*. Fortaleza: Typographia do Libertador, 1883.

Tocantins, Leandro. *O Rio Comanda a Vida. Uma Interpretação da Amazônia*. Rio de Janeiro: Livraria Civilização Brasileira, 1961.

Tollenare, L. F. *Notas Dominicais*. Salvador: Livraria Progresso Editora, 1958.

Valverde, Orlando. "O Uso da Terra no Leste da Paraíba." *Revista Brasileira de Geografia* 17, no. 1 (1955).

———. "O Nordeste da Mata Pernambucana (A região de Timbaúba)." *Boletim Carioca de Geografia* 13, nos. 1–2 (1960).

Valverde, Orlando and Mesquita, Miriam Gomes Coelho. "Geografia Agrária do Baixo Açu." *Revista Brasileira de Geografia* 13, no. 3 (1961).

Varnhagen, Francisco Adolpho. *História Geral do Brasil*. 3d ed. São Paulo: Edições Melhoramentos, n.d.

Vasconcelos Sobrinho. *As Regiões Naturais de Pernambuco, o Meio e a Civilização*. Rio de Janeiro: Livraria Freitas Bastos, 1949.

Velho, Otavio Guilherme. *Frentes de Expansão e Estrutura Agrária*. Rio de Janeiro: Zahar Editores, 1972.

Verdonck, Adrien. "Memória oferecida ao Senhor Presidente e mais Senhores do Conselho desta Cidade de Pernambuco sobre a situação, lugares, bem como de Itamaracá, Paraíba e Rio Grande." *Revista do Arquivo Público* 4, no. 6 (1949).

Vilhena, Luís dos Santos. *Notícias Seteropolitanas e Brasílicas*. Estado da Bahia: Imprensa Oficial, 1922.

Viveiros, Jerônimo. *História do Comércio do Maranhão*. São Luís: Edição da Associação Comercial do Maranhão, 1954.

Watgen, Hermann. *O Domínio Colonial Holandês no Brasil*. São Paulo: Companhia Editora Nacional, 1938.

Index

ABCAR (Brazilian Association of Credit and Rural Assistance), 130
abolition, 46, 71, 78–80, 125, 153, 184–85
Abreu, Capistrano de, 144, 145
Abreu Soares, Manuel de, 142
Acaraú, 26
Acaraú River, 143, 144, 149, 150
Açu, 149, 171
Açu River, 22, 23, 112, 143, 150, 151
agrarian reform, xiii, 87, 88, 190–205 passim; history of 2–5; legislation, 2–4; schools of, 2. *See also individual laws;* Peasant Leagues; unions
Agrarian Review of São Paulo, 211
Agreste, 4, 9, 10, 14–21, 34, 111–40; agriculture, 4–5, 17, 18, 20, 74, 131; *caatinga,* 19–20; cattle raising, 17–18, 20, 59, 112–15, 119, 125–29 passim, 131–35; colonization, 202; deforestation, 18; Dutch occupation, 112–13; labor relations, 35, 126–40 passim; landholding patterns, 87; Peasant Leagues, 209; population, 20; rainfall, 16, 18–19, 20, 21; settlement, 112–13; size, 16–18; slavery, 113; subregions, 16–17; topography, 16–19
Agricultural and Livestock Society of the Planters of Pernambuco. *See* Peasant Leagues
agriculture, 149–56; colonial, 42; commercial, 4, 17, 20, 23, 25, 28, 32, 36, 116, 130, 181–83, 185, 205; diversification of, 126; slash-and-burn, 32, 188; subsistence, 3–4, 17, 23, 25, 28, 32, 45–46, 49, 50, 59, 73, 92, 94, 98, 106, 110, 113,

115, 116, 117, 118, 121, 122, 126, 127, 128, 134, 140, 145, 146, 150, 154–55, 161, 171, 175, 176–79, 181, 185–87, 188, 191; transhumant, 115; *vazante,* 28. *See also individual crop entries*
Água Branca Mountains, 17, 150
Água Preta, 39; colony, 204
Alagoas, 6, 7, 12, 17, 20, 22, 24, 39, 58, 72; cattle raising, 13, 50, 111; coconut cultivation, 72–73, 103; colonization, 191–92; deforestation, 12–13; irrigation, 13; labor relations, 96, 139; Peasant Leagues, 209; population, 57; rice cultivation, 13; Sertão in, 17; slavery, 79
Alagoinhas, 17
Albuquerque, Jerónimo de, 43, 45, 179
Albuquerque Coelho, Duarte de, 43, 44
Albuquerque Coelho, Jorge de, 43
Alcântara, 179
Alliance for Progress, 195
Amado, Jorge, 110
Amaraji, 92, 208
ANCAR (Rural Credit Agency for the Northeast), 203
animal husbandry, colonial, 42. *See* cattle raising
Apodi River, 112, 143, 144
Apodi-Mossoró River, 24
Aquidamã, 17
Aracaju, 17, 89
Aracati, 171
Arapiraca, 20
Araripe Mountains, 150
Arcoverde, 203
Areia, 18

Arraes, Gov. Miguel, 205, 218
Association of Brazilian Geographers, ix
Assunção Island, 203

babassu palm cultivation, 5, 27, 31, 32,
    186–87, 196
Bahia, 6, 7, 9, 17–18, 22, 24, 31, 49, 110,
    117, 143, 144, 197–98; Agreste in, 17;
    agriculture, 17, 89, 146; cattle raising,
    14, 50, 109–10, 112; coconut cultiva-
    tion, 72–73, 103; colonization, 192;
    forestry, 14; immigration to, 87, 89;
    population, 57; settlement, 14, 141;
    slavery in, 79
Baixada Maranhense, 31
Baixa Verde Mountains, 26, 150
Balaiada revolt, 182, 184
Balsas River, 31
Bananeiras, 18
bandeirantes, 144
Bank of Brazil, 131
Bank of the Northeast, ix, 7, 130
Barbosa da Silva, Francisco, 143
barbed wire, 151
Barreiros, 39
Batalha, 163
Baturité Mountains, 26, 150
Bebedouro project, 28, 166
beet sugar industry, 82
Belém, 31, 32
Belmonte, 14
Bezerra de Melo economic group, 39, 86
Bezerros, 18, 116, 117, 144
black pepper cultivation, 127
Boa Esperança dam, 31
Bolandeira colony, 204
Bom Jardim, 16, 116, 117
bondage labor, 76–78, 163, 199, 207
Bonito, 92; colonization, 201–2
Borborema Plateau, 10–11, 13, 26, 44, 45,
    103, 112, 147
Botelho, Gov. Diogo de, 47
Branco, Humberto de Alencar Castelo, 3,
    198
Brandão, Avelar, 217
Brasília, 34, 137
Brazilian-African trade, 49
Brazilian-European trade, colonial, 48–49
Brazilian Institute of Agrarian Reform. See
    IBRA
Brazilian Institute of Democratic Action,
    210
Brazilian Institute of Geography and
    Statistics. See IBGE
Brazilwood, 41, 42, 48–49, 50, 57, 112,
    142
Brejo do Madre de Deus, 16

caatinga, 10, 16, 17, 23; defined 19–20
Cabo, colonization, 201–4 passim
Cabo de Santo Agostinho, 49
Cabrobó, 147, 165, 203
cacao, 4, 18, 20, 89, 110
Cachoeira, 14
Caetés Indians, 42, 44
Caldas, Francisco, 143
Camamu, 72
Camaragibe River, 12
Camaratuba River, 50, 111, 143
Camocim, 26
Camocim River, 149
Campina Grande, 34, 116, 117
cannibalism, 44–45
Capibaribe River, 18, 43, 49, 111, 116,
    147
Capoame, 147
Caruaru, 203
Caravelas, 14
Cariri, 27
Cariri Indians, 113, 143
Cariri Mountains, 150
carnauba wax industry, 5, 23, 155–56,
    166–67, 169–71, 173, 185–86
Carolina, 31
cashew industry, 23, 127
Catarina, 28
cattle raising, 4, 5, 9, 63, 73–74, 111–15,
    157, 197; in the Agreste, 17–20, 59,
    112–15, 119, 125–29, 131–35; in
    Alagoas, 13, 112; in Ceará, 164; colo-
    nial, 45; complementarity with rice cul-
    tivation, 109; disease, 21, 113, 158,
    160; Dutch, 49–50; migration, 21,
    131–32, 146–47, 159–60, 169, 181, 185;
    in mountains, 150–51; in Paraíba, 164;
    selective breeding, 131, 132, 159, 189;
    in Sergipe, 14, 112; in the Sertão, 20,
    28–29, 112, 114, 119, 141–51;
    supplementary feeding, 121, 131–33,
    134, 158–60, 167, 169, 185; in Zona da
    Mata, 10
Cavalcânti, Gov. Luís, 190
Ceará, 6, 7, 22, 23, 24, 27, 45, 143, 146,
    147, 150, 153, 209
Ceará-Mirim, 6, 7, 70; labor relations, 95
Ceará-Mirim River, 24
central mills, establishment of, 71–72
Chapada Diamantina, 178
Chapada do Apodi, 24–25, 146; agricul-
    ture, 24–25; cattle raising, 24, 25;
    geographic boundaries, 24; settlement,
    24; topography, 24–25
Chapada do Araripe, 27; colonization, 200,
    204
CHESF (São Francisco Hydroelectric
    Company), 28

church, and agrarian reform, 215–18
CIBRAZEM (Brazil Warehousing Company), 130, 131
CIDA (Inter-American Committee for Agricultural Development), 36
Cimbres, 116, 117
civil war, U.S., 117–19, 154
class society, development of, 59–69. *See also* labor relations
climates: *Af*, 14; *Am*, 11, *Amí*, 11; *As̓*, 11, *Aw̓*, 25; *BSHw*, 25
CNG (National Council of Geography), 6–7
coconut cultivation, 4, 14, 45, 59, 72–73, 103, 113, 141, 200–201
CODEVASF (Development Company of the São Francisco Valley), 107, 108, 166
Coelho de Sousa, Joâo, 141
Coelho Pereira, Duarte, 42, 43, 44, 45, 46–47, 152
coffee, cultivation of, 9, 75, 125, 127, 153; in Agreste, 18, 75, 122–26, 138–39; on Borborema Plateau, 75; in Cariri, 27; labor relations, 138–39; in the mountains, 153; varieties, 123
Colégio, 20
colonization, contemporary, 190–205
Complementary Law Number 11, 98
Consolidated Labor Laws, 3, 97
Constitution of 1946, 205
constitutional reform, 204
cooperatives, consumer, 90, 102
COPERBO (Pernambucan Synthetic Rubber Company), 216
Corrente River, 144
Coruripe, 43
Coruripe River, 12, 18
Cosme, 184
Costa Azevedo economic group, 39
Cotinguiba, 58
cottage industries, 166
cotton cultivation, 5, 10, 58–59, 69, 72, 74–75, 92, 109, 116–22, 127, 131, 153–55, 167, 180, 182
Cotton Custom House, 74, 118
Cotton Inspection Station, 74
Cova da Onça colony, 204
cowboys, 113–15, 133–34, 142, 145, 146. *See also* labor relations
CRC (Resale and Colonization Company), 191, 198–201, 205, 211, 213, 216
crop rotation, 60, 140, 176, 196
Cunhaí, 45, 50
Cupaoba Mountains, 112
Curimataú River, 16
Cururipe River, 111
CVSF (São Francisco Valley Commission), 107

das Velhas River, 142, 144
debt peonage, 97–98. *See also* bondage labor
deforestation, 60, 71, 115, 119, 150, 167, 188, 189
development, vii; obstacles to, ix–xi; regional, 1. *See also* agrarian reform; modernization
Dias d'Ávila family, 49
Dias Lins, Deputy, 39
Dias Lins economic group, 86
Dias Moréia, Belchior, 141
Directorate of Lands and Colonization, 191
disease: animal, 113, 158, 160; human, 102, 186; plant, 119, 123
Divina Pastora, 89
DNOCS (National Department of Works Against the Drought), 192–93
droughts, 29–30, 63, 116, 144, 149, 185
Dutch invasion, 45, 48–53, 111, 112–13, 190
Dutch West Indies Company, 52–53

Eastern Littoral. *See* Zona da Mata and Eastern Littoral
economic diversification, 120, 190–205 passim
emancipation. *See* abolition
engenho, defined, 12*n*
engenhocas, defined, 58
Equatorial France, 179
European trade policies, and sugar, 57
expropriation, 3, 87–88, 195–96, 199–200, 201, 204–5, 213

factories, sugar, 89–103 passim
Feira de Santana, 17
Fernando de Noronha, ix, 7
Ferrari, Fernando, 2
fertilizer, 12, 87, 104, 106, 128, 140, 176, 201, 205, 217
flooding, 28, 63, 180
Flores, 26
Floresta, 28, 147
Food and Agricultural Organization of the United Nations, 36
Food for Peace, 195
Fortaleza, 26, 33, 164, 171, 186
French, expulsion of, 143
Freyre, Gilberto, 48
fruit, cultivation of, 18, 20, 106, 127–28, 180
furão, 101, 171
Furtado, Celso, 196–98, 206, 207

Gama, Gov. Bernardo da, 181
Garanhuns, 116, 117, 203, 204
Garanhuns Plateau, 18

Garcia d'Ávila family, 141–42, 181
garlic, cultivation of, 173–74
General Commerce Company of Grão-Pará
    and Maranhão, 180, 182, 184
GEPA (Executive Group for Food Produc-
    tion), 130
GERAN (Executive Group for the
    Rationalization of Agroindustry in the
    Northeast), 195
German colonists, 190
goat raising, 25
Goiana, 10, 43, 72
Goiana River, 103
Goiás, 31
gold, 42
Golden Law (May 13, 1888). See abolition
Goulart, João, 2, 3, 215, 218
Gouveia, Antônio de ("Padre of Gold"), 44
Grajaú River, 30, 179
Guabiraba, colonization, 201–4
Guarabira, 17
Guaraíra River, 144
Guedes de Brito, Antônio, 142
Guiana Maranhense, 31–32, 188
Gurgueia River, 31
Gurupi River, 31

Heriarte, Maurício de, 179
hides, 181, 182. See also cattle raising;
    leather civilization

IAA (Alcohol and Sugar Institute), 83, 85
IBC (Brazilian Coffee Institute), 125
IBGE (Brazilian Institute of Geography
    and Statistics), 7
Ibiapaba Mountains, 150
IBRA (Brazilian Institute of Agrarian Re-
    form), 3, 88. See also INCRA
IFOCS (Federal Inspectorate of Works
    Against the Drought), 154
Igaraçu, 42, 50, 74
Imperatriz, 31
Inajá, 147
INCRA (National Institute of Colonization
    and Agrarian Reform), 3, 37, 88, 198
INDA (National Institute of Agricultural
    Development), 3
inflation, 195
Ingàzeira, 203
Indians: alliances, 45; colonial period, 46;
    conquered, 142–44; Dutch allies, 51;
    free, 56; French allies, 112, 178–79;
    hostilities, 42, 46, 142–44; removal,
    184; resettlement, 115–16
industrialization, x, 39–40, 60, 82–87. See
    also agrarian reform; modernization;
    migration, rural-urban
Industrial Revolution, 74, 117, 180

Inspectorate of Cotton, 118
Ipanema River, 16, 112
Ipojuca River, 18, 43, 49, 111, 116, 147
irrigation, 5, 13, 23–24, 28, 29, 87, 91,
    106–7, 164–65, 166, 173, 175, 192–94;
    colonial, 43
Itabiana, 17, 20
Itabiana Mountains, 17
Itabuna, 110
Itamarcá, 41, 178
Itapecuru River, 30, 144
Itapecuru Valley, 141, 178, 179, 180, 181
Itapecuru-Mirim Valley, slavery in, 184
Itapetinga, 18
Itiubá Mountains, 150

Jaboatão River, 43, 111
Jacarecica River, 13
Jacaré dos Homens, 163
Jacuípe River, 144
Jacuípe, 39
Jaguaribe River, 22, 23, 24, 143, 144
Jaguaruana, 22
Jatinã, 28, 147
Jequié, 18
Jequitinhonha River, 141
Jews, in colonial period, 47–48, 53
Jiquiá River, 12
Joaquim Nabuco Institute of Social Re-
    search, ix
João VI, 117, 182
João do Vale Mountains, 26, 150
João Pessoa, 193–94
Julião, Francisco, 93, 199, 207–18 passim
Jundiá, 39
Junqueiro, 12
Jurema, 20
Jurema, Federal Deputy Aberbal, 207
"just war," 113

Kubitschek, Juscelino, 2, 173

labor legislation. See individual laws
labor relations, rural, 56. See individual
    entries under state headings
labor systems, vii–viii, x–xi, xiii, 1–5. See
    also slavery; wage labor
Lagarto, 20
Lajedo, 20
land grants, 42, 43, 77, 84, 113, 141–43,
    145, 150, 167, 175
landholding patterns, 4, 34, 35–40, 87,
    157, 167, 168, 175, 188, 190–99 pas-
    sim, 204–18 passim
Land Statute, 3, 88, 198
Laranjeiras, 14
latifundia: dissolution, 84; foundation of,
    43–44

leather civilization, 145, 181
Limoeiro, 10, 17, 116, 147, 171, 203
livestock raising, 31, 32, 59, 110, 184–85.
    See also cattle raising
Luís Correia, 186
Luís Gomes Mountains, 26
lumbering, 110, 180. *See also* deforestation

Maceió, 193–94
Mafrense, Domingos Afonso, 142
Major Isidoro, 163
Mamanguape, 43, 72
Mamanguape River Valley, 12, 16, 59, 75,
    90, 111, 112, 143
Manguaba River, 12, 43
Marabá, 32
Maragogi, 39
Marajó Island, 31
Maranhão, 5, 6, 7, 27, 30–32, 34, 144; cat-
    tle raising, 181; colonization, 188, 192;
    cotton cultivation, 182; migration to,
    87; rice cultivation, 189; settlement, 5,
    45, 178–79
Mariano, Severino, 217
Martins Mountains, 26, 150
Maruim, 14, 43, 89
Massapê, 22
Mata Grande Mountains, 17, 150
Mearim River, 30, 179
Meira, Mauritônio, 216–17
Melo, Antonio, 5, 216
"Memories of Recife" (Manuel Bandeira),
    6
Mendes, Eliseu, Bishop of Mossoró, 173
Meneses e Siqueira, Diogo de, 47
Meruoca Mountains, 26, 150
middle class, rural, 127, 194
Middle North, 9, 33, 178–90; agriculture,
    182–83, 185; cattle raising, 174–81,
    184–85, 188–89; cotton cultivation, 180,
    182, 183, 185, 187; deforestation, 32;
    French in, 178–79; irrigation, 31; labor
    relations, 183–89; rice cultivation, 180,
    182, 183, 187, 188, 189; settlement,
    178–83, 188; sugar cultivation, 179–80,
    181, 182–84; tobacco cultivation, 181;
    topography, 30–32
migrant workers, 93–94, 98–102, 110, 128,
    138–39, 164, 176, 218; in Agreste, 93,
    98, 100; in Alagoas, 99–101; in
    Ceará-Mirim, 99; and coffee, 139; in
    Paraíba, 99–101; in Pernambuco, 99–
    101; in Sergipe, 99; in the Sertão, 93,
    98; and sugar cultivation, 94; in Zona
    da Mata, 136–37
migration: Indian, 46; landowner, 153;
    livestock, 21, 25, 27, 31, 70, 131–33,
    151–59; rural, 14, 20, 118, 136–37,

195–97; rural-urban, 1, 4, 34, 87, 89,
    125, 136–37, 186
minerals, search for, 141
Ministry of Agriculture, 88, 207
Ministry of Labor, 2, 217
miradouros (springs), 27
modernization, vii–viii, 3, 126, 177, 189,
    190–205; obstacles to, ix–xi; regional
    differences, 1, 4–5; of rice cultivation,
    107; technical, 24; of sugar industry,
    58–69, 69–72, 80–82, 85, 87, 190–205
    passim
Morais, José Ermírio de, 86
Mossoró, 22, 171
Mossoró River, 22, 23, 112, 149
Moxotó River, 16, 144
Mundaú River, 12, 13, 18
Munim River, 179

nascente (springs), 27
Nassau, Maurício de, 51, 56, 190
Natal, 143, 171, 193–94
National Council of Geography. *See* CNG
National Institute of Agricultural De-
    velopment. *See* INDA
National Institute of Colonization and
    Agrarian Reform. *See* INCRA
Negreiros, Monsignor Emerson, 217
Northeast: boundaries defined, 6–9;
    drought, 6–7; landholding patterns,
    32–40; populations statistics, xi, 32–40;
    settlement, 41–44, 57; subregions,
    9–32, 33–34; topography, 7–9. *See also*
    individual subregions

olhos d'água (springs), 27
Olho d'Água colony, 204
Olinda, 23, 42, 44, 45, 50, 51, 111, 141,
    144, 147; during Dutch conquest, 49
Oliveira Ledo, Teodósio de, 143
Oliveira Porto, Manuel de, 142
onions, cultivation of, 28, 164–65, 173–74,
    203
Orobó, 16
outlaws, 51, 77
Ouricuri, 203

Pajeú River, 26, 112, 144, 147
Palmares colony, 204. *See also* *quilombos,*
    Palurares
Palmeira dos Índios, 163
Pão de Açúcar, 163
Paraguaçu River, 141, 178
Paraíba, 6, 7, 9, 10, 16, 17, 18, 22, 24, 25,
    26, 39, 45, 58, 137, 143, 147; cattle
    raising, 73; coconut cultivation, 72–73,
    103; colonization, 192; labor relations,

95, 162; Peasant Leagues, 209; slavery, 78–79; sugar cultivation, 10, 45, 70–71
Paraíba Valley, 75, 90
Paraíba do Meio River, 12, 13, 18
Paraíba do Norte, 49, 103, 111
Paraíba do Norte River, 45, 112, 144
Paramirim River, 144
Paraná, 34, 137; migration to, 89
Parnaíba, 186
Parnaíba River, 24, 30, 31, 144, 149, 178, 186
passion fruit juice industry, 191
paternalism, vii–viii
Pau–Brasil colony, 204
peasants, 92, 93, 190–205 passim
Peasant Leagues, 5, 93, 163, 199–201, 205–18 passim
Peixe River, 143
Peixoto Viegas, João, 142
Penedo, 108, 109
Pernambuco, 5, 6, 7, 10, 11, 16, 17, 18, 20, 22, 24, 26, 27, 39, 41, 43, 57, 58, 147, 149; Agreste in, 18; agriculture, 146; climate, 11; coconut cultivation, 103; colonization, 190–92; conquest of, 179; cotton, 182; Dutch conquest, 48–53; geographic subregions, 12; labor relations, 95, 96, 97; landholding patterns, 11, 92; modernization, 197–98; rural unions, 218; slavery, 46, 76, 79; sugar cultivation, 70, 90, 103; topography, 10–12; vegetation, 12
Pesqueira, 16, 18
Petrolândia, 28
Piató Lake, 171
Piauí, 7, 24, 30–32, 145; agriculture, 146; cattle raising, 181; labor relations, 162; Peasant Leagues, 209
Piauí River, 13, 31, 144
Pilão Arcado, 147
Pindaré River, 30, 179
Pindaré River Valley, 184
Pindorama colony, 191
Pinto, Gov. Magalhães, 216
Piranhas River, 26, 143
Piranhas-Açu River, 24, 144
Pirapama River, 43
Pium colony, 191
plow, introduction of, 69
Pombal, Marquis de, 180
Ponta Grande Lake, 171
population density, 192. *See* migration
populism, 2
Porta Alegre Mountains, 26, 150
Porto Calvo, 39, 43, 49, 72
Porto Seguro, 14, 110
Portuguese-African relations, 48, 59
Portuguese-European trade, 119

Potengi, 50
Potengi River, 143
Poti River, 31
Potiguare Indians, 45, 112
Preto River, 144
Program of Land Redistribution and Stimulus to Agroindustry in the North and Northeast. *See* PROTERRA
Propriá, 17, 20
PROTERRA, 3, 40, 88, 195

Quadros, Jânio, 2
quilombos, 47, 51, 61, 184; Palmares, 47, 113

railroads, 17, 43, 81, 84–85
Rãs River, 144
Real River, 141, 144
Recife, 4, 10, 17, 22–23, 33–34, 51, 53, 56, 58, 69, 72, 111, 116, 117, 137, 147, 164, 171, 182, 191, 193–94, 204, 207
Recôncavo, 6, 14
Rede Ferroviária do Nordeste, 84
reforestation, 13, 88
renters, x, 4; unionization of, 2
Riachuelo, 89
Ribeiro Coutinho economic group, 39
rice cultivation, 5, 32, 106–10, 127, 180; in Alagoas, 13
Rio Capibaribe, 18
Rio de Janeiro, 1, 34, 89, 109, 110, 137, 171, 182
Rio Formoso, 39, 43, 72; Peasant Leagues, 210
Rio Grande do Norte, 6, 7, 9, 10, 22, 24, 25, 26, 39, 45, 58, 146–47, 149; cattle raising, 73, 111; coconut cultivation, 72–73, 103; colonists in, 191; livestock, 59, 143; population, 57; salt, 150; slavery, 78; sugarcane cultivation, 10, 45; unionization of rural workers, 217
Rio Largo, 13
road building, 147, 186, 189, 196
rubber, exploitation, 14, 110, 199
rural workers: compared with urban, 206–7; organization of, 130; proletarianization, 96–97. *See also* migrant workers; sharecroppers; unionization
Rural Labor Statute, 2–3, 98, 138, 218
Rural Social Service Agency, ix
Russas, 24, 171

sabotage, agricultural, 214
Salgueiro, 203
saltworks, 147, 150, 166, 171
Salvador, 4, 17, 33, 69, 110, 117, 137, 141, 142, 147, 182, 193–94
Sampaio, Gov. Cid, 198–99, 205

Santa Maria de Boa Vista, 28
Santo Amaro, 14
Santo Antão, 59
Santo Antônio River, 12
Santos, 109
São Bento do Norte, 22
São Bento do Una, 16
São Cristóvão, 43
São Francisco River, 5, 7, 13, 24, 25,
    27–28, 43, 49, 59, 73, 111, 141–42,
    144, 178
São João dos Pombos, 17
São Jorge dos Ilhéus, 110
São José do Egito, 203
São Luís Island, 32, 179, 180
São Miguel de Campos, 13
São Miguel Mountains, 26
São Miguel River, 12, 59, 144
São Paulo, 1, 7, 29, 34, 89, 119, 137, 143
São Pedro, 147
São Sebastião Island, ix
Second National Development Plan, 2
Sergipe, 6, 7, 13–14, 17, 22, 24, 49, 110;
    cacao cultivation, 14; cattle raising, 14,
    50, 59, 73, 88; coconut cultivation, 14,
    72–73; migration from, 89; population,
    57; rubber exploitation, 14; rural-urban
    migration, 14; slavery in, 79; sugarcane
    cultivation, 14, 88, 103; tobacco culti-
    vation, 14
Sergipe River, 13, 144
Seridó Valley, 25
Serinhaém River, 43, 49, 103, 111
Serra das Russas, 17
Serra de Ororobá, 18, 147
Serra Negra, 18
Serra Talhada, 147, 203
Sertão and Northern Littoral, 5, 9, 10, 16,
    22–30, 33, 35, 44–77; agriculture, 23,
    24, 26, 45, 149–56; carrying capacity,
    26; coffee cultivation, 153; colonization,
    202; conquest, 50; cotton cultivation,
    23, 74, 153–55; deforestation, 23;
    drought, 22; economic evolution, 156;
    erosion, 26; labor relations, 152–77
    passim; livestock raising, 59, 141–51,
    156–64, 175; Peasant Leagues, 209;
    population centers, 26; settlement,
    141–49; size, 21; slavery in, 44; subre-
    gions, 22–23; sugarcane cultivation, 70,
    151–53, 165; topography, 22–25
Sertãozinho colony, 204
sharecroppers, x, 4, 79, 108, 130, 142–43,
    145, 161–65, 171, 172, 185, 207, 213;
    unionization of, 2, 35, 37
silver, 42
Sinimbu factory, 13
Siriji River, 75

sisal, 123, 127
slavery, 5, 41, 60–69, 73, 74–80, 113, 119,
    120–24, 142, 143, 145, 152, 153, 179,
    180, 181–85, 205; cost, 46, 76; disease
    and, 78; during Dutch occupation,
    48–55; Indian, 42, 43, 44, 45, 46, 50,
    51, 179, 183; "just war," 113; mortality
    rates, 46–47; Negro, 44, 45, 46, 47, 51,
    59; revolts, 47. *See also* abolition;
    quilombos
small farmers, 128–31
Soares, Gabriel, 141
Soares Guimarães, Fábio Macedo, 6
Soares Moreno, Joaquim, 143
social welfare, rural workers and, 98. *See*
    Rural Labor Statute
sorghum, 2–7, 23–24
Sousa, Tomé de, 49, 141
squatters, 80, 92, 94–98, 121, 125–26, 132,
    138, 146–47, 155, 163–64, 175, 201–18
    passim
SUDAM (Superintendency for Develop-
    ment of the Amazon), 188, 189
SUDENE (Superintendency for Develop-
    ment of the Northeast), 5, 7, 28, 29,
    36, 87, 166, 188–213 passim
sugar industry, 83, 85, 100–107, 111, 127,
    147, 149, 151–53, 175, 181, 190, 200–
    201; in the Agreste, 18, 20, 85, 112,
    116–17, 120–21, 137–38; in Alagoas,
    12–13, 82–83, 85–86, 103; in Bahia, 83,
    103; on Borborema Plateau, 85; in
    Capibaribe-Mirim Valley, 86, 119; in
    Cariri, 27; in Ceará-Mirim, 83, 100,
    151; colonial, 42, 45; in Coruripe, 100;
    Dutch, 48–54, 56–59; evolution of,
    38–40, 43, 50–51, 58–59, 80–87; in
    Jiquiá Valley, 82; in Maranhão, 83; in
    Middle North, 179; modernization of,
    38–40, 73, 80–82, 89, 152; in moun-
    tains, 151; in Mundaú Valley, 82, 85,
    119; in Paraíba do Meio, 119; in Pa-
    raíba do Norte, 82–86, 103, 119; in
    Pernambuco, 81–86, 103; in Piauí, 83;
    in Rio Grande do Norte, 82, 86; along
    Rio São Francisco, 103; in Sergipe, 14,
    82–83, 103; in the Sertão, 35, 165, 176;
    in Siriji Valley, 86, 119; in
    Tracunhaém, 119; trade, 41; varieties
    of cane, 69–70, 91, 151; in Zona da
    Mata, 10, 35, 103
sun-dried meat, 147–49
Superintendency for Development of the
    Northeast. *See* SUDENE
Superintendency of Agrarian Reform. *See*
    SUPRA
SUPRA, 3
Surubim, 20

Tabajara Indians, 42, 45
tabuleiro vegetation, 9
Tabuleiros do Litoral, colonization, 200
Tacaratu, 147
Taipu, 17
tarefa, defined, 101
Tavoura, José de, 217
Teixeira, João Pedro, 210
Teixeira Mountains, 26, 150
Terceiro, José, 217
Teresina, 31, 186
Terra Preta colony, 203–4
Timbaúba, 203
tobacco cultivation, 14, 18, 20, 89, 123–27, 139–40, 180, 181, 203; as specie, 59
Todos os Santos Bay, 14
toque ("carbuncles"), 158
tourism, 110
Tracunhaém River, 75
trade, international, 180, 182, 184. *See* Brazilian-African trade; Brazilian-European trade; Portuguese-African trade; Portuguese-European trade
transportation, 72, 180–81. *See also* road building
Triunfo, 26
truck farming, 129
Tupinambás Indians, 178
Turiaçu River, 31

Una River, 18, 43, 50
unemployment, 1–2, 88–89
unions, 2, 5; of rural workers, 98, 205–18 passim

urbanization. *See* migration, rural-urban; modernization
usina, defined, 12n

Valença, 72
Vargas, Getúlio, 2
Vaza Barris River, 13, 144, 178
Verde River, 144
Vertentes, 20
Vicência, 208
Vitória da Conquista, 18
Vitória de Santo Antão, 92, 201–4

wage labor, x, 4, 5, 93, 101, 165, 205, 218; development of, 153, 154; freed slaves, 79–80; organization of, 2, 34, 37. *See also* Peasant Leagues; rural workers; sharecroppers; squatters; unionization
wine production, 28, 166

Young University Catholics, 216

Zona da Mata and Eastern Littoral, 4, 9–14, 16, 18, 33, 41–110; agriculture, 4, 14, 35; colonization, 193, 202; exploration and settlement, 10, 41–44; geographic boundaries, 9, 14; labor relations, 102–10; landholding patterns, 36, 87, 88; livestock raising, 59; Peasant Leagues, 209; population, 14; rainfall, 9–10; vegetation, 9–10
Zé Doca, 197

A Note on Author and Translator

Manuel Correia de Andrade is a professor of economic geography in the Federal University of Pernambuco, Recife. He is a leading authority on the Northeast and has served on professional and governmental groups dealing with the region. Andrade revised the 1973 edition of his book to accommodate Johnson's English-language translation.

Dennis V. Johnson, who was a visiting professor of geography in Brazil for two years, is assistant professor of geography at the University of Houston.